"In an age of hyper-parenting and frenetic, over-scheduled families, Susan Sachs Lipman offers up an encyclopedia of wonderful activities that will help every family slow down and smell the roses."
—Alvin Rosenfeld, MD, coauthor of *The Over-Scheduled Child*

"Susan Lipman provides parents a fail-safe guide to slowing down in our frenetic world. With doable activities that often require nothing more than our imagination, *Fed Up with Frenzy* gives readers very doable ways to reclaim family connection with simplicity. It's every parent's answer to 'Mom! I'm bored!'"
—Christine Louise Hohlbaum, author of *The Power of Slow: 101 Ways to Save Time in Our 24/7 World*

"Susan Sachs Lipman's new book *Fed Up with Frenzy* is a must for all parents and families today—and is a great guide to parenting and life. She gives us a toolkit of ideas for dealing with the frenzy of today's lifestyle and encourages us to practice slow parenting, including 'time for beneficial unstructured play' for children and families. I strongly agree with her assertion that 'families who have unstructured time and play are joyful and close.' As the 16th Director of the National Park Service and Co-Chair of the U.S. Play Coalition, I believe Susan's book will help us all achieve more happiness and success in life."
—Fran P. Mainella, Visiting Scholar Clemson University, 16th Director of the National Park Service, and Co-Chair of the U.S. Play Coalition

"Susan Sachs Lipman not only encourages parents to slow down and connect with their kids, but also shows them how—laying out simple, low-cost, or free ways to do it. Dip into any chapter and you'll find lots of ideas for sure-fire, kid-tested fun."

—Regan McMahon, author of *Revolution in the Bleachers: How Parents Can Take Back Family Life in a World Gone Crazy Over Youth Sports*

"Today's parents have the deck stacked against them, with conflicting demands on their time, attention, and finances as they struggle to raise their children to be happy, healthy people. Too many fall into the trap of over-scheduling their children—and themselves—to the point where no one gets the time or chance to just *be*, and, more importantly, just be together. In *Fed Up with Frenzy*, Susan Sachs Lipman details countless opportunities and activities for bringing families closer together and allowing creativity, bonding, imagination, and wholeness to blossom, in each child and parent and in the family as a whole. By turns clever, personal, and entertaining, *Fed Up with Frenzy* is ultimately wise, and any parent who reads it will feel the same after adopting Lipman's recommendations. May the Slow Parenting movement bloom!"

—Phil Catalfo, author of *Raising Spiritual Children in a Material World* and coauthor of *The Whole Parenting Guide*

"If this inspiring book has one message, it's 'Slow down!' But how? *Fed Up with Frenzy* isn't just a manifesto, it's a practical guide that shows parents how to reclaim play for your children and yourself, how to reconnect with the natural world, and how to carve out space and time for the community in which you live. *Fed Up with Frenzy* is a blueprint for any family that feels overwhelmed by the pace of contemporary life."

—Darell Hammond, founder and CEO of KaBOOM!

"The natural world is the ideal setting for slow parenting. From your own backyard to the local urban park, nature and wildlife are all around us, providing kids time to slow down and escape into a world of wonder where they can imagine, dream, and fulfill their curiosity about the natural world."

—Patrick Fitzgerald, Director of Education Advocacy, National Wildlife Federation

"For every parent who wants to slow down and reconnect but doesn't know where to begin, *Fed Up with Frenzy* will bring you exactly where you long to be. Like a new-fangled version of the *Things to Make and Do* books from the '60s and '70s, Suz Lipman has packed her heartfelt book with a bounty of games, activities, rituals, and slow tips on every page to help families find slow connection within the confines of their own families and their own communities. I heartily recommend leaving this book where every member of the family can easily access it!"

—Bernadette Noll, mother of four and cofounder of Slowfamilyliving.com

"Suz Lipman has written a honey of a book that gently and thoughtfully extends the essential, ongoing conversations about the benefits of "slow living" right into the heart of the home. *Fed Up with Frenzy* is a love letter to families everywhere, with practical tips and strategies that are accessible and easy to accomplish."

—Pamela Price, founder of RedWhiteandGrew.com

"Put down that mobile phone and pick up *Fed up With Frenzy*. Stop being frazzled, slow way down, and start enjoying your family. If you want to really experience life, your kids, and those treasured moments, then make this book your new guide. In this fast-paced world, Susan Sachs Lipman has it right. Slow Parenting is where it is at!"

—Jennifer Carden, author of *The Toddler Café* and founder
of *Playful Pantry*, playfulpantry.wordpress.com

"This book is a wonderful resource for parents, grandparents, and caregivers to reintroduce you to the simple pleasures in life with its practical activities that connect you to the seasons and with each other as a family."

— Kari Svenneby, founder of activekidsclub.com

"Childhood today is often viewed through the rearview mirror, as busy parents shuttle even busier children from activity to activity. In her charming and inspiring book, *Fed Up with Frenzy*, author and self-proclaimed "Slow Mom" Susan Sachs Lipman tempts us all to slow down and simplify the way our families are living. With recipes, activities, ideas, and tips galore, *Fed Up with Frenzy* is a practical, fun guide to unplugging your family and really connecting. It's a must-have for anyone with children."

—Bethe Almeras, aka *The Grass Stain Guru*
Writer, speaker, educator, and childhood advocate

"As a mother of three school-aged children with my own fair share of a hectic life, Suz Lipman's book reads like a deep breath of fresh air and helps us embrace the joys of parenting through connections to nature. *Fed Up with Frenzy* provides a healthy dose of inspiration along with a lot of fun and easy ideas for how to explore and play close to home. I recommend this book to all caregivers who are looking for a way to invite nature back into their families' lives."

—Rue Mapp, founder and CEO,
Outdoor Afro, outdoorafro.com

Fed Up with *Frenzy*

*Slow Parenting™ in
a Fast-Moving World*

Susan Sachs Lipman

Illustrations by *Lippy.*

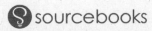 sourcebooks

Published by Sourcebooks, Inc.
P.O. Box 4410, Naperville, Illinois 60567-4410
(630) 961-3900
Fax: (630) 961-2168
www.sourcebooks.com

Library of Congress Cataloging-in-Publication Data
Lipman, Susan Sachs.
  Fed up with frenzy : slow parenting in a fast-moving world / Susan Sachs Lipman. — 1st ed.
     p. cm.
  (trade paper : alk. paper) 1. Parenting. 2. Parent and child. I. Title.
  HQ755.8.L547 2012
649'.1—dc23

2012011800

Printed and bound in the United States of America.
VP 10 9 8 7 6 5 4 3 2 1

For Michael and Anna, my champions and teachers, whose love and laughter make me want to slow each memorable day.
and
For my parents, who encouraged me to jump in rain puddles and see life as a continuous adventure.

Contents

Chapter 3: Slow Crafts   107

Chapter 4: Slow Kitchen   137

Chapter 5: Slow Garden   165

Chapter 6: Slow Nature   197

Chapter 7: Slow Seasons   227

Chapter 8: Slow Celebrations   269

Chapter 9: Slow Travel   303

Chapter 10: Everyday Slow   321

Chapter 11: Slow Parenting   335

Resources   346

Foreword

My parents always said I was named Anna for a reason. They told me that Anna was a special name because it had been my great-grandmother's name, and it was also easily understood in most countries. I've known from the beginning that my family was special, too. My mother and father are happy people who have always lived by their values. The strongest value they passed on to me was to slow down and embrace what Mother Nature has given us.

I was raised in nature. When I was little, my dad used to tell me that the forest around us was my backyard. My parents encouraged me to explore my surroundings, to be prepared for—and not afraid of—the unexpected. Now I feel confident and prepared for everyday life. I can walk in nature or in a city by myself and feel like I know what to do.

We were always walkers. I walked to school, my mom walked to the market, my dad walked to the library. My parents also taught me the joy of biking, and I bike everywhere I can today. I learned that being slow can be good for the environment and that you enjoy life more when you look around. I learned that gardening and cooking can take time, love, and patience, but make you happy.

When I was little, it was also impressed upon me that I could make a difference, but that in order to do so, I had to make sacrifices. I did not always do every activity, rushing from practice to practice. I did not always have the newest things, but instead bought less and re-used things. I learned to rely on myself.

My mom made sacrifices, too. Always putting others before

herself, my mom made sure that I was aware of my surroundings and cherished the beautiful world I was raised in. My mom was an avid Girl Scout leader who always took us girls on gorgeous hikes and fun adventures. She instilled in me the fact that time is a gift, to cherish what I have, and to love the Earth and give back more than I take.

As a little girl, I took what she said for granted, never thinking thoroughly about the gifts of knowledge she was giving me. Now, as I have grown older, I realize how privileged I am to have grown up in one of the most beautiful places in the world, with one of the most beautiful mothers. Beautiful on the inside.

My mom is a very special person and I can't imagine what I would have done without her. She's an amazing human being, and I have been privileged to have been raised by such a kind and giving person. I am so proud that she has channeled her love of teaching and slowing down into a lovely book. I love her so much, and even though all her ideas can't be put into a single book, I still think this one is pretty good.

Anna Lipman, age 16
Mill Valley, CA

Introduction

A t soccer games and birthday parties, in school hallways and other places parents congregate, our conversations are often the same: many of us feel that we are running around and doing more together than ever, yet somehow enjoying our family time less. We often find ourselves isolated, distracted, plugged into electronic devices, performing chores, driving, and multitasking—and our family lives tend to reflect that. Chaos, rather than calm, is the norm.

A decade ago, when my daughter, Anna, entered elementary school, I distinctly realized that something wasn't right. Our lives, and the lives of many families around us, were off balance. Parents seemed frazzled and hurried, spending more time transporting our children and dropping them off than actually playing or even being with them. Our children seemed to do specific, monitored, often goal-oriented activities instead of playing freely. There were arranged playdates, lessons, and sports practices; yet despite all the organizing and hovering, many of us went about the task of parenting relatively alone and unfulfilled.

I yearned for a life filled with creativity and play; true connection with my family, my community, and myself; and an enjoyment of small observations and moments that comes from slowing down enough to notice them. I wasn't experiencing those types of connections and moments because I was too busy planning, scheduling, and driving. I was too busy with the future to notice the present, too busy with the calendar and the to-do list to stop and chat in the market or between activities.

And, frankly, others seemed quite busy, too. I began to wonder just what the rush was, and whether slowing down might help me and my family become more connected and calm.

My family had experienced some of the connection and community I sought during Anna's preschool years—so much so that the pace and expectations of elementary school life seemed jarring. It was as if the ground beneath us had transformed from a meandering, woodsy path into a rapidly moving walkway. We suddenly struggled to keep up.

Anna's preschool, Kumara School, had emphasized process over product. For the most part, the children directed their own play, in nature and with art materials that were simple and often natural or recycled. Anna spent about a year being fascinated with adhesive tape—pulling, cutting, and laying it down on paper, creating cardboard box-and-tube cameras and "candy machines." She didn't seem to need or want anything more expensive, complicated, or "educational" than that. I've found that this and similar observations often occur when we slow down, adjust our ideas about what is normal or expected, and let our children and our own instincts guide us.

Even with a small child, society sometimes informed us that we'd better hurry and get on a schedule, or else she would be left behind, from kindergarten on up to college. We had visited other preschools in which kids sat on specific cushions and learned the letters of the alphabet, in order to get ready for kindergarten. I instinctively felt that Anna would learn best by playing and that traditional academics could wait. I was well on my way to entering a slower parenting style that didn't adhere to schedules of education and child development, which had sped up dramatically since my own childhood.

As a young family with a preschool child, we had time to garden, visit farms, make jam, create art, and celebrate the seasons. With Anna's school community, we welcomed each summer and winter solstice and many holidays with songs, stories, rituals, and food, much the way people have been bearing witness to the changing seasons and honoring life's mysteries for thousands of years. We connected with a burgeoning group called Sustainable Mill Valley that was championing better use of resources, local food, and other goods; stewardship of our beautiful land and town; and community gathering and bartering. We had friends of many generations, professions, backgrounds, and beliefs.

And then something changed. With elementary school, we entered a world that seemed frenzied and heavily scheduled. Parents appeared to be models of efficiency, whipping out day planners to plan their kids' playdates, carving time from busy schedules for the many child-centered appointments, activities, and meetings. Although I knew Anna couldn't stay a preschooler forever, I missed the ease, fun, and organic community that that period of her life had offered our family and wondered whether this new way was the sole alternative.

My feelings of unease mounted one morning as I sat in my car near the school drop-off curb, engine running, waiting my turn to deposit Anna at school. Other parents inched up, one per car, in the chaos of traffic—some honking, some cutting in aggressively, some visibly upset. Passenger car doors opened and slammed shut. A volunteer parent hustled children out of their cars and onto the sidewalk. The youngest children, who appeared dwarfed by their brightly colored backpacks, wound their way into the school in a sort of daze.

This ritual is a necessary feature at suburban schools across America that offers busy parents the opportunity to let their children out of their cars without having to park, leave the driver's seat, or turn off the ignition. The drop-off, and the pickup at day's end, are designed for maximum efficiency. Signs tell us, "Drop, Don't Stop."

The abrupt transition didn't feel right to me. I decided that, even though I was a busy working and volunteering parent, my schedule wasn't so packed that I couldn't find fifteen minutes to help my daughter (and, by extension, myself) make a more graceful transition to school. I started parking the car a few blocks from the school and walking in with her. We felt the change immediately. In those few minutes walking to and from school, we made observations and talked about the day. We enjoyed the smells of wild onions in the spring and wood-burning fireplaces in the winter and fall. We met people who lived in the neighborhood, and we greeted fellow parents and students as they poured through the school's gates.

I believe that that small act profoundly changed our lives. As Anna became older, we walked longer distances, then she walked and biked to school by herself. There were still hurried mornings when I was grateful for the drop-off curb. But we also found community and created memories and joy by intentionally sidestepping frenzy, by choosing to slow one particular part of our day and routine to get something back that was incredibly full. To this day, the smell of the wild onions near the school will remind us of the fun we had walking that little bit and the lifelong friends we made during that special period.

A few years later, when Anna was in the fourth and fifth grades, her Girl Scout troop would meet down the street from her school at the conveniently located Scout Hall. This provided another opportunity for neighborhood walking, and the girls loved to walk the few safe blocks to the hall. It was wonderful for them to have fun together and get a little exercise and fresh air after school. Along the way, they marched, sang, and waved to shopkeepers and at passing drivers, who waved back. I saw the girls learn things about their town and neighbors, things that you can learn only when you slow your pace enough to allow for observation and connection, as well as for roots to form.

For some of the girls, scout meetings offered a rare opportunity to walk in their town. Yet parents invariably arrived at the school at meeting time, offering to drive everyone the few blocks to Scout Hall. They thought the meeting could start more quickly that way, that time would be used more efficiently. They could drop the girls off, run errands, and pick them up again at meeting's end, and no one would have to walk. I protested: Walking was part of the meeting. It provided the girls with fun, relatively unstructured, and meaningful time together. Walking, as an activity, had value. In time, the other parents, especially those who walked with us, began to agree.

When well-meaning parents experience their days as a race against time, much is actually lost. Many of us want more connection and meaning in our families' lives, but we remain too busy to even think about achieving those things. Nearly half of Americans bring work home with them regularly. Working mothers spend a whopping 40 percent of their waking hours multitasking. Children have roughly half the free time that they did thirty years ago.

And then there are a great number of us who are constantly plugged into electronics. How many times have you been somewhere and seen a whole family, each of whom is individually texting or playing a game on his or her own device? Perhaps you've wished your own family was more connected to one another and less to technology. Instead of freeing us, technology, for work and for pleasure, has created a culture in which many of us are afraid to unplug, for fear of missing something. It turns out that, instead, what we wind up missing is a life of family connection and joy.

Slowing down has offered me, my family, and the kindred spirits in my community the blessings of greater family memories and closeness, more enjoyment of lost arts and activities, and, more often than not, the kinds of happy and successful children that we had hoped to foster through our unintentional anxiety and over-scheduling.

The threads of encouraging free play; using resources wisely to help the planet and ourselves; getting better in touch with our food, land, and lives; reclaiming lost, tactile arts; and forming healthy communities and loving families have all woven loosely together into something called the Slow Movement. Many trace the Slow Movement's origins to Italy and the Slow Food movement, which came about as a response to quickly prepared and consumed fast food. The Slow Cities movement, also from Italy, followed, to encourage thoughtful urban planning and use that is designed to get people walking, convening, enjoying local goods and services, and slowing down as a result. Today, there are designated slow cities all over the world. Carl Honoré wrote *In Praise of Slowness: How a Worldwide Movement Is Challenging the Cult of Speed*. More books and slow groups followed. More people decided to try something different. And their ideas took on the force of a movement.

While exploring the slow life for my own family, I came across and learned from a community of authors and mentors. Those resources are included in the Resources section of the book.

The more I read, the more I talked to people who desired to take a similar path, and the more I tried to walk that path myself, the more my family experienced enhanced presence, community, spontaneity, play, and simply time together. By making choices to eliminate a couple of organized activities and commitments, we made time to take long family hikes, make televisions out of shoe boxes, and float origami boats down a local creek after the spring rains. By shifting away from the culture of hurriedness, we made time to open our lives to enhanced wonder, connection, and joy.

As Carl Honoré writes, the Slow Movement is not about crawling at a snail's pace. Rather, it is about doing things at the right speed for you. It's about choosing how to spend time and then savoring the moments, rather than rushing through them.

In the years since my family has slowed down, I've noticed a slight change in other families, too. Perhaps a critical mass of us also felt off balance. Perhaps many of us have even decided to say "Enough!" to super-parenting and consumerism and running around (I call it "racing to yoga") and not being happy anyway. Perhaps you count yourself in this group.

Why Become a Slow Parent?

Many of us probably know instinctively that slowing down is good for our families and ourselves, and many experts affirm this. Here are a few specific benefits that come from slow parenting.

☀ Slow Parenting Creates Successful Children

A whole host of positive character traits—resilience, optimism, confidence, empathy, and better performance in school—flourish when parents and children have time to be together and experience one another's positive support and unconditional love. Dr. Kenneth Ginsburg, author of *Building Resilience in Children and Teens: Giving Kids Roots and Wings*, writes, "The most valuable and useful character traits that will prepare…children for success arise not from extracurricular or academic commitments but from a firm grounding in parental love, role modeling, and guidance."

☀ Slow Parenting Improves Physical and Psychological Health

Slowing down, for as brief a period as six minutes, can reduce stress for people of all ages. Activities like reading, listening to music, enjoying tea, and going for a walk significantly lower our heart rates and other stress indicators. Getting out in nature, something we often do when we slow our pace, has also been found to bring profound benefits to every aspect of children's development—intellectual, emotional, social, spiritual, and physical. In addition, slow parents tend to make time to allow kids to run, jump, and play; to use their bodies to be active, to dance to music, to march to a beat, and to express the joy inherent in being alive.

✳ Slow Parenting Allows Time for Beneficial Unstructured Play

It turns out that kids actually need free play and unscheduled time for their cognitive, physical, social, and emotional well-being. Unstructured free play has been found to benefit creativity, problem solving, self-discipline, cooperation, flexibility, and self-awareness. Kids who have time to play are less stressed, less aggressive, and happier. Families who have time to play experience vital bonding.

Sometimes play is when we can most be ourselves. Unstructured play allows us get in touch with our imaginations and our inner worlds in a way we can't during competitive sports or more passive leisure activities. Slow parents can foster their children's play simply by making time for it and then choosing when to join in and, importantly, when to get out of the way.

> *"Play is where children show us the innermost experiences that they can't or won't talk about."*
> —Dr. Lawrence J. Cohen, Playful Parenting

✳ Slow Parenting Allows for Valuable Downtime

Dr. Ginsburg notes, "Some of the best interactions occur during downtime—just talking, preparing meals together, and working on a hobby or art project, playing sports together, or being fully immersed in child-centered play." Time and again, we've noticed this, on family walks or sitting around the kitchen table stringing beads. Something happens when time is allowed to expand, when the family is no longer rushing. Interesting and deep conversations occur, and we feel a genuine closeness. In the very small moments, the world can seem marvelous, because we actually have a chance to notice this. Our children can reveal things because they are calm and relaxed. In our busy lives, we often miss out on downtime, both because we over-schedule our time and because we rush through everyday tasks and moments, like gardening, bathing a pet, or running errands, which could provide time to be together in a simple and unhurried way.

✳ Slow Parenting Fosters Irreplaceable Connection and Learning

Although we may think that some of the best enrichment for our kids comes from educational videos and materials, research shows that children who watch DVDs, like *Baby Einstein*, actually learn fewer words and score lower on cognitive tests than do children who learn through human interaction, language, and play. Videos and other tools can also end up replacing vital parent-child bonding time. When we spend time holding our kids in our laps and reading to them, we're doing more than transferring words. We're transferring affection and the idea that they are important to us and that we value the time spent together. "There is no substitute for a parent's attention and time," says Dr. Rebekah A. Richert, who researched videos and word learning. The many hours my family spent reading together helped create an intense bond that lasts to this day, a bond due both to our physical closeness and to the wonderful books we all discovered together.

> *"There are no more valuable means of promoting success and happiness in children than the tried, trusted, and traditional methods of play and family togetherness."*
> —Dr. Kenneth Ginsburg

✳ Slow Parenting Allows Us to Be Fully Present

With a 2010 study reporting that the average American child spends an astonishing fifty-three hours per week plugged in to some form of electronic media, many of us rightfully worry about our children allotting too much time to electronics. But parents' multitasking and media use can be just as extreme and disruptive to parent-child bonds.

"Today's parents might not even realize how their divided attention plays out with kids," says Dr. Sherry Turkle, director of the Massachusetts Institute of Technology's Initiative on Technology and Self and author of *Alone Together: Why We Expect More of Technology and Less of Each Other*. For children, she says, "shared attention can feel like no attention at all." In more than three hundred interviews with children over five years, Dr. Turkle unearthed countless stories of children feeling neglected for media. Although she recognizes the pressure adults feel to make themselves constantly available for work and other communications, she believes that a greater force drives them to keep checking their screens.

I confess to finding the screen very compelling. When I volunteered in schools, and now that I rely on the Internet for work, there were and are always new emails to answer and fascinating things to see and read. For that reason, I refrain from checking my devices when I'm having family time. I try to be present and to "single task," knowing that the electronics can wait and that my divided attention wouldn't end up being satisfactory to anyone.

✳ Slow Parenting Fosters Discovery and Wonder

Time is necessary for discovery, wonder, observation, imagination, and creativity to flourish. The psychologist Carl Jung wrote that we are all born creative. If we don't use the creativity we're given, our souls and spirits become deprived and unfulfilled. "Imagination is more important than knowledge," said Albert Einstein. It is extremely important and natural to young children especially. Rudolf Steiner, the philosopher whose work laid the groundwork for Waldorf schools, advocated that children be allowed to remain in the peaceful, dreamlike realm of the imagination for as long as possible. There's time enough for the concrete, and there is a time when children's brains are developmentally prepared for it. Slow parents can foster discovery and wonder by providing materials for art and pretend and nature play and then either guiding the projects as much as needed or getting out of the way and letting kids supervise their own play. We can foster these qualities by taking the time to observe and share, whether we're walking in our neighborhoods, playing in nature, or performing chores.

"By simplifying, we protect the environment for childhood's slow, essential unfolding of self."
—*Kim John Payne*, Simplicity Parenting

"If a child is to keep alive his inborn sense of wonder, he needs the companionship of at least one adult who can share it, rediscovering the joy, excitement, and mystery of the world we live in."
—*Rachel Carson*, The Sense of Wonder

✳ Slow Parenting Creates Family Memories

The warmest and most potent family memories often come from moments that seem small at the time. Small gestures and jokes that arise during shared activity, downtime, and play can have a way of becoming repeated family sayings and microrituals, which add to life's texture and enter the family memory bank.

One memorable time, out of the many sessions we had engaging in one of our favorite hobbies, making jam, we were crushing berries in a food processor when one lone berry ended up on top of the unit, plump, uncrushed, and seemingly looking down at the rest. Anna, who was three years old, said, "That berry looks like he's saying, 'OK, every berry. I'm going to say who gets made up into jam.'" We laughed that she had created a sort of boss of the berries. I wrote the saying down on a piece of paper that went up on the refrigerator, and the saying became one of our gentle family traditions—to this day, when we're gathering to go somewhere, we are likely to call out, "OK, every berry."

✳ Slow Parenting Helps Create and Pass On Beloved Family Traditions

Many traditions arise from a combination of intention and awareness, two qualities that slow parenting fosters. My friend Cynthia has a tablecloth onto which she has guests write their names after special gatherings. She then embroiders over the writing so that the tablecloth has the memories of multiple generations and gatherings literally stitched into it. When I use the soup ladle given to me by my childhood friend Sandy, which was her own mother's, it triggers an opportunity to tell Anna stories about our families and the times when we were growing up.

✳ Slow Families Experience Purpose and Connection

Slow families tend to enjoy a greater sense of purpose, as well as a better connection to nature, the seasons, their neighborhoods, and the daily rhythms of life. They often practice enhanced routines and gratitude, which in turn helps children feel secure and helps parents respond to their children's needs with grace.

> *"Once you understand the importance of creating rhythm in the life of the child, and then provide appropriate opportunities for his or her creative play and imaginative and artistic development, you'll find that your child is much happier and easier to live with. And nurturing children in this way also nurtures the caregiver."*
> —*Rahima Baldwin Dancy*, You Are Your Child's First Teacher

Making time to enjoy meals together is a hallmark of slow families. Dining as a family at least five times a week is associated with lower rates of teen smoking, drinking, and illegal drug use. Children from families with predictable routines report greater satisfaction with family life and even perform better in school. If our family is any indication, the meals certainly need not be anything special—the special part is that we share them.

Spending time in nature together can also be quite powerful for families. And that doesn't mean you have to pack up and travel to a national park—the nearby nature of a backyard, city park, school playground, or a balcony with growing flowers can provide the same benefits as a wild space. My family and I nearly always feel the incredibly calming and bonding effects of nature. Nature works like magic to allow people of all ages to get in touch with the wonder of the world and their own inner compasses. And that, coupled with the downtime that nature provides, tends to allow us to connect more deeply to one another.

In addition, nature and gardening have provided my family with many memories, from the marigolds and lamb's ears that Anna planted when she was small to the flowers we gathered to make May Day crowns, the games of Tag we played in the park, and the naps we took under canopies of stars.

Getting Started on the Road to Slow

Perhaps you've already experienced a lack of balance and fulfillment in your parenting and in your life but have been unsure how to approach it, or have felt unsupported by partners, friends, work, schools, or the culture at large. Perhaps you've shared my nagging feeling that something is "off."

Most of us entered our roles as parents with dreams and desires for memorable experiences with our children. Many of us yearn to slow down and have more family time to enjoy simple pleasures like skipping stones, making fresh strawberry jam, blowing bubbles, singing campfire songs, or gazing at the stars. Often we're not sure where to start or how to do some of these activities. And of course, our children don't know how either.

In an attempt to slow our family down, I tried many fun pastimes with my family and with scout and youth groups, and in this book I have compiled our favorites. You'll find tons of ideas and instructions that will allow you to slow down; be more present as a parent; improve your connection with your children; and enjoy more of your family, friends, and time. My hope is that the activities in *Fed Up with Frenzy* will help your family regain a sense of connection, joy, and playfulness—and perhaps even discover or rediscover games or crafts from your own or your parents' childhoods.

Using This Book

The activities in *Fed Up with Frenzy* cover a wide range of skills, ages, and moods. Sometimes you will want to complete an activity relatively quickly with man-made materials (slow family or not) and sometimes you'll want to do an activity that calls for a more sustained effort, in which everything is lovingly created from scratch. Sometimes you will want to plan a community-wide event far in advance, and sometimes you will desire something quiet or spontaneous. Please feel free to follow activity directions to the letter, or to use the ideas as jumping-off points. What matters is that you enjoy the act of doing something together that feeds your family members' souls.

Perhaps you'll simply be facing a rare moment of downtime—a rainy day or a school vacation or a slumber party or an afternoon in the backyard or on the living-room floor—and think, "Now what? What activity can I do that is fun and maybe a little unusual, meaningful, or bonding?"

Fed Up with Frenzy is designed to help you exchange the tyranny of time not just for productivity or even serenity, but also for deeper meaning and connection with your children and your own parenting. I firmly believe that the time my husband, Michael, and I spent with our daughter when she was young—putting on puppet shows, baking pies, walking in the woods or the neighborhood, reading to one another each night—truly paid off when she became an older child and then a teenager. The habits that led to closeness were deeply ingrained. Our shared family memories and small moments had served as a powerful bonding agent. *Fed Up with Frenzy* is full of simple, affordable, and delightful activities and tactics to help you be more present with your own children and experience more joy and wonder as you trade a lifestyle of frenzy for fun.

I hope you'll stay in touch and let me know what you think of this book and what worked for you and your family. You can find me through my blog, *Slow Family Online*, at www.slowfamilyonline.com.

1

Slow Activities

Many wonderful activities from simpler times have gotten lost in the shuffle of our busy lives. Yet classic, wholesome activities like singing campfire songs or writing messages in invisible ink are often just the sorts of things that many of us want more of in our own and our children's lives.

These activities, songs, and projects provide fun, time-tested pursuits that can bond families and friends and create lifelong memories. My family treasures our memories of showing outdoor movies, sailing paper boats, blowing bubbles, and playing Flashlight Tag, which we've done ourselves and with neighbors, friends, and large groups. As with many simple activities from slower times, most activities in this chapter are inexpensive to do and require only items you already have on hand.

Make Something That Goes

Blame it on those first wheeled Mesopotamian chariots, the Wright Brothers and their flying machines, or Curious George and his simple paper boat—there's something extra special about building something that moves, whether by wheel, water, or a gust of wind. These projects can make great activities for rainy days, but there's also the added adventure of taking them out into the world. We've taken our homemade boats to local creeks and duck ponds. Our trains and planes provided hours of play, indoors and out.

✳ Juice-Box Train

It is especially rewarding to create something completely new from recycled materials. This juice-box train is easy and suitable for most ages, and it makes a fun toy to play with when done.

You'll need:

- 4–5 individual juice boxes, washed and dried
- Construction paper, markers, crayons, or paint
- Tape
- Scissors
- String

Wrap the juice boxes in construction paper, folding the corners to fit as you would wrapping paper on a present, or paint the boxes. Each juice box, stood on its longer vertical side, will be a train car. The front of each juice box will form one side of each train car.

Poke one hole each in the tops and bottoms of the juice boxes (which are now the fronts and back of the train cars). This is where the train cars will connect.

Continue to decorate your train cars, drawing or painting over the paper wrapping, as desired.

If you'd like, make a smokestack with a cylinder of construction paper folded down the middle, or a cowcatcher with a triangle of construction paper, and attach them to the engine car with tape.

Cut a piece of string approximately 1 1/3 times as long as the finished train and knot the end of it.

Thread the string through each of the train cars until you reach the caboose, leaving 3"–4" or as much space as you would like between cars.

✳ Paper Boat

My family got the idea to make this paper boat from a beloved book, H. A. Rey's *Curious George Rides a Bike*, in which sweet and lovable George secures a paper route, which leads him to make and sail a whole flotilla of folded-newspaper boats. Wondering whether a newspaper boat could really float, we got out some old newspaper, folded it into boats using the directions in *Curious George*, and took our boats down to a local creek, where they indeed sailed along once released, on a gently flowing spring stream. You can make your own boat, using any kind of paper.

You'll need:

- Sheet of any type of paper, roughly the same scale as an 8 1/2″ × 11″ sheet
- Adhesive tape, optional

Place the paper on a surface vertically, and fold it in half, top to bottom.

Fold the paper in half again, side to side.

Unfold the fold you just made.

With the creased side on top, fold both top corners in toward the center crease. This leaves a triangle shape, with a rectangular bar along the bottom.

Fold the bottom rectangles up on each side, creasing at the bottom of the triangle shape.

Place a thumb and forefinger on the inside of the shape, at the center of each triangle, and carefully, completely open out the shape from the middle.

Keep opening the shape until it flattens again into a perfect square. (Your two fingers should now be on opposite sides of the square.)

Lay the square on the table like a diamond.

Fold each side in half, width-wise, bringing each bottom

triangle up to the point at the top. (This will result in a triangle shape.)

Place a thumb and forefinger into the center of the triangle, as before. This time, as you pull the bottom opening apart, use the other hand to stretch out the two top triangles from the other side of the figure, so that they become the bow and stern (back and front) of the boat.

Flatten the inner triangle slightly to create a sail.

If you'd like, you can line the bottom of the boat with adhesive tape, which may make it more waterproof and help it float longer.

✳ Cork Rafts and Sailboats

Ahoy! Cork is a wonderful, buoyant material that is perfect for very small seagoing (or bathgoing) vessels.

You'll need:

- Corks
- School or craft glue
- Flat toothpicks
- Construction or other paper
- Ruler
- Markers, crayons, or colored pencils
- Scissors

For the raft:

Arrange corks in a square or rectangle, with long sides touching each other.

Glue the sides of the corks together and let the glue dry.

Draw a small rectangle (approximately 1" x 4") on the paper with the ruler and cut it out.

Fold the paper in half, so that you have two rectangles approximately 1″ x 2″.

Draw your country's flag or flags from your imagination on each outer side of the paper.

Glue the toothpick into the inner fold on the back side between the two flags, and let the glue dry. When dry, glue the two halves of the paper together to secure the flag.

Affix the toothpick flags into one cork or several corks and set the raft in water.

For the sailboat:

Glue corks together, following the instructions for the raft, or simply use a single cork.

Draw a triangular sail shape on the paper (approximately 1″ long) on the side that will be glued to the toothpick.

Decorate your sail, if desired.

Glue the sail to the toothpick on its 1″ side and let the glue dry.

Affix the toothpick sail into the cork or cork base and set sail!

✳ Popsicle-Stick Airplane

Popsicle sticks are great to have on hand for a variety of projects. They are inexpensive and can be purchased, plain or colored, from craft stores. Everyone loves to make and fly airplanes, and the rounded popsicle-stick ends make for a fairly safe, satisfying, and easily assembled flying machine.

You'll need:

- 5 popsicle or craft sticks per plane
- Glue
- Paint, if desired

Stack three popsicle sticks and then fan them into a triangle, so that one end of each stick is still touching the others. Glue the tops together.

Weave a fourth popsicle stick over the first stick, under the middle stick, and over the third stick.

Weave a fifth popsicle stick the opposite way—under the first stick, over the middle stick, and under the third stick.

If you'd like, add a dot of glue at each juncture for extra security, and let the glue dry.

Paint your airplane or leave it natural.

Fly as you would a paper airplane. Hold the middle stick and try to launch it decisively and parallel to the ground.

Slow Tip: Make a kite! Cut a piece of plastic (grocery bags work) in the shape of the plane. Glue it onto one side. Tie 4" of fishing line to the center stick in 2 places. Tie a length of line to that. Go outside and catch a breeze.

Put on a Show

Thespians have been entertaining others with plays ever since their namesake, Thespis, dragged a handcart around ancient Greece, complete with masks that the pioneering actor donned to perform plays about daily life. Children of all ages love the various aspects of plays—creating, improvising, singing, dancing, wearing costumes, and acting out scenarios for an audience.

Anna particularly enjoyed making tickets and programs and luring family and friends to see her shows. When she was about three years old, she would call, "The show is about to begin! Coming to the show!" (her words), carnival-barker style, sometimes for periods of time that went longer and were more elaborate than the actual shows. Other children respond to the dress-up aspects of theater, and still others unleash their creativity by taking a character through make-believe events. Drama, role-play, and dress-up allow children to engage in important imaginative play and fantasy with family and friends, and of course, they can be a source of wonderful bonding and memories.

WANT TO MAKE A QUICK COSTUME?

Tunic: Cut a hole for a head in a 1-yard piece of fabric.

Cape: Fold over an inch of a piece of fabric that is at least 24″ long. Sew a seam, leaving a casing to string elastic or a tie through.

Animal ears: Cut out felt ears and tape them to a plastic headband. Crease the ears slightly at the bottom to make them stand up.

Tutu: Cut strips of tulle approximately 4″ wide and 20″ long from a roll or a 4-yard piece. Loop each strip around a waist-sized piece of elastic or a headband. Thread ends of tulle through the loop and pull to tighten.

Crown: Wrap a strip or sheet of paper around a child's head and tape the ends to attach. Cut a zig-zag shape around the top and decorate the outside.

✳ Start a Costume Trunk

One of the easiest ways to encourage theater play is to start a costume trunk or box, filled with pieces collected from closets and thrift shops. These items can include scarves, hats, ties, belts, capes, purses, petticoats, high-heeled or other unusual or period shoes, hard hats, aprons, Halloween costumes, costume jewelry, and clothing and accessories of all types. It's remarkably simple to transform a child into a character with just an item of clothing and a touch of imagination. Collecting fun costume items, and having a place for them, will make it easy to dress up and try on new characters.

❋ Make a Sock Puppet

When Anna was small, we witnessed firsthand the power of the simplest of puppets. A sweet purchased washcloth puppet gave us the idea, and perhaps the liberty, to create on-the-fly washcloth puppets for that first one to interact with. We spent many a bath time holding plain washcloths over our hands and giving them distinct voices to put on puppet shows. When Anna was very little, she talked to the puppets and told them things it seemed she might not have been able to articulate to us. "OK, puppet show…" her tale would begin. The puppets seemed to give her freedom and safety as well.

We later had the extreme fortune to meet Frank Gonzalez, a very playful artist and educator who delights both in sock puppets and in creating community art and experiences out of recycled materials. With Frank, we made many sock puppets, with materials on hand or readily available. As with many creative endeavors, we found that sock puppets can be simple creations or as limitless as one's imagination. Frank's were affectionately named Señor and Señorita Worm.

Slow Tip: You don't need an expensive or complicated puppet theater. Make a puppet show above the back of a couch, or between two tablecloth "curtains" under a table, or by hanging an adjustable shower rod in a doorway and looping and attaching two sheets or lengths of fabric over it for curtains.

You'll need:

- Sock
- 2 buttons, pom-poms, or craft eyes

- Red construction paper and/or felt
- Yarn, pipe cleaners, costume jewelry, or other decorations, optional
- Tacky or craft glue

Make a fist with your hand and place the sock over it and down your arm, with your thumb in the heel of the sock, to form a mouth. This will give you an idea of puppet positioning.

Sew or glue the buttons, pom-poms, or craft eyes to the sock puppet for eyes.

If you'd like, cut a construction paper or felt oval and fold it in half for a mouth. With the sock flat, glue the mouth in place.

Cut and glue a tongue of felt or paper. Sew or glue on yarn or pipe-cleaner hair, a felt flower headpiece or ears, and pipe-cleaner glasses, if desired. You can even adorn your sock puppet with costume-jewelry earrings!

Slow Snippet: Young children don't mind seeing the puppet master. Some won't notice, since they get so caught up in the story. Others find comfort in knowing that an adult is making the puppets move and talk.

✳ Make a Shoe-Box TV

This fun project uses basic recycled items and can awaken the storyteller in any of us. I remember making shoe-box TVs as a child, and my husband, Michael, being an animator by trade, particularly enjoyed creating them with Anna. You can make multiple story scrolls and change them through the back of the box. In doing so, you'll join nearly every ancient civilization in telling stories using scrolls, starting with the Egyptians, who created them on papyrus.

You'll need:

- Shoe box or a square-shaped box and lid
- Cardboard tubes (from paper towels, foil, or plastic wrap) or 3/4″ or wider wooden dowels, approximately 3″ longer than the height of the box
- 4–10 pieces of printer paper (8 1/2″ × 11″)
- Drawing materials
- Scissors, craft knife, and tape

Cut a large square or rectangle opening for the TV screen into the bottom of the box, leaving an even border of 1″ or more around all sides.

Holding the box with the TV screen facing you, cut one hole on each side of the top surface, each about 2″ from the side and 2″ back from the cutout section. Place the cardboard tubes into the holes so that they touch the inside of the box at the bottom.

Cut two bottom holes that line up with the top ones and run each tube through the bottom hole, leaving some tube sticking out of the top hole as well.

Cut the cardboard tubes, if necessary, so that about 1/2″ sticks out on the bottom and 1″–2″ on top. Leave the tubes out of the box.

Decide on a story you want to tell that primarily uses pictures.

Place the paper horizontally on a table or other drawing surface (cutting, if necessary, to fit the tube length—the paper's height should be slightly shorter than the tube). Draw one picture on each page, adding words, if desired. Leave at least 1″ on each paper edge and at least 2″ on the left edge of the first picture and the right edge of the last picture.

Lay the pictures out, left to right, in the order they will appear. Turn them over and, keeping the order, run a piece of tape down each back seam where two pictures come together.

Tape the beginning end of the paper story scroll to a tube or dowel. Holding the tube in your left hand, with the story starting on the left, gently roll the tube to the right, so that the paper begins to roll around it. You should see the pages, in their correct order, rolling around the tube. When you have a few sheets left of unrolled paper (a length that is longer than the width of the box), tape the closing end of the story scroll to the second tube. Holding that tube in your right hand, roll the tube to the left, so that the paper begins to roll around it. If the first tube was wound around the back of the paper, the second tube should wind around the front of the paper.

Place the tubes into the holes and gently tighten the paper story. Replace the lid box on the back. Decorate the front of the TV, if desired.

Gently turn the tubes to make the pictures move.

 Slow Tip: You can also use images from magazines or comic books to create your story.

Create a Secret Code

The ancient Spartans wrote secret messages on ribbons, which could only be read when wrapped around a precise-sized cylinder. Since then, people have been fascinated with coded messages as a way to share secrets with someone close. Have fun creating, sending, and decoding your own secret messages.

❋ Number Code

Number codes are some of the simplest codes to create.

You'll need:

- Paper
- Pen or pencil

Write each letter of the alphabet on a piece of paper.

Next to each letter, write the numbers 1 through 26 in order. If you want to create a more complicated code, assign numbers to the letters that are not necessarily in order.

Decide what you want your message to be.

Find the first letter of your message and write its corresponding number.

Continue writing the numbers that correspond to the letters in your code until you are finished. Put a dash between each number to avoid confusion between, say, 1, 5, and 15.

✳ Code Wheel

You'll need:

- Cardboard
- Drawing compass
- Scissors
- Two-pronged paper fastener
- Pin
- Pen or pencils

Draw two separate circles with the compass, one that is 3″ in diameter and one that is 4″ in diameter.

Cut them both out.

Place the smaller circle on top of the larger one and place a pin through both, at their center.

Draw twenty-six lines, as evenly as you can, around the circle going from the center of the small circle, out to the outer edge of the larger circle, creating wedges. If using the compass to create even lines, each angle from the center will be approximately 14 degrees.

Write the letters of the alphabet on the outer edges of each circle, one per wedge.

Place the paper fastener through the center of the two circles, leaving enough give for one to spin on top of the other.

Use the outer circle for the letters in the text in your code and the inner circle for the set of letters that will substitute for that text. For example, if the outer *M* falls over the inner *C*, then every time your message calls for an *M*, you would write the letter *C*.

Slow Tip: If you're cracking a code, start by trying to seek out the most common letter. In English, it is *E*. Other common letters are *T, A, O, I*, and *N*.

Make Your Own Invisible Ink

I first did this project with a troop of Brownie Girl Scouts, and then we continued to make invisible ink at home. Why not? It's fun to know that only a select few will be able to read your message. Here are two kinds of invisible ink, both of which are very easy to make and use.

☀ Lemon Invisible Ink

You'll need:

- 6–12 lemons, depending on the size of your group
- 1 cup per person or pair
- Paper
- Sticks, paintbrushes, or cotton swabs
- Flashlight or working lightbulb

Juice one lemon into each cup.

Dip the stick, paintbrush, or cotton swab into the juice and use it to write your message on the paper.

Allow the paper to dry.

To reveal the secret message, hold the paper up to the flashlight or lightbulb, or to the sun, if you are outdoors.

> ***Slow Snippet:*** What makes it work? The acid in the lemon juice weakens the paper and then turns brown when heated.

☀ Baking Soda Invisible Ink

You'll need:

- 1 cup baking soda
- 1 cup water
- Container, approximately 1 pint
- 1 cup per person or pair
- Paper
- Sticks, paintbrushes, or cotton swabs
- 1 cup grape juice concentrate

Pour equal parts water and baking soda into the container and mix well, then pour a little bit into each cup.

Dip the stick, paintbrush, or cotton swab into the baking soda mixture and use it to write your message on the paper.

Allow the paper to dry.

To reveal the secret message, use the stick or other item to spread a light layer of grape juice concentrate over the message, and watch it become revealed.

Slow Snippet: What makes it work? The acid reaction between the baking soda and the grape juice causes the message to appear.

HOW TO BLOW BIG, LONG-LASTING BUBBLES

» Make sure the bubble mix covers the entire opening of the wand or tool.

» Make sure the bubble and bubble tool touch only wet surfaces.

» If the day is too windy for big bubbles, seek a windbreak and form bubbles near that.

» Blow or wave the wand gently, just enough for the film inside to catch some air. Blowing too hard can cause the bubble to break or can create many small bubbles instead of one big one.

Blow Bubbles

Just the sight of a bubble floating by overhead can make even the most harried person stop and smile. Part science, part wonder, a bubble is simply a thin skin of liquid surrounding a gas. But you needn't know any bubble science to enjoy this fun and inexpensive activity. Best of all, bubbles can be made using ingredients you have around the house. When the weather's nice, I often make a bucket of bubble solution and leave it outside with wands and other fun equipment so Anna and others can make bubbles whenever they'd like. It's always fun and magical to create bubbles and run around to watch them trail behind you in the breeze.

✳ Recipe for Great Bubbles

There's no need to spend money on commercial bubble mixes. The best mixes come from ingredients that are inexpensive and easily available. You can leave a large batch in a bucket or tub for days without the solution losing its ability to form bubbles. Bubble mixes are best made at least a half hour before you need them, so they can settle.

You'll need.

- 6 cups (or parts) water
- 2 cups (or parts) Dawn dishwashing detergent
- 3/4 cup (or part) light corn syrup
- Measuring container
- Tub, bucket, or pan (large enough for the wands to fit inside)

If you can, use Dawn brand dishwashing detergent, for large, firm bubbles. Joy is second best.

If you're using the same container to measure both the water and the detergent, measure the water first to prevent the detergent from foaming in the container.

If your water is very hard, you may want to use distilled water.

Stir in the corn syrup gently. The solution should be smooth, not sudsy or foamy.

✳ Make Your Own Wand or Bubble Maker

There are wonderful commercial wands with very large, whimsically shaped openings; they're often available at toy stores and fairs. You can also make your own homemade wand.

> *You'll need:*
>
> - 2 or more wire hangers

Bend a clothes hanger into the shape of a circle and twist a couple of times to secure it.

Unfold a second hanger as straight as you can and attach it to the first to form a handle.

MORE BUBBLE FUN

Bubble Clusters: Put a small amount of bubble solution in a pie tin or on a cookie sheet. Blow into it with straws to create multiple bubbles in clusters.

Bubble within a Bubble: Put a small amount of bubble solution in a pie tin or on a cookie sheet. Blow a bubble with a straw. Gently lift the straw from the bubble to remove it. Making sure the straw is wet, gently insert it into the top of the bubble, so it enters at a 45° angle. Blow gently to form another bubble.

✳ Create a Bubble-Window Maker

You'll need:

- Cotton string with some absorbency
- Plastic straws cut into pieces

Run a length of string through the straws in a continuous line.

Leave some string between each straw and knot the string ends together.

You can make many shapes with the straws. Try a "bubble window." To make the window, lift the solution out of the bucket or pan in one plane and at an angle, which will help the film remain inside the shape made by the straws, so that it resembles a window. Put two wet hands through a bubble window and shake hands!

Slow Tip: Search around your house for other good bubble makers. Six-pack rings, strawberry baskets, funnels, cookie cutters, mason-jar rings, rubber bands, pipe cleaners, strainers, even fly swatters can all make fine bubbles. Often items with many smaller openings will produce masses of fun bubbles. Your hands are another wonderful bubble maker—especially if they are wet.

Run a Lemonade Stand Like a Pro

Lemonade is the quintessential old-fashioned, slow-summer drink. It's been enjoyed by people from medieval Egyptians to sailors and gold miners, many of whom drank lemonade to stave off scurvy, colds, and other diseases. It's refreshing, thirst quenching, and simple to make—and of course, it's the iconic beverage behind the time-honored lemonade stand. When Anna was small, one of her favorite things to play was shopkeeper, so it's no surprise that, when the time came, we got busy running many a thriving lemonade stand and creating fun memories in the process.

You'll need:

- Card or portable table, if there isn't one at your spot, and a tablecloth
- Chairs, optional (good for longer sales)
- Cash box, pencil box, or shoe box, and plenty of change, especially quarters and dollar bills
- Recipe ingredients (recipe follows) and ice
- 1 or more big pitchers or containers
- Cups
- Napkins and plates if you're selling baked goods
- Cooler for storing extra lemonade, optional
- Trash bags, if there isn't a can nearby
- Cover for the pitcher, if bugs or leaves are a problem
- Sunscreen, hats, or visors, optional

Tips to Help Your Stand Run Smoothly

Involve Everyone in the Planning

Even the youngest kids can help make a shopping list, count change, make lemonade, and be involved in all aspects of the stand. Get some neighbors to help too, to create a wonderful community activity.

Choose a Location

The three top determinants of a successful business? Location, location, location. If your street doesn't have much foot or car traffic, sell on a local corner or near a public place, such as a community or recreation center, school, library, grocery store, sports field, or residential open house. We've had great success at a natural stopping point on our local bike path. If your city requires a permit (yes, some do, even for kids), be sure to get one.

Advertise

Make a big, bright sign for your stand advertising the lemonade and any other goodies, along with their prices. Consider adding helium balloons. Of course, the best advertising is simply yelling, "Lemonade for sale!" in your loudest voice.

Follow Precautions with Cash

As profits mount, have an adult or older child put large bills in a fanny pack or purse.

Decide Whether You Want to Sell Anything Else

Baked treats and lemonade go together. Cookies, brownies, blondies, Rice Krispies treats, fruit bars, and other goodies can be made from scratch or a mix, or be store bought. Make and bag your own gorp. (See the recipe in the Camp in Your Backyard section. If you use chocolate, be sure to keep the gorp out of the sun.)

Make Some Other Key Business Decisions

Decide on a price for your lemonade and other items. Add up the expenses of starting the stand, and price accordingly to make a profit.

Consider raising money for a particular item or trip, or donating some or all of your proceeds to a worthy charity. Let your customers know if that's what you're doing.

Think about any other factors that will attract customers—the appearance of the stand, cleanliness, professionalism, and a friendly attitude. Greet each customer with a smile, and be sure to thank everyone for their business.

Take Some Safety Precautions

Wash your hands and tie back long hair before preparing food, and use clean equipment. Adults or older kids should handle sharp knives. Baked goods may be best prewrapped for individual sale. Check with your venue to find out whether there are local health requirements for making or selling food. Children should sell with a buddy, if not an adult. Always be aware of traffic.

Make and Taste Test Your Lemonade

The following is a good old-fashioned lemonade recipe that rides the line between tart and sweet.

✳ Classic Country Lemonade

This is a tasty, natural lemonade.

You'll need:

- 1 1/2 cups lemon juice (approximately 8 large lemons)
- 1/2 cup sugar
- 5 cups cold water
- 1 large lemon, cut into slices for decoration
- Pitcher
- Ice cubes

In a large pitcher, combine lemon juice, sugar, and 2 cups of cold water.

Stir briskly to dissolve sugar.

Add remaining water and ice cubes and stir briskly again.

Add decorative lemon slices, if desired.

Yield: Approximately 8 cups

Slow Snippet: On the January, 2004, debut show of *The Apprentice*, Donald Trump issued the challenge of which team could establish the best lemonade stand.

Camp in Your Backyard

Camping out in sleeping bags is fun any time of year—in a backyard, on a porch or balcony, even on the living-room floor. We camp on our deck as often as possible, with or without a tent. Anna especially enjoys camping out during sleepovers. Wherever you roll out the sleeping bags, these traditional activities can make the act of doing so even more of a fun adventure.

✳ Make Yummy Camp Treats

There's something about cooking and eating outdoors that enhances the entire experience, from the taste of the food to the joy of the company. Many people, when asked to recall the outdoor adventures of their childhoods, remember cooking over a fire. Doing so uses most of our senses, which tend to already be heightened merely from being outdoors. Luckily, the following camp and portable treats are just as much fun to make and taste just as good when on a hike, in the backyard, or in the house as they do out in the wilderness.

Edible Campfires

Eat a campfire? Why not! This fun and educational snack is easy to make and will help young campers remember that a real campfire is made with tinder, kindling, and fuel. They'll pick up a couple of safety precautions as well. I've made these many times with my family and with scout and youth groups. It's always very engaging and memorable. After you make it, you can eat the campfire or put it on display.

You'll need:

- Paper plate
- Spoon

- 1 cup water
- 1 cup cocoa powder
- Handful of pretzel logs or bread sticks
- Handful of raisins, chocolate chips, or minimarshmallows
- Handful of shredded wheat cereal, or similar cereal
- Handful of red hots or red licorice
- Handful of thin pretzels or baby carrots
- Handful of candy corn

On a paper plate, which represents a clearing in the ground, set up the "rocks" for your fire ring with a large circle of raisins, chocolate chips, or minimarshmallows.

Shape the pretzel logs or bread sticks into an *A* shape to create a base frame for the campfire.

Place shredded cereal—the tinder, or fire starter—in a teepee shape or mound inside the logs.

"Light" the tinder with a couple of red hots or pieces or licorice.

Place a layer of thin pretzels or baby carrots over that, to represent kindling. Don't forget to leave room for air to circulate just as you would with an outdoor campfire!

Add candy corn to represent an even larger fire.

Place more pretzel logs or bread sticks over the existing fire to give it more fuel.

Add more candy corn, if desired.

Have your separate cups of water and cocoa powder and your spoon handy, as you would buckets of water, dirt, and a shovel to put your fire out in an emergency.

Hobo Popcorn

Popcorn is extra fun to make outdoors over a fire, using one of the oldest cooking tools around—a stick.

You'll need:

- 1 tablespoon popcorn kernels
- 1 square heavy-duty foil, approximately 18" x 18"
- 1 teaspoon cooking oil
- Butter, salt, or Parmesan cheese, optional
- Skewer or stick

Place the popcorn and oil into the foil square.

Bring all the corners of the foil together to form a pouch.

Fold the foil to seal the pouch, making sure to leave room for the popcorn to pop, and tie the pouch to the skewer.

Hold the pouch over the fire and shake until all the corn has popped.

Open carefully and add butter, salt, or cheese, as desired.

Gorp

Some say that the word *gorp*, for the longtime campers' standby of trail mix, comes from the acronym "good ol' raisins and peanuts." Others claim that it stands for "granola, oatmeal, raisins, and peanuts." The word even appears in early twentieth-century dictionaries, with the meaning "to eat greedily," which is what one may be tempted to do with this salty/sweet snack.

The best gorp keeps well and provides plenty of energy while hiking or camping. One time we packaged and sold gorp, along with lemonade and cookies, on a local bike path, where it was very popular!

You'll need:

- Small containers
1 cup each of your choice:
- Raisins

- Dried cranberries
- Chopped dried fruit, such as apricots, apples, papaya, pineapple, dates
- Banana chips
- Nuts, such as peanuts, cashews, almonds, walnuts
- M&Ms
- Chocolate or carob chips
- Yogurt-covered raisins
- Sunflower seeds

Combine all the items together. (Skip the chocolate if you will be somewhere hot.) Divide into containers to take on a group hike.

Banana Boats

This gooey, easy, and fun camp treat is one of my family's favorites. Banana boats are tasty and super-filling as well.

You'll need:

- Banana
- Minimarshmallows
- Chocolate pieces or chips
- Peanut butter, caramel sauce, crushed cookies, or mint patties, optional
- Foil

Peel the banana down one side only.

Cut a trough down the peeled side of the banana or scoop a section out of the middle.

Fill the trough or section with chocolate and mini marshmallows, or other treats, as desired.

Place the peel back over the open part and wrap the banana in foil.

Cook on a grill or in the oven for about five minutes or until the chocolate has melted.

> **Slow Tip:** Stuck inside? You can still make banana boats in a conventional or toaster oven. Even the classic s'more can be cooked indoors by lining a small metal baking pan or toaster oven pan with foil and non-stick cooking spray. Place marshmallows on the pan and bake in a broiler or toaster oven, turning them halfway through cooking. Watch them to prevent burning.
>
> When the marshmallows are cooked, place them between squares of milk chocolate and graham crackers and enjoy an indoor camping treat!

✳ Make a Box Oven

Simple to make and lots of fun to use, box ovens employ one of the oldest energy sources of all, solar power. Although people have dried food in the sun for centuries, it took French-Swiss scientist Horace de Saussure to truly harness solar power for cooking. He used glass to trap heat and create convection while his peers in the 1700s were still burning mirrors. Anything that you can cook in a regular oven can be cooked in a box oven, though it's best to stick with recipes that don't require raw meat or eggs, until you're proficient.

You'll need:

- Outdoor space
- Large, sturdy cardboard box, with four sides and a bottom (no top or lids), such as a box for 10 reams of paper
- Heavy-duty aluminum foil

- Duct tape
- Cookie sheet or large cake pan
- 4 tin cans, filled with water to weight them
- Charcoal briquettes
- Charcoal chimney and fire starter, optional
- Matches
- Disposable foil tray or pie tins
- Tongs
- Small stone
- Recipe and cooking items
- Bucket of water for fire safety

Choose a hot day with full sun.

Completely line the box inside and out with foil, shiny side out. Tape only on the outside of the box (to avoid tape fumes getting into the food).

Choose a flat surface away from flammable objects and cover it with foil.

Use the tin cans as "feet" to hold the cookie sheet or cake pan, which serves as the oven tray.

Fill the foil tray or pie tins with briquettes, approximately one for every 40° of desired oven temperature, and light, or place briquettes into a charcoal chimney.

Light the charcoal or firestarter, if using.

Place the item to be cooked on the oven tray. Cupcakes, biscuits, English-muffin pizzas, and other items that don't require long cooking times all work well in box ovens.

Slide the briquettes under the oven tray when ready (indicated by their white color), using tongs to spread them if they have been in a chimney.

Place the box oven down over the items, using a small rock to lift part of the box off the ground for ventilation.

Follow your recipe for cooking times.

Box Oven Pineapple Upside Down Cake

You'll need:

- 2 boxes yellow cake mix, prepared
- 1 ounce butter or margarine
- 1 8-ounce can pineapple
- 1/2 cup brown sugar
- Dutch oven or large cake pan
- Second pan or cookie sheet

Place butter or margarine in the Dutch oven or pan and melt in the box oven.

Stir brown sugar and pineapple into the melted butter.

Pour prepared cake mix over the pineapple mixture.

Bake for 25 minutes or more, until cake is golden brown.

Remove from box oven and invert onto second pan or cookie sheet.

✳ Sing around the Campfire

Your campfire might be a beach bonfire, in a fireplace hearth, or even in your imagination. In any case, singing songs and creating music in a group are simple and surefire ways to add warmth to any occasion and make people feel closer to one another. Something magical happens when people lift their voices together. In times past, generations of family and friends regularly gathered around glowing fires, living-room pianos, and elsewhere to make music together. Music has provided some of my and my family's favorite memories.

Of course, you needn't limit your singing to the outdoors. I used to sing my favorite childhood camp songs to bond with

Anna and make her bath time more fun. I was once in a foreign country on a train car that broke down and went completely dark at night. A group began singing, and others joined in—it was a wonderful experience that proved both communal and calming.

HOW TO GET ANY GROUP SINGING

You don't have to be a fantastic singer to lead a group in songs. You just need some enthusiasm, a few good songs under your belt, and the following time-tested song-leading techniques:

» Be enthusiastic and project a confident attitude—and have fun yourself!

» Try to find a midrange key that is not too high or too low, and give the group a starting note.

» Know the songs in advance and practice leading them.

» Prepare the group to sing. If they've been sitting down, get them moving with an action song.

» If there's a song everyone knows, start with that.

» When you introduce a new song, sing a verse or chorus first, then teach it phrase by phrase. Sing one phrase and have the group sing it back to you. String more phrases together as the group gains confidence, then sing the whole song through.

» Maintain eye contact with many different people in the group.

» Choose a variety of songs that suit the mood you want to foster, perhaps rowdier action songs for the beginning of a singing session and quieter songs to end it. You'll want to mix up song types too, or gauge what the group might need to stay interested.

» If you are singing a round, have the group sing it all together first, before dividing into smaller groups. Direct with your hands to tell each group when to come in.

These traditional and newer songs are appropriate for all ages and many have familiar, chantlike tunes. As with many traditions that are passed down orally, there are variations in lyrics from group to group and person to person. I've included just a few of my favorite campfire songs to reflect different moods. You can also find many of the tunes online.

Action Songs

Action songs are a great way to start a singing session. In addition to being fun, participatory, and often silly, they get any nervousness about singing out of the body and allow younger children to move around before settling in.

Go Bananas

This super-silly song is popular with scout and camp groups. It's easy to sing because it sounds like a cheer, and the actions go well with the words. Start the song by calling out, "Did somebody say bananas? Bananas of the world unite! Bananas Split!" (see actions below).

Peel bananas, peel, peel bananas
Peel bananas, peel, peel bananas
Go bananas, go, go bananas
Peel, peel, peel, peel, peel
Peel, peel, peel, peel, peel
Go, bananas!
Bananas of the world unite!

Actions for each callout:
Unite—Clasp hands over head.
Split—Jump legs out and open arms straight out.
Peel—Raise alternating arms, thumbs facing behind you.
Go bananas—Dance crazily.

More lyrics:

Eat bananas—substitute *eat* for *peel* and pretend to sing with your mouth full.

Squish bananas—Substitute *squish* for *peel* and make a motion to squish the banana with two hands.

Cut bananas—Substitute *cut* for *peel* and make motions to chop the banana with alternate hands.

Other fun action songs include "Bazooka Bubble Gum," "Bingo," "John Brown's Baby," "Little Cabin in the Woods," "Once an Austrian Went Yodeling," and "When I First Came to this Land."

Add-On Songs

Add-on songs are fun because singers have to remember and sing what came before, in addition to any newly introduced lyrics.

She'll Be Coming 'Round the Mountain

Many people know this song from campfires past. More than 150 years old, it probably began as an African American spiritual, in which "she" was a train that would come to carry slaves to freedom. The lyrics have a way of building up excitement, and the repetition makes them easy to remember and sing.

> She'll be coming 'round the mountain when she comes (toot, toot!).
> She'll be coming 'round the mountain when she comes (toot, toot!).
> She'll be coming 'round the mountain, she'll be coming 'round
>   the mountain,
> She'll be coming 'round the mountain when she comes (toot, toot!).

Add rejoinders to the ends of new verses, so that by the last verse, you say them all. For example, on the next verse, you say the new rejoinder (whoa back) and then the old one (toot, toot): She'll be driving six white horses when she comes (whoa back, toot, toot!).

More verses:

Oh, we'll all go out to meet her when she comes (hi, babe, etc.).

She'll be wearing red pajamas when she comes (scratch, scratch, etc.).

We will all have chicken and dumplings when she comes (yum, yum, etc.).

We will kill the old red rooster when she comes (cock-a-doodle-doo, etc.).

She will have to sleep with Grandma when she comes (snoring noise, etc.).

Oh, we'll all shout "Hallelujah" when she comes (hallelujah!, etc.).

End by repeating, "She'll be coming 'round the mountain," with all the rejoinders.

Other memorable add-on songs include "Old MacDonald Had a Farm" and "There Was an Old Lady Who Swallowed a Fly."

Call-and-Response Songs

Call-and-response songs, or "echo songs," are by nature repetitive and easy to learn. They tend to get even reluctant singers to participate.

Boom Chicka Boom

This nonsense song is especially easy. The tune is a simple cheerleader-type chant. Singers will enjoy getting louder and singing in different styles, as well as moving around and being as sassy as they want to be.

Leader: I said a boom chicka boom!
Group: I said a boom chicka boom!
Leader: I said a boom chicka boom!
Group: I said a boom chicka boom!

Leader: I said a boom chicka rocka chicka rocka chicka boom!
Group: I said a boom chicka rocka chicka rocka chicka boom!

Leader: Oh yeah?
Group: Oh yeah?
Leader: All right.
Group: All right.
Leader: Let's get louder!

The leader then calls out various styles instead of "Let's get louder!" and changes the words accordingly:

Leader: Oh yeah?
Group: Oh yeah?
Leader: All right.
Group: All right.
Leader: [Fill in] style!

Photographer Style
I said a zoom clicka zoom! (repeat)
I said a zoom clicka, watch the birdie, smile a clicka zoom!

Surfer Style
I said a dude chicka dude! (repeat)
I said a dude chicka wipeout chicka whoa chicka dude!

Thunderstorm Style
I said a boom crasha boom! (repeat)
I said a boom crasha flasha crasha flasha crasha boom!

Barnyard Style
I said a moo chicka moo! (repeat)
I said a moo chicka watch your step, don't track it in the room!

Janitor Style
I said a broom push-a broom! (repeat)
I said a broom push-a mop-a push-a mop-a push-a broom!

Valley Girl Style
I said, like, boom chicka boom! (repeat)
I said, like, boom chicka rocka chicka gag me with a spoon!

Looking for more great call-and-response songs? Try "Princess Pat" and "Sipping Cider through a Straw."

Rounds
Rounds are often what people think of when they imagine singing around a campfire. For centuries, people have found them quite pleasing and pretty to sing, as two, three, or more parts weave together like threads. To sing a round, divide your group into two or three sections and have each one come in (and finish) one line after the previous group. Teach everyone the song in unison first.

I Love the Mountains
This rousing song of gratitude and recognition of the physical beauty that surrounds us has been popular for generations:

I love the mountains.
I love the rolling hills.
I love the flowers.
I love the daffodils.
I love the fireside,
When all the lights are low.
Boom dee ahda, boom dee ahda,
Boom dee ahda, boom dee ay,
Boom dee ahda, boom dee ahda,
Boom dee ahda, boom dee ay.

Rose, Rose

Tweens and teens, especially, love singing this somewhat mournful but very pretty song, which conjures images of wandering minstrels and troubadours of the Middle Ages. Many just sing the first verse:

Rose, Rose, Rose, Rose,
Will I ever see thee wed?
I will marry at thy will, sire,
At thy will.

Rose, Rose, Rose, Rose
Will I ever see thee wed?
What shall be the name of the lad, Rose?
Name of the lad?

Ding, dong, ding, dong
Church bells chime on an April morn.
Dawn will see thee married today, Rose,
Married today.

Come, come, come, everyone,
Join us in our happy home.
Celebrate the birth of our son,
Our firstborn son.

Other rounds include "Are You Sleeping?," "Kookaburra," and "Make New Friends."

Slow Snippet: The first known round is believed to be "Sumer Is Icumen In," or "Summer Has Come In," sung in Latin and Middle English.

Quiet Songs

Quiet songs help signal the close of singing time. Sometimes they occur when the campfire or natural light has become low. Often they follow the rhythm of the session. Young children, especially, can be energetic when they first come together and then calm down after a period of singing in a group. If this is a sleepover event, the calming effect can help everyone make the transition to bedtime. Singing quiet songs to officially close a circle or a day can also be very pleasing to people. (For more ideas about closings, see chapter 8.)

Day Is Done (Taps)

My scouting cohort traditionally ends campfires, activities, and even meetings with this song, just as my troop did when I was a child. It's very pleasing and adds a nice cap to events. It originated as an army bugle call to signify "lights out" and was popularized during the American Civil War. "Taps" today is sung in many languages, from Samoan to Icelandic.

> Day is done,
> Gone the sun,
> From the lakes, from the hills, from the sky.
> All is well,
> Safely rest,
> God is nigh.

More classic quiet songs include "Blowin' in the Wind," "Dona," "Five Hundred Miles," "Freight Train," "Michael Row Your Boat Ashore," "Today," and "Where Have All the Flowers Gone?"

Slow Tip: People sometimes feel especially safe sharing in the dark. With certain kinds of groups, you might want to ask questions or share thoughts around a circle.

Show an Outdoor Movie

Watching a movie outside is a special event. It provides the magic opportunity of watching lights flicker in the dark, combining aspects of the ancient campfire with the novelty of viewing a movie outdoors. For many summers, my family hosted movie nights in our driveway, where our family and friends sat on borrowed folding chairs, and at the neighborhood community center, where folks rolled out blankets on a lawn under starry summer skies. Either way, you'll want to have popcorn, snacks, and drinks on hand. You can even make your own posters or tickets!

You'll need:

- Movie on DVD or other format
- Player and powerful speakers or a guitar amplifier
- Projector (you can often borrow this from friends or rent one from camera or party-supply stores)
- Table or other steady surface for the projector
- Power source (and extension cord and surge protector, recommended)
- Plain wall or 1–2 white bedsheets, fabric, or a tarp for a screen
- String
- Hammer and nails or hooks
- Scissors

- Stapler or staple gun
- For frame: Wooden poles or PVC pipes, premade or home-made patio umbrella stands, heavy-duty tape, optional (See Make a Stand for a Movie Screen on this page.)

Choose the location for your movie, taking into account screen size and placement, space for viewers, and availability of electricity.

Plan to start the movie during dusk.

If you don't have a large exterior wall (or a fence to hang a screen), prepare your screen. You can staple two king-sized bedsheets together for an extra-large screen.

Fold the top of the sheet down about 2″ and staple to create a casing. Run string through the casing, leaving a few feet of string on each side.

String up the screen between two trees, and tie the screen to one or more nails or hooks in each tree.

If there are no trees in your location, decide which type of stand to make or use for each side of the screen (see instructions below). Be sure to properly anchor whichever type of stand you choose.

Practice with your setup at least once before the actual show-time, in case you need to make adjustments.

Make some popcorn and sit back and enjoy being a big-screen impresario, as well as the unique experience of outdoor movies.

✳ Make a Stand for a Movie Screen

Premade patio-umbrella stands are easy to find and relatively inexpensive. To make a movie screen stand out of them, you need two umbrella stands and the correctly sized wooden, metal, or plastic poles to fit inside them. Secure the ends of the sheet to the poles with electrical or other heavy-duty tape and place the poles so that the screen is taut. Prefer to do it yourself?

There are two quick ways to create stands and frames for your movie screen.

You'll need:

- 2 wooden or PVC poles, long enough to accommodate your screen height and anchoring method
- 2 buckets or household trash cans
- Mixing bucket and quick-setting concrete or sand (available at garden or hardware stores) and water, or 2 large wood squares, 2 foot-pad hardware pieces, a drill and screws, and sandbags, optional
- Electrical or heavy-duty tape, stapler, hammer and nails, string

If using concrete, prepare it in a bucket, according to directions. Set the poles into the buckets or pots. Have one person hold a pole while the other pours concrete around it. Let it set for at least twenty-four hours. Try to prepare these close to where you will show your movie, as they will be heavy when dry.

Slow Snippet: The first drive-in movie theater was created in the early 1930s by Richard Hollingshead, of Camden, New Jersey, who mounted a projector to the hood of his car and showed the images on a tree-mounted screen.

If using sand, pour it into the buckets or cans. Wet the sand and drive the poles into each center.

If using wood bases, nail or drill a foot pad sized to your poles into the center of each base. Place a pole into the opening of each foot pad.

For all methods:

Secure the ends of the sheet to the poles with electrical or heavy-duty tape. If possible, staple or nail the screen fabric to the poles or cut holes in it at intervals and tie them to the poles. Place poles so that the screen is taut.

Weight wooden or other bases with one or two sandbags each, if desired.

Slow Tip: Invite your neighbors to the viewing party—they will probably hear the movie anyway!

✳ Make Hand Shadow Puppets

This is a great activity to round out a movie night or campout. Have someone project a flashlight onto a wall or other surface. Hold your hands between the light and the wall in various shapes to create shadow puppets. Give your puppets voices and have them tell funny or scary stories. It can be amazing to experience the power that comes from simply adopting a voice: you might discover new characters and situations and enact whole shadow plays.

Slow Snippet: Shadow puppetry started two thousand years ago in China, where it was performed by oil-lamp light.

It can take some practice to make the shapes and place them in the beam of light so that they look like various animals. Here are a few classic shadow puppets:

Rabbit—Make a fist with one hand. Place the other palm over it and make a peace sign (for ears) with two fingers.

Hawk—Link your thumbs together, with your hands facing away from you. Stretch out your fingers and hands and flutter them like wings.

Spider—With palms facing you, cross your hands at the

wrist. Press your thumbs together to form the spider's head. Wiggle your fingers in a climbing motion.

Wolf or dog—Place your palms together, fingers facing away from you. Put your thumbs up to form ears. Let your pinkie drop to form a mouth. Bend your index fingers to create a forehead.

Camel—Lift one arm. Hold your hand in a loosely curved position. Hold the pinkie and ring finger together. Hold the other two fingers together, thumb pressed in. Curve both sets of fingers and hold them wide apart to form a mouth. Your arm, from the elbow up, will be the camel's neck.

Slow Tip: Backyard campouts call for Flashlight Tag. Follow the rules for basic Tag, tagging other players using a beam of light. Tagged players become the next "it."

Tell Fortunes

Nearly everyone enjoys having their fortune told. A fun activity during an indoor or outdoor gathering, fortune-telling offers a hint of mystery and just the right amount of interesting play. It allows everyone to have a turn being in the spotlight. Because fortune-telling is so personal, my family has found it to be especially wonderful during slumber parties. (For more slumber-party games, see chapter 2.)

✳ Nuts 'n' Bolts

Chances are that you've never considered the fortune-telling properties of common snack foods. Neither had I, until I got this idea from Tia Smirnoff, a longtime scout and youth leader in my community. Better yet? This activity serves multiple purposes—it gets a group settled, gives them something fun to do, serves as an icebreaker, and gives them a snack when the fortune-telling is over.

> *You'll need:*
>
> - Pretzel sticks
> - Cheerios or other round cereal
> - M&Ms in various colors
> - Small cups or bowls
> - Plates
> - Poster board and markers

Before the event, make a poster-sized chart titled "Tell Your Fortune." Divide the chart in half, length wise. On the left half, draw between eight and ten combinations with three possibilities each from the snack foods. Use simple symbols and colors to denote pretzel sticks, Cheerios, and M&Ms. Examples include the following:

Red M&M, green M&M, Cheerio
Cheerio, pretzel stick, Cheerio
Cheerio, yellow M&M, pretzel stick
Pretzel stick, pretzel stick, blue M&M

On the right half of the poster, next to each three-piece combination, write a fortune, such as:

You will make a new friend.
You will invent something.
You will run for office.
You will take a trip soon.

The combinations and fortune-telling possibilities are nearly endless.

Prepare cups or bowls with a scoop each of various snack foods, or have participants scoop their own.

Instruct participants to take three items from their cups and lay them out on plates or in their hands to see if the combination matches up with one of the fortunes. If they don't have a fortune, they keep drawing items one by one from the cup until they do. Once they've gotten a fortune, they are free to have their snack!

✳ Numerology

Numerology goes back thousands of years and was employed in many ancient civilizations around the world. It was the Greek philosopher Pythagoras, and his secret society, who invented the system of numerology that is closest to the one we use today. Numerology is more a predictor of personality and destiny, using one's birth date and name, than a fortune-telling device. It's fun and simple to do, and great for all ages (except the very young).

You'll need:

- Paper and pencils

Write down your birthday with the month, day, and year in numbers. For example, May 17, 2003, is written as 5, 17, 2003.

Add each separate digit together, to reach one total. For example, $5 + 1 + 7 + 2 + 0 + 0 + 3 = 18$.

Add any remaining digits together until the sum is one digit. For example, $1 + 8 = 9$.

What do the different numbers mean?

1—Leader: Initiates projects and follows through

2—Peacemaker: A good team member, diplomatic and well liked

3—Social butterfly: Charming, idealistic, friends with many

4—Rock: Likes routine, tradition, hard work, and nature

5—Freethinker: Enthusiastic explorer of ideas and places

6—Friend: Supportive, caring, loyal, and enjoys art

7—Individualist: Seeks answers to life's questions, large and small

8—Worker: Likes business, problem solving, and hard work

9—Achiever: Creative, energetic, able to act on ideas

Slow Tip: You can also add up the letters of your name to find your number. Write the numbers 1–9 across the top of a piece of paper. Under that, write the letters of the alphabet in three rows, with one letter under each number, so that A–I are under 1–9, J–R are under 1–9, S–Z are under 1–8. Write the letters of your name and assign each letter a number. Add up the digits together until you get down to one digit.

✳ Card Reading

Cartomancy, or fortune-telling with cards, was especially big in eighteenth-century Europe. Even Napoleon was said to have consulted the cards.

You'll need:

• Regular deck of playing cards

Remove the cards numbered 2 through 6 for each suit. That will leave a thirty-two-card deck with the aces, face cards (king, queen, jack), and cards numbered 7 through 10 for each suit.

Shuffle the cards and spread out the deck on a flat surface, facedown. Instruct the person who's having his or her fortune read to choose any three cards.

Lay those cards in a row, faceup. The cards represent, from left to right, the past, the present, and the future.

Ask a question of the cards and see what answer you think is revealed. Here are some common meanings of the cards:

Hearts—Love and Home
Ace—Happy home, friendship, a love letter
King—A fair-haired man
Queen—A fair-haired woman
Jack—A kind, fair-haired friend
Ten—Good luck
Nine—A wish come true
Eight—Visitors and parties
Seven—Harmony and calm

Diamonds—Business, Travel, and Change
Ace—Good news
King—A fair-haired man
Queen—A fair-haired woman
Jack—A kind, fair-haired friend
Ten—A change bringing good fortune
Nine—A new project, gift, or travel
Eight—A pleasant journey
Seven—Surprise news or gift, resolution of a small argument

Clubs—Business and Power
Ace—Happiness and wealth
King—A dark-haired man
Queen—A dark-haired woman
Jack—A kind, dark-haired friend
Ten—Luck with money or friends, travel
Nine—Achievement, possibly through a helpful friend

Eight—A small amount of money, the need to surround the self with
trusted others

Seven—Success from hard work, resolution of a small problem

Spades—Fate and Caution

Ace—Possible conflict

King—A dark-haired man

Queen—A dark-haired woman

Jack—A dark haired friend who may be untrustworthy

Ten   Resolution of a problem

Nine—A new beginning

Eight—The need to be careful and flexible

Seven—Advice that is best not taken

2

Slow Games

We are a huge game family. We'll play Boggle at breakfast, Monopoly at night, and card games in between. We also enjoy games while walking, traveling, being outdoors, and when by ourselves and with groups—in short, anywhere and everywhere we want to add an element of fun. Games allow us to break the ice with new people in a low-key way, to pass the time enjoyably, to challenge ourselves, and to create memorable occasions when neighbors and friends all come together for old-fashioned, unplugged fun. Games have a terrific bonding element to them as well—years later, our family still talks about the hilarious and memorable moments we have had playing games. Games also have a way of evaporating the day's cares and making any family more playful by allowing family members to truly be in the moment.

In addition, many games can be enjoyed by players of all ages in a variety of settings and don't require a lot of instruction or equipment.

Card Games

Playing cards are wonderfully portable and versatile. It's no wonder they've captured people's imaginations since the tenth century in China, when they depicted coins instead of today's symbols. I usually pack a deck in a backpack for family outings, and it keeps us busy for hours. Chances are you have a deck of cards somewhere in your home or can buy an inexpensive one at a nearby store. Your child will no doubt enjoy discovering the card games of your own childhood, as you enjoy playing together. We have very happy memories of a phase of especially epic crazy-eights games during our family card nights.

These are a few of our favorite child-friendly card games that can be played with two or more players.

❉ Slapjack

This fun, noisy game inspires hand-eye coordination and thinking on one's feet.

The Deal: Cards are all dealt, one at a time, to all players. It doesn't matter if some players have more cards than others.

Object: To win all the cards, by being first to slap each jack as it is played to the center.

Players take turns lifting one card from their pile and placing it face up in a common pile at the center of the table. Players must be careful not to see their own cards first. Whenever a jack is turned over, the first player to slap it takes all the cards in the common pile and places them in his or her own pile.

When more than one player slaps at a jack, the one whose hand is directly on top of the jack wins the pile. If a player slaps at any card in the center that is not a jack, he or she must give one card, facedown, to the player of that card.

When a player has no more cards left, he or she remains in the game until the next jack is turned. That player may slap at the jack in an effort to get a new pile. If the player fails to win that next pile, he or she is out of the game. Play continues until one player has won all the cards.

❉ I Doubt It

This easy game incorporates some of the bluffing aspects of poker. If you're playing with a large group, use two decks.

The Deal: The dealer gives two or three cards at a time to

each player in rotation. On the last round of dealing, the cards are dealt out one at a time as far as they will go.

Object: To be the first player to get rid of all of his or her cards.

The first player places between one and four cards facedown on the table and announces that he or she is putting down as many aces as the number of cards. For example, the player may put down three cards and say, "Three aces." Each player in rotation discards similarly, announcing the number of cards and their rank in descending order (e.g., ace, king, queen, jack, ten, nine). Discarding players may or may not be telling the truth. Any player at the table may say, "I doubt it," after any discard, and the player who put the cards down has to turn them faceup. If the player who discarded turns out to have made a true statement, the doubter must take the cards in question, along with all the other cards in the pile.

If the statement is false, the player who didn't tell the truth must take all the cards on the table, including those just put down, and add them to his or her hand. If two or more players doubt the statement, the one who spoke first is the doubter. When a statement is not doubted, the cards remain facedown in the pile until they are subsequently picked up. When the play gets down to twos, the next player begins again with aces. The first player to get rid of all of his or her cards wins.

✳ Crazy Eights

This fun game involves wild cards and a little memory and strategizing.

The Deal: Deal seven cards to each player. Place leftover cards facedown in the center to form the stock. One card from the stockpile is turned up to form the starter pile.

Object: To be the first player to get rid of all of his or her cards.

The first player must lay faceup onto the starter pile a card of the same suit or the same rank as the first one. Players follow in turn. If someone has no match, he or she must draw cards from the stockpile until a match occurs. If there is no stock, a player who is unable to play any card in the hand must pass. All eights are wild. A player putting down an eight gets to call the suit that the eight represents. The next player must put down a card of the designated suit or another eight. The first player to get rid of all his or her cards wins.

Board Games

There are so many fun, creative board games available. It's great to have some classic and newer ones around to play during gatherings of friends and family. These are just a few that I recommend (consult the packages for directions): Apples to Apples, Cranium, Pictionary, Taboo, and Scrabble are all great fun and come in junior versions. Bingo, Yahtzee, mancala, backgammon, Sorry, Boggle, and checkers are more classic games that have kept my family busy for hours. Trouble, Slamwich, and Hi Ho! Cherry-O are great for younger players. Set is a wonderful matching card game that is enjoyable and makes you think.

Charades

The extremely popular game of Charades can be enjoyed by people of all ages, playing as individuals or teams. It likely began as a riddle game in the royal courts of Europe—the word *charade* comes from the French for "chatter" or "gossip"—and spread to Victorian England. There, it was a popular parlor game that is essentially the same one we play today.

Object: To get the opposing team to guess a predetermined title, by acting it out without using any words.

You'll need:

- Strips of paper
- Writing utensils
- Hat or envelope
- Timer, optional

Divide into two teams. Tear or cut paper into ten or more strips per team. Each team writes a title of a book, movie, television show, or other item on each piece of paper. When done, the papers go to the opposing team, in an envelope or hat. Players take turns drawing papers and wordlessly acting out each title for their team to guess. You may opt for a time limit. Teams score points by successfully guessing the titles.

Charades usually follows an order. First, the team guesses what kind of title is being mimed (e.g., book, movie). This can be followed by the number of words in the title, the order of the current word being acted out (e.g., first, second), and the number of syllables in that word.

There are many standard and more unusual charade gestures:

- Movie—Hold a movie camera to one eye and crank your other arm, as you would with an old-fashioned movie camera.
- Television show—Draw a TV screen in the air with your fingers.
- Play—Sweep one arm in front of you to indicate a stage.
- Book—Place hands together in front of you and then open them, as if opening a book.
- Song—Pretend to belt out a song.
- Computer or video game—Hold thumbs up to a pretend console and move them up and down.
- Job or career—Pretend to hammer.
- Animal—Pretend to roar like a lion.

- Number of words in title—Hold up the corresponding number of fingers.
- First, second, or third word—Once players have guessed the total number of words in the title, hold up the corresponding number for the order of the word you are playing.
- Syllable in word—If you are trying to get people to guess one syllable, lay the number of fingers for that syllable (e.g., one for first, two for second) across one forearm.
- Sounds like—To get players to guess a word that sounds like the ultimate one, tug at one ear.
- Shorter—To get players to guess a shorter version of the word they are saying, make a chopping motion.
- Longer—To get players to guess a longer version of the word they are saying, draw your arms out.
- Short word—To get players to guess a short word like *an* or *the*, pinch a thumb and forefinger closer together.
- On the nose—When a player guesses the correct word, nod and touch your nose, to indicate that he or she guessed the word "on the nose."

 **Slow Tip:** Seeking a variation on charades? Have players act out activities that the group has enjoyed. This can be especially fun on New Year's Eve, to get people thinking about the past year.

More Timeless Games

There's no time like the present to learn some tried-and-true games. People have enjoyed these classic games for generations, and they are so much fun that they're ripe for a comeback.

✳ Marbles (Ringer)

They can be called plainsies, peewees, bumblebees, clouds, swirlies, cat's eyes, or beach balls. They can be made of glass, clay, agate, or steel. Although marbles and marble games seem to evoke another, slower era—and indeed, people have been playing marbles since ancient times in Pakistan, Egypt, and Rome—people of all ages play and even compete today. In the United States the National Marbles Tournament has been held on the Jersey Shore since 1922. The British and World Marbles Championship, played annually on Good Friday, goes all the way back to 1588, when two young men duked it out with marbles to determine who would win the hand of a local milkmaid. There are many marbles games, but ringer is the classic.

> *You'll need:*
>
> - 13 standard-sized marbles and 1 larger shooter marble for each player
> - Flat surface
> - Sidewalk chalk or string and tape

Draw a chalk circle at least 3' (and as large as 10') in diameter on a sidewalk or driveway, or tape a string circle in place on a carpet. The larger the circle, the more challenging the game. Place the thirteen smaller marbles in the center of the circle, in the shape of an *X*, or scatter them randomly. The first player sits just outside the circle and shoots his or her large marble (or shooter) into the circle, aiming at one or more smaller marbles, with the intent of knocking the smaller marbles outside of the circle but leaving the shooter inside the circle. To shoot, place one or more knuckles on the ground and flick the shooter marble with a thumb. If one or more marbles are successfully knocked out of the circle, and the shooter is left inside, the player collects the marbles that he or she shot outside the circle and shoots again from the place where the shooter landed. If the shooter lands outside the circle as well, the next player is up. The second and subsequent players do the same. Shooter marbles stay where they landed during each round. Players can also choose to shoot the shooter marbles of others further away from the circle so that that player will have a more challenging place to shoot from during the next round. Play continues until all the marbles have been knocked out of the circle. Players count their marbles to determine a winner.

Slow Tip: As with bowling, pool, softball, croquet, and other games that require hand-eye coordination, shooters should keep their eyes on the marble they are aiming at.

Slow Tip: You can make your own marbles, the ancient way, using polymer clay. Roll solid or multicolored pieces of clay into the shapes of marbles and bake according to package directions. Don't forget to make a few larger shooter marbles.

✳ Jacks

This simple classic game never goes out of style, and although it can be challenging at first, players do get better with practice. Sets of jacks can be found in many markets.

> *You'll need:*
>
> - 10 metal jacks and a bouncy ball (usually sold in a set)
> - Hard, level surface

Scatter the jacks onto the floor, asphalt, or other hard surface.

With your dominant hand, throw the ball up (approximately 6"; this can vary) near the jacks. After the ball bounces and is in the air again, scoop up one jack along with the ball. Put the jack aside. Repeat, this time picking up two jacks. Keep increasing the amount of jacks you pick up. If the ball bounces more than once on that turn, play moves to the next person. When there are no more jacks left on the playing surface, players count their jacks to determine a winner.

✳ Dominoes (Draw)

I've long been fascinated by dominoes, and I'm not alone. Domino sets date back a thousand years, to China, where they derived from five-thousand-year-old dice. Dominoes were originally carved from ivory or bone that were inset with small, round dots (called pips) of ebony. The Chinese version of dominoes morphed into the extremely engaging game of mahjongg. Dominoes enjoyed a resurgence in the United States in the 1950s, particularly in San Francisco and Texas. Although there are many dominoes games, draw is the standard.

> *You'll need:*
>
> - Set of dominoes
> - Flat surface
> - Paper and pencil for scoring

Place all the dominoes in a set facedown on the table or other surface. If two players are playing, each chooses seven dominoes. If there are more than two players, each player chooses five dominoes apiece. Don't show the other players your dominoes. The remaining dominoes stay off to the side and become the boneyard. The player with the highest "double" domino (e.g., six and six, or five and five) goes first and lays his or her domino on the table. The next player has to find a domino that matches the value on either side of the double domino. If the player has a match, he or she places the domino perpendicular to the double domino to begin a chain. The next player then has to match one of the values on one of the domino halves that are already on the table, adding to the chain. (Double dominoes are always placed perpendicular to the existing dominoes; dominoes with different values on each half are placed the long way, as if forming a train.) If a player doesn't have a domino of matching value to play, he or she takes a domino from the boneyard and keeps taking one until he or she finds a match. If there are no more dominoes left in the boneyard, the player passes his or her turn. The first person to run out of dominoes is the winner, and that player's score consists of all the points on the other players' unplayed dominoes. Sometimes, everyone has to pass because no one has a playable domino. In that case, the person with the lowest total on his or her remaining dominoes is the winner.

Slow Tip: Another fun thing to do with dominoes? Stand dominoes in an S shape or other pattern, just far enough to tip into each other, let one go, and watch the others topple in order.

☀ Pickup Sticks

It's called *Spillikans* in Canada, *Plockepinn* in Sweden, *Mikado* throughout Europe, and *Kau cim* in China, where the sticks were used as a fortune-telling device. Canisters of pickup sticks can usually be found in toy and variety stores, or you can even use twigs when outside.

You'll need:

- Set of pickup sticks, or approximately 41 sticks
- Flat surface

Hold the pickup sticks in a bundle, then release them so that they land in a pile. Players take turns trying to remove one stick at a time, without disturbing any other sticks. When a stick from the pile is disturbed, the next player takes a turn. Some players use a designated stick to remove other sticks. Commercial sets of sticks are often color coded, so that some sticks have higher point values. When all the sticks have been removed from the pile, players total either their number of sticks or the values of the sticks on the basis of their colors, according to package directions.

Jump-Rope Games

Jumping rope has gone in and out of fashion since ancient Egypt, when both men and women jumped over vines. It wasn't until the twentieth century that jumpers incorporated singsong games and rhymes. Many of these are passed down through the generations like oral history, with different regions using different chants. I learned many of these from my mom and passed them down to my daughter. Around the world, people play similar games, and the style is recognizable and universal.

You'll need:

- 1 regular jump rope for one person, or a longer jump rope for two turners to turn while a jumper (or more) jumps.

The jumper jumps over the rope each time it hits the ground. Jumpers can execute one jump each turn or take one big jump followed by one smaller jump each turn. A turn ends when the jumper fails to jump over the turning rope. The following are classic, easy jump-rope games. They don't have tunes so much as chants, so they are especially easy to pick up.

✳ A, My Name Is Alice

This is a fun add-on game that also calls for a little creativity and is different every time.

The first jumper starts with the letter *A* and fills in the blanks in the following sentence, however he or she chooses:

A my name is _____ and my husband's name is _____ and we live in _____ and we sell _____.

For example: A my name is Alice and my husband's name is Al and we live in Albuquerque and we sell apples.

If the jumper hasn't tripped up, he or she moves on to the letter *B*: B my name is Betty and my husband's name is Bob and we live in Boise and we sell beans.

Jumpers move through the alphabet as long as their turns last. New jumpers usually start with *A*, which makes it easy to compare how far each jumper gets, and choose new names.

 Slow Tip: A, My Name Is Alice can also make a fun travel game, no jump rope required!

✳ Teddy Bear, Teddy Bear

This jump-rope game is a little more advanced, as it requires players to pantomime the activity they are singing about (to the best of their abilities) as they jump.

Teddy Bear, Teddy Bear, turn around.
Teddy Bear, Teddy Bear, touch the ground.

Teddy Bear, Teddy Bear, tie your shoe.
Teddy Bear, Teddy Bear, that will do!

Teddy Bear, Teddy Bear, go upstairs.
Teddy Bear, Teddy Bear, say your prayers.
Teddy Bear, Teddy Bear, turn out the lights.
Teddy Bear, Teddy Bear, say good-night!

The following games involve counting as far as jumpers can get during each turn.

✳ Mabel, Mabel

Mabel, Mabel, set the table.
Do it as fast as you are able.
Don't forget the red (pause) hot (pause) *peppers*!

On the word *peppers*, start turning the rope doubly fast, counting a point for each turn. The jumper jumps until he or she misses and is out.

✳ Cinderella

Cinderella, dressed in yella,
went downstairs to kiss a fella.
By mistake
she kissed a snake.
How many doctors did it take?
1, 2, 3…

Count each turn of the rope successfully jumped.

✳ Apples, Peaches, Pears, and Plums

Apples, peaches, pears, and plums.
Tell me when your birthday comes.
January, February, March…

Count one month for each turn of the rope successfully jumped.

Hand-Clap Games

Hand-clap games are another traditional activity that people really enjoy. In many parts of the world, people of all ages and boys, as well as girls, participate. It's social, requires no special equipment, and can be done most anywhere. As with jump-rope games, the chants and claps can vary by region.

The following is a basic clap for two people. Stand or sit across from your partner. First, clap your hands to your thighs at the same time. Then clap your hands together at the same time. Reach your right hand diagonally in front of you to clap your partner's right hand. Clap your own hands together again. Reach your left hand diagonally in front of you to clap your partner's left hand. Clap your own hands together again, and then clap your hands to your thighs at the same time that your partner does. Keep repeating the clap to the beat of your chant.

✳ A Sailor Went to Sea

A sailor went to sea, sea, sea,
To see what he could see, see, see.
But all that he could see, see, see,
Was the bottom of the deep blue sea, sea, sea.

Slow Tip: The first diagonal right hand clap should occur on the first syllable of *sailor*. At the end, for "sea, sea, sea," clap both hands with your partner, straight across, at the same time.

✳ Miss Susie

Miss Susie had a baby.
She named him Tiny Tim.
She put him in the bathtub
To see if he could swim.

He drank up all the water.
He ate up all the soap.
He tried to eat the bathtub
But it wouldn't go down his throat.

Miss Susie called the doctor.
The doctor called the nurse.
The nurse called the lady
With the alligator purse.

In walked the doctor.
In walked the nurse.
In walked the lady
With the alligator purse.

Mumps said the doctor.
Measles said the nurse.
Nothing said the lady
With the alligator purse.

Out walked the doctor.
Out walked the nurse.
Out walked the lady with the alligator purse.

Slow Tip: The first diagonal right hand clap should occur on the first syllable of *Susie*. Add "purse, purse, purse" onto the end and clap both hands with your partner, straight across, at the same time.

☀ Say, Say, Oh, Playmate

This is a sweet, old-fashioned chant about friendship and play.

Say, say, oh, playmate,
Come out and play with me,
And bring your dollies three.
Climb up my apple tree.

Slide down my rain barrel,
Into my cellar door,
And we'll be jolly friends
Forever more, more, more!

I'm sorry playmate.
I cannot play with you.
My dolly's got the flu.
Boo hoo, hoo, hoo, hoo, hoo.

Ain't got no rain barrel.
Ain't got no cellar door.
But we'll be jolly friends
Forever more, more, more.

You can use the same three-clap ending mentioned previously for "more, more, more."

> **Slow Snippet:** As a child, my friends and I said, "rainbow" instead of "rain barrel," and "chocolate door" instead of "cellar door"!

Playground Games

Children on playgrounds and in fields and parks are usually thrilled to play one of these fun, easy games that require little or no equipment and have been creating memories for generations. I learned these in the classic settings of school playground and camp, and I have enjoyed them with my own family, scout troop, and other groups in parks, playgrounds, campgrounds, and neighborhood gathering spots.

✳ Red Rover

Because it's a game of strength, Red Rover should be played with a few precautions, which are noted. One benefit of the sometime-controversial game is that the game ends when everyone ends up on the same side, so there are no winners or losers.

Divide into two teams. Each team forms a line, approximately 30′ from the other. Team members all hold hands.

The first team decides who they are going to call over. They then call out, "Red Rover, Red Rover, let (player's name) come over."

The person named breaks free from his or her line and runs as fast as possible between any two players on the opposing team, in an effort to break through those team members' arms.

If the runner breaks through, causing those opposing

players' hands to drop, he or she chooses one person from the opposing team to join his team, and they both go back and join in their line.

If the runner fails to break through, he or she joins the opposing team's line.

Each team alternates calling people over until all the players end up on one side.

Note: To prevent injury, players should join hands, and not arms, so that they can easily unlink, and keep their hands at waist level. Players should be roughly the same size.

✳ Duck, Duck, Goose

South Asians know it as *Kho Kho*, Ghanaians as *Antoakyire*. German children play a version called *Plumpssack*, which involves dropping a handkerchief at one player's spot. Young children play this timeless game around the world.

Players sit in a circle, facing each other. Choose a player to be "it." "It" walks around the outside of the circle, tapping each person on the head and saying, for each tap, "duck," "duck," "duck." Finally, "it" taps a person on the head and says, "goose" and begins to run around the outside of the circle. The person who is tapped as a goose gets up and chases "it" around the circle. If the goose is able to tap "it" before he or she sits down in the goose's spot, then that person is "it" again. If the goose does not tag "it," then the goose becomes the new "it."

✳ Red Light, Green Light

Another game played around the world, Red Light, Green Light has many charming variations. In the Czech Republic it's called *Cukr, káva, limonáda, čaj, rum, bum!* ("Sugar, coffee, lemonade, tea, rum, boom!")

One player is chosen to be the stoplight. That person turns

his or her back to the group, which forms a line approximately 30'–90' away (depending on the ages of players). The stoplight calls out, "Green light!" and the players advance toward the player who is the stoplight as quickly as they can. When the stoplight wishes, he or she calls out, "Red light!" while turning around to see the runners. The runners must stop immediately. Any player caught moving after a call of "red light" has to go back to the starting line. "Green lights" and "red lights" are repeated until the first player reaches and tags the stoplight and is declared the winner. If all the players are out before they reach the stoplight, then the stoplight wins that round. The winner becomes the new stoplight.

Slow Snippet: Many cultures count, "One, two, three," and then shout a particular word instead of saying "red light." In Mexico, it's *calabaza* (pumpkin); in Israel, *herring*; in Italy, *estrella* (star); and in France, *soleil* (sun).

✳ Mother (or Father), May I?

Mother (or Father), May I? has both random and whimsical aspects that speak to small children, in addition to requiring some creativity in thinking up and executing new steps.

One player is chosen to be the mother. The other players form a line approximately 30'–90' away (depending on the ages of players). The first player calls out, "Mother, may I take (number and type) of steps?" Mother answers either "Yes, you may" or "No, you may not," and the player advances or stays where he or she is. (Some people play that Mother can offer an alternative number and type of step.) Players continue to inquire and take various steps. The first one to reach the mother wins and is the new mother.

Steps can include the following:

- **Baby steps**—as small as possible
- **Newborn baby steps**—crawling
- **Giant steps**—as big as possible
- **Backward steps**—with back toward the mother
- **Bunny steps**—two-footed hops
- **Scissor steps**—feet cross or uncross on each step
- **Robot steps**—stiff and robotic
- **Cinderella or princess steps**—balletic twirls
- **Tornado steps**—crazy twirls
- **Umbrella steps**—starting by standing with legs apart and facing the side of the field instead of the front, then each step begins with the back leg and makes a 180° arc so that the player moves forward and faces the opposite direction on each step

✳ Capture the Flag

Another game from many of our childhoods, this one works on a playground, field, or neighborhood street.

You'll need:

- 2 flags or bandannas

The games works best in an area with varied terrain, such as trees or other landforms.

Divide into two teams. Mark a line in the center of the play area. Each team's territory, or base, is on either side of the line. Each team also picks a spot for its jail, usually far from the flag. Determine a time period (5–10 minutes) during which each team hides its flag in its own territory, usually in the part farthest from the opponent. Once flags have been hidden, the teams meet in the middle.

Each player tries to enter the other team's territory and find its flag. In addition, the player has to bring the flag back into his or her own team's area without getting tagged by an opponent. Tagged players go to jail and sit out the game until tagged by a teammate, at which time they can rejoin the play by walking back into their own territory first. Players can be tagged only within the enemy's base. If a player is tagged while transporting the flag, the flag is dropped at that spot. The game is won when an opposing flag is successfully captured and brought to the home base.

❋ Kick the Can

My husband, Michael, has fond memories of epic games of Kick the Can in his Pennsylvania neighborhood growing up. They'd continue for hours, as good games often do, with kids hiding behind trees in the conjoined backyards, strategizing and running, sometimes long after dark, on leisurely summer nights.

You'll need:

- Large can or bucket
- Flashlight, optional

Place a can on the ground and designate an area near it as a jail. Choose an "it," who counts to a high number (usually between fifty and one hundred) while the other players hide. When the number is reached, "it" moves away from the base and starts to look for the other players, who in turn are attempting to return to the can to kick it. If the person who is "it" sees a player, he or she calls out that person's name (while shining a flashlight on the player, if at night) and tries to kick the can first. If that happens, the player goes to jail. If the player reaches the can first and kicks it, then that player can hide again and any jailed players are freed. The game ends when everyone except "it" is in jail.

✳ Four Square

Not sure what to do with that four-square court painted on your local or school playground? This classic game couldn't be easier or more inclusive. If you don't have a four-square court, you can easily draw your own with chalk.

> *You'll need:*
>
> • Standard-size rubber playground ball
> • Four-square court, or chalk to draw one

If there isn't a court, draw a large square, approximately 16″ × 16″. Divide that into four squares, each 8″ × 8″. Letter the squares clockwise, from A to D. The player in the A square begins by bouncing the ball once in his or her own square, then hitting it underhand so it bounces into the D square. The receiving player then hits the ball into another square, with play continuing until the ball bounces more than once or goes out of bounds. When that happens, the player who didn't hit the ball in time, or hit it out of bounds, moves to the D square, and the other players move up in the alphabet. If there are more than four players, a waiting player in line replaces the one who would have moved into the D square, and that player goes to the back of the line. Play continues without anyone having to permanently leave the game.

✳ Spud

Reminiscent of Dodgeball, another game from a past era, Spud offers a more intricate, playful, and hopefully gentle version of that game.

> *You'll need:*
>
> • Rubber playground ball or other soft ball

Players stand in a circle, with one in the middle holding the ball. Those around the circle count off by going around the circle and each saying a number, from one to the amount of players in the circle. The player in the middle throws the ball up in the air as high as possible and yells out one of the numbers.

Everyone scatters as far away from the circle as possible except the person whose number was called. That player catches or picks up the ball and simultaneously yells, "Spud!" At that moment, the other players freeze. The player with the ball then takes up to three giant steps toward any other player. He or she then throws the ball at that player, who must keep his or her feet planted but can move any other body part to avoid being hit. If the player is hit, he or she gets an *S* and becomes the next "it." If the thrower misses or the ball is dodged, then the thrower gets an *S* and is "it" again. When a player accumulates the letters to spell *spud*, that person is out of the game. The last person left, or the one with the fewest letters at a set end time, is the winner.

Tag Games

Based on the simple premise of chasing and catching, Tag is one of the most common and enjoyable games around the world. It's great for giving players an opportunity to run around. There are tons of creative and cultural variations to Tag, which is called Tip, Tig, Dobby, and Chasey in other parts of the world. To play, simply choose an "it" who counts to a set number before chasing others. When "it" tags a player, that person becomes the new "it." Some play with a safe, tag-free base. Here are a few of the many variations on basic Tag.

❋ Freeze Tag

Once players are tagged by the person who is "it," they are frozen and must stay perfectly still. They become unfrozen when another player runs up to them and tags them. If a frozen player moves before being unfrozen, and is seen and called out by "it," that player is out of the round.

Slow Tip: Want to play Statue Tag? Freeze in an especially dramatic pose, like a statue.

❋ Blob Tag

Once a player is tagged by the person who is "it," the two join arms and become a blob, which chases players together to try to tag them. Other players who are tagged also join arms and become part of the blob. Some play a version in which, when the blob reaches four people, two split off to become a new blob. The last person standing alone becomes the new "it."

❋ Octopus Tag

You'll need:

- Soft ball or rolled-up pair of socks, optional
- Playing area marked with two ends

Players all start at one end of the playing area. The person who is "it" stands in the middle and calls, "Fishes, come swim in my ocean!" Players try to run toward the other side without being tagged or having a ball successfully thrown at them by "it." Once tagged, players become tentacles—they stand in the spot where they are tagged but stretch out their arms in an effort to help tag others. Players who reach one side can be safe or can proceed back to the other side. The last person standing becomes the new "it."

Slow Tip: Try Octopus Tag in a swimming pool.

✳ Pizza Tag

Choose two players to be "it." The remaining players start at one end of the playing area and count off, in order, "pepperoni," "mushrooms," "sausage," "olives," and "cheese." The two people who are "it" are pizza makers, and they take turns calling out a topping. Players who are that topping try to run past the pizza makers to the other side of the playing area, where they are safe. Once tagged, players sit or stand and stretch out their arms in an effort to help tag others. Players who reach one side can be safe or can proceed back to the other side. The last two people standing become the new pizza makers.

✳ TV Tag

When players see the person who is "it" approaching, they must crouch down and say the name of a TV show to be safe. Show names can be used only once per round. If a player can't think of a TV show in time, he or she becomes "it." The person who is "it" must move once a player crouches down. You can also play variations of TV Tag with girls' names, fruits, animals, or any other category you'd like.

✳ Everybody's It

In this game, everybody is "it," which means that anyone can chase and tag anyone else. If a player is tagged, he or she freezes by bending over forward. Players can unfreeze the frozen players by running through the hoops they make with their bodies. This game usually ends when everyone is tired.

Slumber-Party Games

Slumber parties lend themselves to certain types of games—silly, scary, revealing, bonding—that might not occur anywhere else. Our family has wonderful slumber-party game memories, as do I, from my own childhood. Our funniest memory may have been the time Michael was telling the girls a scary story and the doorbell rang with a pizza delivery. The girls just about jumped out of their skins! The following games and activities will entertain party guests, create classic memories, and help break the ice for those who don't know one another well. Try to be prepared with a list of games and any required equipment, especially for younger children. With kids about eleven and older, be sure to allow them some downtime for talking and sharing. With any age group, switch gears if a game isn't working.

✸ Freeze Dance

This game gets everyone up and dancing to favorite music. Choose the music in advance of the party.

> *You'll need:*
>
> • Music and player or radio

The leader or parent plays music and players dance to it. The wilder the better! When the music stops, dancers stop in place. If any move at all, and the leader catches them, they are out. Music and dancing continue until there is one person left.

✳ Makeup Race

Girls' slumber parties just seem to call for a game involving makeup.

You'll need:

- 2 or more cosmetic bags or dopp kits, with a top opening, or a lunch bag
- Box or bag of cotton balls
- Cosmetic items, such as lipstick, lip balm, powder compacts, mascara, and eye shadow
- 2 or more spatulas or oven mitts
- Blindfold

Divide the group into two or more teams. Each team places a cosmetic bag in front of them. Scatter equal amounts of cotton balls and cosmetic items on the floor around each bag. Players take turns being blindfolded and attempting to scoop up the items with one hand and in one scoop, using either the spatula or the oven mitt, and placing them into the cosmetic bag. The cotton balls are especially tricky to feel. Team members who are not blindfolded can shout directions. The first group to get all their items into their bag wins.

✳ Celebrity Dream Game

This game offers a chance to turn your dream celebrity into the real thing.

You'll need:

- Magazines with pictures of celebrities
- Scissors

Before the party, go through magazines and cut out pictures of celebrities who may be interesting to the guests. Try to have more photos than guests. There can be more than one photo of the same person. Close to bedtime, lay out the pictures for the group to see. Have each guest choose a photo to put under his or her pillow and in the morning, ask whether anyone had a celebrity dream.

✳ I Hope To—I Would Never

Slumber parties are also fun times to reveal and learn about one another. This game provides a fun, entertaining, and safe way to do that.

> *You'll need:*
>
> • Paper and writing utensils
> • Kitchen timer

Each player divides a piece of paper into two columns and labels them, "I hope to" and "I would never." Give guests ten minutes to write down five things in each column: things they hope to do and things they would never do. When the time is up, gather the sheets and shuffle them. Hand a sheet to each player. If someone receives his or her own sheet, it goes back into the pile. Players then read the answers on the sheet they hold. Others call out the person they think wrote each, and the player writes down the guessed names and the numbers and names of people guessing. When that's done, players reveal who wrote what. If guests wish to play for points, points go to the person who stumped the most people and to the person who guessed the most correctly.

✳ Murder in the Dark

This is another classic slumber-party game—a little scary, a little silly—and it has lots of variations.

> **You'll need:**
>
> • Deck of cards with one ace and as many other cards as there are players

Deal one card to each player. The person who receives the ace is the murderer. Players keep their identities secret. Predetermine the area of play, whether it's one room or more. Choose one player to turn out the lights. Players begin walking around in the dark. The murderer creeps up to other players and taps them on the shoulder. When tapped, players fall down "dead," as dramatically as possible. Murderers try to kill as many victims as they can. If a player runs across someone who has been murdered, he or she yells out, "Murder in the dark!" and the lights get turned back on. Players who are still "alive" take turns guessing who the murderer was. The first person to guess correctly wins the game.

Slow Tip: A less active, but perhaps trickier, version of this game can be played in a circle, with the lights dimmed and the murderer winking at victims to kill them. Victims count to five before dying. If someone guesses who the murderer is, he or she wins.

For other slumber-party activities, see the sections Tell Fortunes in chapter 1 and Slumber-Party Crafts in chapter 3.

Team-Building and Icebreaker Games

This group of games is especially helpful for scout troops, field trips, large groups, groups with time on their hands, and even ordinary groups that are a little, well, high-maintenance. They focus less on winning, being "it," and elimination than they do on participation, creativity, getting acquainted, cooperation, and fun. I learned many of these through Daisy Kiehn, a marvelous Girl Scout trainer, who in turn learned many of them from the 1974 *The New Games Book* by the New Games Foundation.

✳ Icebreakers

These are great to bring out to help people loosen up, start playing, and get to know one another.

Instant Replay

This is a cute game to play that helps players both introduce themselves and learn one another's names.

Players stand in a circle. The first player steps into the middle and performs an expressive action (e.g., jumping, outstretching his or her arms, bowing, making a funny face) while calling out his or her name. The other players step in and do the same action while saying the person's name. This is repeated until everyone has gone in.

Punchinello

A similar game to Instant Replay, Punchinello was a favorite of mine when I was a Brownie scout and of my troop when I was a Brownie leader.

Players stand in a circle, with one person in the middle. Everyone around the circle sings a song.

What can you do?
Punchinello, funny fellow.
What can you do?
Punchinello, funny you.

The person in the middle then does something physical, such as jumping up and down, skipping, or patting him- or herself on the head. Players around the circle begin to do the same action while singing:

We can do it, too.
Punchinello, funny fellow.
We can do it, too.
Punchinello, funny you.

The person in the center then shuts his or her eyes and spins in a circle, with a finger pointed out toward the players, who sing:

Who do you choose?
Punchinello, funny fellow.
Who do you choose?
Punchinello chooses you.

The person who is pointed at is the next Punchinello and comes into the center.

Human Knot

Cooperation is a hallmark of Human Knot, a classic team-building game. Use it to set the tone for a group event.

Players form a circle, with their shoulders touching. Each player puts one hand into the center and takes the hand of another player. Don't worry if there are an uneven number of hands. Each player then puts another hand in and grasps a different hand, so that everyone has at least one hand held. Players then try to untangle themselves and come out into a circle without letting go of any hands. Yes, it can be done!

✳ Games That Invoke Laughter

Laughter loosens people up and helps create memorable experiences. These games travel easily from field to slumber party, from younger children to slightly jaded preteens.

Ha-Ha

This super-silly game is great at gatherings where people already know one another.

Players lie down in a way that allows each person to rest his or her head on someone else's stomach. When everyone is situated, the first player says, "Ha." The second says, "Ha, ha." Each player adds a "ha" on his or her turn. The object—and the challenge—is to get through everyone's turn without someone cracking up with laughter.

O-Kee-Fen-O-Kee

A feature of "new games" is that they can foster imaginative play. This game certainly does. We have had a lot of good dramatic fun with it.

> *You'll need:*
>
> • Parachute or bedsheet

Players form a seated circle, holding the parachute or bedsheet, which represents the Okefenokee Swamp, chest high. Someone is chosen to be an alligator, and that person slides under the sheet. The players begin to chant, "O-kee-fen-o-kee, O-kee-fen-o-kee," over and over, in silly or scary voices. The alligator grabs one of the players by the ankle, and that person has to join the alligator in the swamp. While going under, it's most fun when players scream and make very dramatic noises. Once in the swamp, the victim becomes another alligator, who can also grab people and pull them under. The game continues until everyone is in the swamp.

Poor Kitty

Sometimes the silliest games have a lot of longevity. This is another game I played when I was young, and it still manages to amuse new generations.

Players form a circle. One person is chosen to be the kitty. The kitty goes up to each player, one by one, and meows, purrs, and otherwise very hammily acts out being a kitty. The player has to pat the kitty on the head, three times, while saying, "Poor kitty, poor kitty, poor kitty," without laughing, regardless of how outlandish the kitty acts. The first person to laugh or smile at the kitty's antics and not be able to get through saying "poor kitty" three times is the next kitty.

✳ Active Games

These physical games are good to have on hand when the group needs to move around.

Catch a Puppy's Tail

I've watched this easy game become a new favorite of many groups.

> *You'll need:*
>
> • Bandanna

Players form a train with hands on the hips of the person in front. The last player sticks the bandanna out of a back pocket or pants waist. The person in the front of the line tries to steal the bandanna while the person in the back of the line tries to protect it. Those in the middle help however they can, all while not letting go of one another. When the tail is stolen, the person from the back moves up to the front and the game begins again.

Islands

Strategy and cooperation are required for this game.

You'll need:

- 6 or more (depending on group size) paper plates, Frisbees, or hula hoops

Toss plates or other objects around a large playing area. A designated person yells, "Go!" and players walk, without knocking anyone, to a plate (island), and touch it, also without knocking or touching anyone. Players who touch another player are out. Plates are removed, one at a time, and play is repeated until there are only two islands left.

I Like My Neighbors

This game provides a fun twist on Musical Chairs and the added benefit that no one is ever out.

You'll need:

- 1 fewer chair than there are players

Players sit in a circle of chairs. The person who is "it" stands in the middle and says, "I like all my neighbors except those wearing socks" or "those who had cereal for breakfast" or "those with brown hair" or any other characteristic. Anyone with a named trait gets up out of his or her seat and tries to sit in a different open seat, as does "it." The one without a seat becomes the next "it."

Slow Tip: Seeking a noncompetitive Tag game? Try Blob Tag or Everybody's It.

Safe, Fun, and Drama-Free Ways to Choose Teams

Some games require teams. Some groups fall into teams nicely, whereas others can use a little help. Over the years, I've learned and utilized a lot of ways to divide groups into teams that avoid hurt feelings and end up being as much fun as the subsequent game.

✳ Birds of a Feather

I got this idea from a naturalist at our local Audubon Center. It's so clever (and even teaches about the flocking characteristics of birds), that I've used it many times.

> *You'll need:*
>
> • Index cards and pen

In advance of the activity, decide how many groups or teams you'll need and designate each one to a type of bird whose call you know. Write each bird type and its distinctive call on the appropriate number of cards.

Some birds and their calls:

- **American robin**—cheerio cheerio cheep
- **Black-capped chickadee**—fee-bee fee-bee
- **Dark-eyed junco**—dit dit dit
- **Hermit warbler**—zwee zwee zwee zeet zeet
- **Lapland longspur**—tee-lee-oo tee-lee-oo
- **Northern cardinal**—who-eet who-eet wheet wheet wheet
- **Red-shouldered hawk**—keee-ah keee-ah
- **Western scrub jay**—swee-tie swee-tie

Distribute the cards evenly and explain that participants will say their calls repeatedly while trying to "flock" with other birds who sound the same. Those will be their teammates. Make sure to tell them to try to really sound, and perhaps act, like a bird.

☀ Vowels

This game uses the same "flocking" concept as Birds of a Feather.

Everyone gathers together. People start chanting the first vowel in their names while searching for others who are saying the same vowel. Players gather with their vowel mates. If you end up with too many or unbalanced teams, then combine some together.

☀ Count Off

This system really mixes people up, because no one is teamed with the person they stand next to. (Shhh—don't tell.)

Players stand in a circle and count off, alternating saying "one" and "two" if two teams are needed. (Add more numbers if more teams are needed.) The ones become one team and the twos become another.

✸ Birthday Lineup

This game can serve as an icebreaker, too.

Have players begin to line up according to the order of their birthdays, from January through December (or any months you choose). This calls for some cooperation, as people determine their order. When they're done, find the halfway point in the line and divide the group.

Chants for Choosing It

Just as with teams, there are those times when a game needs an "it" to start. Like jump-rope and hand-clap games, there are lots of old-fashioned ways to choose "it." Most employ one person doing a simple chant while alternately pointing between him- or herself and another player on each word. You can rest on one knee, with one foot out and alternately tap yours and the other players' feet. These chants don't really have tunes and are easy to pick up.

✸ Engine, Engine, Number Nine

Engine, Engine, Number Nine
Going down Chicago line.
If the train should jump the track,
Do you want your money back?
(Second player answers yes (or no.)
Y-E-S (or N-O) spells yes (or no) and
You are not it.

✳ My Mother and Your Mother

My mother and your mother
Were hanging out clothes.
My mother punched your mother
Right in the nose.
What color was the blood?
(Second player says a color, like "red")
R-E-D spells red and
You are not it.

3

Slow Crafts

Passing simple crafts down from generation to generation is a time-honored way to gather together. Although it's no longer common to have sewing circles or quilting bees, a lot of us yearn for the kind of closeness and time together that such circles can foster. Crafting together can help your family discover the joy of making something, whether it's a safety-pin bracelet or muffin-tin crayons. There's also something wonderful that happens when everyone is engaged, side by side, in a craft activity—time expands just a bit, new conversations occur, and family memories are created, along with fun, useful items.

Crafts have brought my family together many times, especially on slow weekend afternoons when we've gathered to tie-dye clothes (no white items were safe), make special candles and soap that we later gave as gifts, create simple dried-bean mosaics, or make flower fairies and fairy accessories that later became beloved play items.

We also learned that it really doesn't matter what you're creating or how simple or complicated the project is, as long as those participating enjoy the process. Some days we choose a project that we can complete in less than an hour, whereas other days call for longer projects that luxuriously spill into other days and nights. The only constant that I've seen is that crafting brings families and groups together time and again.

A note on these craft activities: Age range and length of time required for each project varies widely. Please read the instructions completely to decide whether a project is right for you. Most of the projects use inexpensive materials that are available in your home, outdoors, or at most grocery or craft stores.

Classic Scout Crafts

My family and I have had a long relationship with scouting, all having spent many formative years as scouts. I had the privilege of being a leader for Anna's troop for seven years. Just like the best youth groups and nature clubs, scouting get kids outdoors and out of their usual environments, to meet new people, try new things, and explore the world and themselves. Some of the best aspects of scouting (and certainly the traditional craft projects) can of course be done by family and other groups as well.

✳ Sit Upons

Sit-upons are easy to make. Although many of us made them as kids, sit-upons remain a practical item for Scouts or for any of us who find ourselves outdoors and in need of a portable, cushioned seat. When I led a troop of six- and seven-year-old Brownie Girl Scouts, this was one of the first crafts we did as a group. Gathering around a picnic table to craft brought everyone together and helped the girls get to know one another in a low-pressure way. Each girl was proud of her accomplishment and happy to have made a useful item that she would take out even years later, any time the troop was outdoors. Once you make a sit-upon, you'll be surprised just how often you use it.

You'll need:

- Vinyl tablecloths or other durable and waterproof fabric (see size, below)
- Standard hole punch
- 3 yards of thick yarn or plastic lace

- Newspapers, cut into 13 1/2" squares
- Tape, optional

Cut two 14" squares of vinyl or other fabric, or one piece that is 14" × 28".

Lay two sides on top of each other, with the right sides facing out, or fold the long piece in half, with the right sides out.

Use the hole punch to punch all around the open sides every 1/2"–1", and about 1/2" from the edge. (Adults may need to help with this.)

Starting at one corner, thread the yarn into a hole and knot it on one end. Use an overlay or whip stitch (around the back and up through the next hole) to stitch the yarn around the open sides. Use tape to thicken the yarn end, such as on a shoelace, if necessary.

Slide in newspaper to the desired thickness and stitch up the fourth side.

Tie the ends of the yarn together and trim.

✳ Tie-Dyed Bandannas

Tie-dyeing may feel like it came onto the scene in the 1960s, with ultrabright rainbows and sunbursts, but it actually dates back five thousand years, to Indian Bandhani dyeing. Although the earliest designs were big on solid dots, you can use any system of folding and tying with rubber bands to create unique patterns and designs. Once hooked, you may want to turn all your white cotton items into colorful, tie-dyed creations. One year, in addition to tie-dyeing shirts and bandannas (and, yes, underwear), we tie-dyed a laundry bag for Anna to take to sleepaway camp. Not only was it a fun project on a large canvas; the bag was sure not to be confused with anyone else's.

Bandannas are a great project if you have a large group or a short amount of time.

You'll need:

- White bandannas or other items to dye (cotton or other natural fabric is best)
- Dye packets in desired colors, available at fabric, craft, and specialty stores
- 1 bucket of water per dye color
- Sticks for stirring
- Salt (to add to the dye)
- Rubber gloves
- Rubber bands
- Trash bags, if needed for ground cover

Begin to fold the bandanna accordion style by making a narrow fold up from the bottom of your bandanna.

Turn the bandanna completely over so the fold is at the top, facedown.

Make another narrow fold in the opposite direction. Continue until your bandanna is completely folded.

Once you have a long, narrow item with many folds, tie rubber bands in the places where you don't want the dye to come through. Don't want too much white? Loosen some of the folds.

Wearing rubber gloves, follow package instructions to create dye.

Dip the bandanna in the various colors, along its length, with lighter colors first. To achieve a rich color, keep the fabric in the dye for fifteen minutes or longer. If using single colors, stir when possible to ensure even distribution of color.

When done, carefully wring out any excess water and rinse in cold water until the water runs clear. Hang to dry. Wash separately the first time to be sure the colors don't run.

Slow Snippet: During the 1920s and 1930s, the U.S. government distributed pamphlets suggesting tie-dyeing as a thrifty alternative to buying new clothes. Clothing, curtains, and tablecloths were made from flour and sugar sacks and dyed using blackberries, onionskins, marigolds, and red cabbage. Dye companies jumped in and encouraged housewives to dye their old corsets.

Slow Tip: Want another pattern? Bunch fabric sections into log-shaped pieces, tie rubber bands along their lengths, and dip in one color or many for a classic bull's-eye look. To create small rings, wrap a piece of fabric around a marble and tie off with a rubber band before dipping.

☀ Talking Sticks

Just as in Native American councils, the talking stick can be a powerful tool for keeping order in a group by reminding everyone to honor and respect the person who holds the stick and is speaking. Traditional talking sticks were often covered in animal hides.

You'll need:

- Small tree branch you can comfortably hold
- Sandpaper
- Knife or scissors
- 4″–6″ thin strips of leather, hemp, or cord
- Paint

- Beads
- Feathers, optional

Remove any extra bark, twigs, leaves, and moss from the branch and sand it so it is fairly smooth.

Paint your talking stick, if desired (ideas below).

Tie the leather, hemp, or cord to one end of the stick.

Add feathers or beads to the cord and knot to secure them.

In Native American tradition, the type of wood used for the talking stick has meaning. For some, white pine symbolizes peace; birch, truth; maple, gentleness; elm, wisdom; and evergreens, growth. Of course, you'll be limited to the type of trees you have nearby. The colors used on the stick also have meaning. Think about the qualities you would like and use those colors in your paint or your beads. Different Native American groups use different colors as symbols of specific qualities:

Red—Life

Yellow—Knowledge

Blue—Wisdom

White—Spirit

Purple—Healing

Orange—Kinship with all living things

Black—Clarity and focus

Many traditions also use colors to represent the four directions:

Yellow—East (sunrise)

Red—West (sunset)

White—North (snow)

Green—South (earth)

In some traditions animals also represent certain characteristics. You may wish to paint these:

Buffalo—Abundance
Elk—Stamina
Deer—Gentleness
Horse—Perseverance
Rabbit—Keen hearing

Slow Snippet: Scouting began a century ago as the "Woodcraft and Scouting Movement."

Whimsical Crafts

My family, like many, has a very soft spot for anything whimsical. Our crafted fairies and mushrooms, whether for play or display, never fail to put us in mind of enchanted woodlands and gardens and the joy of make-believe.

❋ Flower Fairies

Magical, enchanting fairies define whimsy, and this project of pipe-cleaner fairies with unique flower skirts provides a terrific way to bring a delightful array of fairies into your life. With a few simple accessories, your fairies can offer hours of creative play, all from things you made yourself.

You'll need:

- 2 or more artificial flowers per fairy, with distinct layers of petals (available in craft stores)
- Colorful pipe cleaners
- Round wooden beads, 14–20 mm, with holes

- Wire cutters or scissors
- Fine-tip marker
- Craft glue

Slide the flower-petal layers up the stems with your hands to remove them.

Draw a face on one side of the wooden bead with your marker to make the fairy's head.

Cut each pipe cleaner in two pieces, one that is 1/3 of the length and the other 2/3 of the length.

Fold the longer pipe-cleaner piece in half. Twist the looped end slightly and thread it through the bead's hole, leaving a small bit of pipe cleaner sticking out at the top.

Place a dot of glue around the looped end of the pipe cleaner, and attach one flower petal layer over it, and on top of the bead, to create a hat for the fairy.

To make the fairy's collar, run another flower-petal layer up the folded pipe cleaner until it reaches the bottom end of the head bead.

To create the fairy's arms, place the smaller pipe-cleaner piece behind the main one, and fold in half. Twist once around the main one, and reseparate.

Continue adding flower petals to the body of the fairy, under the arms, to create layers of a skirt. When you're done, bend the pipe-cleaner legs so the fairy can sit or stand. Fold or bend the arms or legs again to create hands or feet, or to remove sharp edges.

✳ Fairy Furniture and Accessories

Make furniture and accessories for the fairies using pipe cleaners, household items, or twigs and other objects found in nature. A shoe box, a tree hollow or base, or a secret corner in your home can make a nice habitat for your fairies to settle in.

Fairy chair—Glue or tie four twigs (or pipe cleaners) into a square. Attach four sturdier twigs at right angles to each corner to create legs and three more to one of the twigs to create a chair back. Weave smaller twigs, grasses, flowers, fabric, or other items into the seat and back.

Fairy stool—Glue three small twigs extending from the center of a small flat piece of bark or the top of an acorn. Glue a piece of felt to the bark or acorn for a seat.

Fairy table or footstool—Glue two or four small rocks to a large flat rock or piece of bark to make a table with feet.

Clothesline—Tie string or fishing line to two twigs of about the same size. Cut the shapes of dresses or other items from scraps of fabric.

Mirror—Glue four twigs into a square. Cut out a piece of cardboard that is the same size as the square. Cover it with aluminum foil, wrapping the foil over the edges of the cardboard. Glue the twigs to the front of the mirror for a frame.

Powder puff—Glue a circle of felt or a small bit of cotton to the inside of an acorn cap.

✳ Felt Mushrooms

This simple craft was a favorite of Anna's when she was small. Many years after making them, we still have mushrooms, faded from seasons of sun and rain, scattered around our garden.

You'll need:

- Styrofoam balls or eggs
- Felt squares, at least two colors
- Pipe cleaners

OR

- Styrofoam cone, pointy end cut off
- Needle and thread

- Tacky or other heavy-duty glue
- Stick pins, optional

Fold each of two pipe cleaners into thirds with the middle piece on a work surface and the two remaining thirds of each piece sticking up. The two middle pieces should overlap in an X.

Bend each of the four upper thirds of each pipe cleaner inward toward the others.

Poke all four pipe-cleaner ends into the Styrofoam ball, keeping the base level.

If you'd like, use a flattened Styrofoam cone for the mushroom base instead of pipe cleaners. To do so, glue felt over the cone, tucking the ends in to wrap. Glue the mushroom-top ball to the cone (flattening the ball's bottom end, if need be).

Cut a circle of felt large enough to drape over the Styrofoam ball.

Cut polka dots out of the second piece of felt and glue or sew them to the main piece.

Glue or pin the decorated felt piece to attach it over the Styrofoam ball.

✳ Magic Wand

Magic wands instantly confer colorful events and talents at wizardry. They're fun to play with after you've made one and can be used for magic shows and castle and other imaginative play. They also make inexpensive and memorable party favors.

You'll need:

- Wooden dowel or large twig, 12" long, 1/4" diameter, or your choice of size, or cardboard tube from a dry-cleaning hanger, painted gold

- 2 different colors of ribbon, 1/4" wide, or your choice of width, 3 times the length of your wand
- Gold or other paint, if using a hanger tube
- Piece of cardboard
- Glitter or glitter glue
- Small bells, charms, sequins, or beads, optional
- Craft glue
- Scissors

Cut a star, moon, heart, or other shape out of cardboard. Trace that shape onto a second piece of cardboard and cut out the identical shape. Spread glue on one side of each piece of cardboard. Add glitter, or decorate using glitter glue. Let dry.

Add a big drop of glue to the back of one cardboard shape and affix the shape to the dowel.

Add the other shape so that it mirrors the first and glue the two together with the dowel in the middle. (If the wand is too thick, use one piece of cardboard.)

Cut a length of ribbon of each color, equivalent to about twice the length of the wand.

Add a dot of glue to the bottom end of the wand and affix one end of one ribbon to it. Allow the glue to dry.

Wind the ribbon up and around the wand. When you reach the top, secure the ribbon with a dot of glue on the underside, tie a knot, and let the remaining ribbon hang down in a stream.

Repeat the process with the second ribbon piece, winding it in the same direction as, or a different direction from, the first.

Cut the ribbons at the desired hanging length and knot each end to prevent fraying. Add small bells, charms, sequins, or beads, if desired.

Tie more ribbon strands around the top of the wand (perhaps two of each color). Glue and knot.

✳ Teacup Candles

This charming twist on traditional candle making is one of my family's favorite crafts. It's lots of fun and naturally slowing—crafters have to be patient because the wax can take a long time to melt. This craft is also a great way to rescue old or mismatched teacups. None in your cupboards? Teacups can often be found at secondhand stores, flea markets, and garage sales for less than a dollar apiece. Many of the other items are available at craft and specialty stores. Each of your creations will be unique and will make a lovely and unusual gift. Note: This craft requires adult help.

You'll need:

- Assorted teacups, washed and dried
- Approximately 4–6 ounces paraffin, soy, or bees wax per teacup, or as needed to nearly fill each one
- Pretreated candle wicks with metal tabs at the bottom and at least 2″ more than needed at the top
- Wax wick adhesive
- Wax color chips, optional
- Essential oil or fragrance oil and dropper, optional
- Double boiler, or equivalent
- Dedicated craft or candy thermometer
- Dedicated wooden craft spoon
- Small craft scoop or toothpicks
- Newspapers, to cover work surface

(Many of these items are available at craft and specialty stores.)

Place a small dot of wax adhesive on the bottom of the metal wick, and place it in the center of the teacup.

Break or chop wax into small chunks and place in a double boiler, or in a glass, metal, or other nonflammable container inside a larger pot containing water. Bring the water in the outer pot to boil.

Watch over the melting wax, stirring occasionally and adding more wax if needed. (Wax should never be left unattended. It's also a good idea for candle and soap makers to have dedicated tools, if possible, so that soap and wax don't get onto the utensils you use for food.)

When the wax has completely melted (this can take up to twenty minutes, depending on the type and size of the wax pieces), use the candy thermometer to ensure that it has reached 180°.

Stir in one color chip at a time until the desired color is achieved, or leave natural.

Remove from heat and stir in one drop or more of essential or fragrance oil, if desired.

Carefully pour hot wax into the prepared teacup and let cool for at least one hour. Trim the wick if needed.

Do not pour the remaining wax in your drain. Instead, try to remelt and reuse it.

Handicrafts

Handicrafts often come to mind when people think of slowing down and sharing crafts with one another. Because so many items are no longer made by hand and have instead been turned over to machines, creating handmade objects, especially with others, can help us feel like we're part of a slower and less mechanized time. Often meditative, handicrafts done in a group can allow for conversation or quiet, camaraderie or getting lost in one's own creation.

My family has been involved in several knitting and quilting groups, and one of our favorites is the craft circle of my dear friend Victoria. Members of Victoria's craft circle are encouraged to bring any craft to do (which is great for us less accomplished knitters and quilters). Her circle is a wonderful tradition that allows family and friends of all different craft abilities and persuasions to come together in a community. So often in our busy lives, we get together only when there is a purpose—a school or neighborhood meeting or concern. The act of getting together and doing something creative can be very comforting and allow people to connect in a warm and casual way.

With your own family, handicrafts can offer an excuse to turn off the TV, play some music, if desired, and sit or be together while engaged in activities. People of any age and skill level can do versions of these timeless handicrafts and projects.

✳ Felted Soap

The act of felting anything, particularly a bar of soap, is completely satisfying to the senses. The combination of soft wool and gentle lather is very pleasing, as is the process of shaping the felt over the soap. If you use a scented soap, your sense of smell will be rewarded as well. My family has been known to spend hours over sinks or buckets, completely immersed in the process of felting soap.

Why felt a bar of soap? Besides providing a great family activity, your felt bar acts as a washcloth and soap in one—the felt tightens as the soap shrinks with use. Felted soaps are also pretty and make great gifts. (To make your own soap, see chapter 4.)

You'll need:

- Bar of soap—most solid soaps, like Ivory, felt well. Goat's milk soap, in a scent like lavender, is especially nice. Look for soaps with rounded corners.

- Wool roving (loose sheets of wool that have been carded, and often dyed, but not spun), in single or various colors, available at craft, knitting, and specialty stores. (You will need enough roving in your main sheet of wool to cover 1 1/3 times the area of the bar of soap, with other small amounts of roving for accent colors.)
- 2 dish towels
- Bowl of warm water or a sink
- Raised screen, dish-drying rack, or other drying surface, optional

Wrap your main piece of roving loosely around the bar of soap, covering both length and width, so that the entire surface of the soap is covered in a loose-fitting package. Leave extra wool at the corners of the soap.

Wrap accent threads around the package in any design you'd like. (The design will change somewhat, as threads will shift in the felting process.)

Drizzle with warm water, either from a bowl or at the sink, enough to barely wet most of the bar.

Begin to mold the package with your hands. The wool will begin to wet evenly and the soap will start to lather.

Keep forming and molding the felt to the soap bar. The felt may appear wrinkly and loose. Scrape away excess lather with your hands.

Occasionally squeeze the bar with a towel to release excess moisture.

Continue to rub in your hands, turning the soap over and evenly smoothing the surfaces. Be careful to keep the corners covered. The felt should begin to adhere more tightly to the soap.

When you are satisfied that the felt has tightened over the soap, wipe the excess lather off. Briefly run cold water over the soap to further tighten the fibers.

Let the soap dry for approximately twenty-four hours on a towel, raised screen, or dish-drying rack.

✳ Safety-Pin Bracelet

Safety-pin bracelets are gratifying and inexpensive to make for yourself or friends. You can create bracelets with patterns, like checkers or stripes, or something even more complex (some ideas are below), or just enjoy a random design. When you're done, you'll have a fun and fashionable bracelet to wear or give as a gift.

You'll need:

- Approximately 100 safety pins per bracelet, 3/4″ 1 1/4″ long
- Seed or small pony beads, 6–10 per safety pin
- Elastic cord
- Craft glue
- Toothpicks
- Paper plate
- Graph paper, optional

Pour a small bit of glue onto the paper plate.

Cut two lengths of elastic cord approximately 6″ longer than your wrist.

Place beads onto each pin, in the order you'd like, leaving enough room to fasten the pin. You can also plan out a pattern in advance (see the easy pattern ideas). It is important to note when you are planning your bracelet that the pins will alternate so that each cord goes through the head of one pin and the bottom of the next, all the way around the bracelet. Place the beads onto the pins to allow for each one to face the correct direction.

When you have enough beads on a pin, use a toothpick to put a dot of glue on the end of the pin, and then close it.

Continue to string beads onto pins until you have at least fifty pins.

Begin to string the beaded pins onto the elastic cord in the alternating manner described above. If you'd like, loosely tie an end of each cord together, so the pins don't slip out as you're stringing them. If you have a design that is centered on your wrist, you might want to add solid pins on each end of your bracelet after you've strung most of the pins.

When the bracelet has reached the desired length, carefully untie the knotted end. Pull the cords on top and bottom until the bracelet's fit is correct. Knot the two top cords and the two bottom cords.

Cut the cords so that there is about 1″ left on each. Place the remaining cords back through the hooks and eyes of the pins. Dot each with glue to hold it there and let dry.

EASY PATTERN IDEAS

Each pin will hold six to ten seed beads, depending on the bead size. You can use graph paper to create your own pattern. Draw a rectangle or square with a length and width of six to ten squares. Color in the squares to correspond with the bead colors you would like to use. A square design can be surrounded with beads in a solid color. Try leaves, pumpkins, snowflakes, hearts, stars, suns, piano keys, candy cane stripes, candy corn, Christmas trees, happy faces, polka dots, butterflies, or flags.

Slow Tip: The smaller the hand, the bigger the bead. Younger children can make a pin instead of a bracelet by stringing large beads onto a few safety pins and then hanging those pins from one longer one.

✳ Finger Weaving (or Finger Knitting)

Finger weaving is a fun group activity that offers tremendous portability and ease. Because the weaving is done by hand using lightweight items, finger weaving can be done sitting in a park, standing in line, or during quiet or conversational time. I've seen my daughter and her Girl Scout troop completely engaged in this activity over whole camping weekends, walking around with strands of colorful woven loops dangling from their fingers. Children as young as six years old can create necklaces, headbands, jump ropes, scarves, or other items by doing this simple craft, which is as satisfying as lanyard making and other weaving but much easier.

> *You'll need:*
>
> - Nylon weaving loops, 100 or more per project. Be sure to get nylon loops, which stretch well, and buy extras—finger weaving can be addicting.

Loop the first loop around your nondominant pinkie.

Twist it a half turn and loop it around the ring finger on the same hand.

Twist it another half turn and loop it around the middle finger on the same hand.

Twist it another half turn and loop it around the index finger on the same hand.

Repeat the above process with a second loop, so that there are two loops wrapped around the fingers of one hand.

With your palm facing you, stretch out the bottom loop from your pinkie. Lift it over the top loop and stretch it over to the back of your pinkie.

Do the same with the loops on the other three fingers. You will have one loop each on your index finger and pinkie, and multiple loops on the other fingers.

Continue weaving, using the colors of your choice. As the rope gets longer, it will go down the back of your hand.

When you get to the desired length, you can knot the ends to finish.

The same loops can be used to create potholders and squares with a metal loom, available at craft stores.

✳ Dried-Bean Mosaic

Dried-bean mosaics are one of those easy, inexpensive, and often overlooked crafts that I've seen work like magic to engage my family and other groups for hours, even at older ages. Because the items store for a long time and don't take up much room, you can buy the supplies ahead of time and save them for a rainy or other free day.

> *You'll need:*
>
> - Variety of dried beans and similar items, available at supermarkets, such as kidney beans, pinto beans, navy beans, lentils, yellow and green split peas, black eyed peas, and others
> - Heavy-duty paper plates or pieces of cardboard
> - School or craft glue
> - Pencil
> - Bowls for the beans, optional

If you want to plan out your design instead of working free-form, draw it with a pencil on the cardboard or plate. This is an especially good idea if you have an intricate line drawing, or if you want the beans to form blocks of color or specific images in your design.

Place a generous amount of glue on a small area or line to be covered with beans.

Begin placing the beans onto the glue, pressing lightly.

Continue gluing beans down to make your design.

When you are finished, let the mosaic dry completely (for an hour or more) before moving it.

Slumber-Party Crafts

Although these crafts are a hit anytime, they are practically guaranteed to work at a girls' slumber party or similar gathering. Crafts are a wonderful warmup activity to start the party, as guests who arrive at different times can join in. They also provide a great activity to calm people down after dinner, games, or scary stories (all of which were always a hit at Anna's slumber parties) while creating memories and a nice party flow. Beware: guests may stay up all night having good giggly fun.

✴ Secret-Message Bracelets and Anklets

Alphabet beads come in a wide variety of shapes and colors and allow you to create jewelry and wear a saying of your choice or a secret message that only you or a select few know about. To ensure your message's secrecy, choose only the first letter of each word in your sentence. The tight-lipped in the group may keep others guessing at their messages all night.

You'll need:

- Small alphabet beads
- Decorative beads, optional
- Embroidery floss, string, or elastic cord, thin enough to pass through the beads' holes; you may want floss in 2–3 colors for braiding

- Clasps, optional
- Ruler and tape
- Bead tray or towel

Decide whether to make a bracelet or an anklet. Measure your ankle or wrist with a piece of string and then cut a piece of cord, string, or floss that is at least 4″ longer than that measurement (the cord will stretch a little). If your string or floss is thin enough, and you want to braid or knot between beads, cut two or three equal pieces.

Choose your secret message and arrange your beads on a tray or towel. If you'd like, add decorative beads between or around the letters of the message. Be sure the alphabet beads will face the right direction and be in the correct order when worn.

Knot a clasp to one end of the string or tape it to a hard surface, like a table.

Begin stringing beads or braiding or knotting the string (embroidery floss braids nicely). You can also make a knot every 1/2″ in string or floss, place a bead, then knot again and leave another 1/2″.

When you have reached the correct length for your anklet or bracelet, have a friend knot it onto your ankle or wrist, or knot a clasp to the finished end, adjusting for size.

Your secret will remain as safe as you want it to be.

Slow Tip: How to braid—With three equal strands of floss or string, place the right string over the middle one, so that that one is now in the middle. Place the left string over the "new" middle one, so that that one is now in the middle. Continue braiding down the length of the floss or string.

✳ Homemade Lip Balm

My family and I love concocting craft, beauty, and other items in the kitchen and sharing that fun with our friends. Most kids love mixing, cooking, and creating things. It's very rewarding, and even novel, to make your own lip balm. You can use all-natural ingredients so you know exactly what's in it, and you can flavor it with anything from peppermint to bubble gum. Small pots of lip balm are wonderful gifts, as well as great party souvenirs. This craft works best with a group of six or less. Adult supervision is required with younger children.

This recipe will produce twelve small pots of lip balm, and can easily be doubled. Many of the items for making lip balm are available in craft and specialty stores; all items should be labeled "cosmetic grade."

You'll need:

- 2 ounces almond, apricot, avocado, grapeseed, or sunflower oil
- 1 ounce mango or shea butter
- 1 ounce beeswax, shavings or pellets
- 1/2 teaspoon flavoring oil, to taste
- 1/4 teaspoon liquid vitamin E, optional
- 1/4 teaspoon lip-safe colorant, optional (food coloring does not work)
- Pipettes or funnels made from paper-cup cones
- Small lip-balm pots
- Stickers to decorate and label the pots (large blank shapes for labeling, tiny stars and shapes for fun additions)
- Double boiler, or equivalent

Decorate your containers, if desired.

Melt oil, butter, and beeswax together over low heat, in the top of a double boiler, or in a small Pyrex container that is placed inside a pan of simmering water.

Stir until thoroughly mixed.

Add flavoring oil (to taste), vitamin E (as a moisturizer), and color, if desired. Stir thoroughly.

Remove the mixture with pipettes, or by spooning into funnels, and place into the lip-balm containers.

Let the mixture harden. Cap and use.

✳ Paper-Bag Autograph Books or Scrapbooks

Scrapbooking has become an extremely popular craft, and as soon as you try it, you'll see why. It's super-satisfying to create a scrapbook or autograph book from paper bags, magazines, and other pictures—and they make a great personal souvenir from a slumber party. If you choose to make your book an autograph book, you can have other guests each write on a page when the book is done, creating another party activity.

You'll need:

- Paper lunch bags, any size, approximately 10 per book
- Solid and patterned paper
- Magazines that can be cut up
- Photographs (this book is not acid-free, so you may want to use duplicates instead of originals)
- Thin markers or colored pencils
- Ribbons
- Standard hole punch
- Glue sticks

- Scissors
- Three-ring binder rings, optional
- Stickers, dried flowers, stamps, and other scrapbooking and decorative items, as desired—craft stores usually have great ready-made scrapbooking embellishments, often in themes

Cut the folded end off each bag, so that it lays flat, with two open ends.

Fold ten or so bags in half. Each bag represents four pages of your book.

Choose a theme. Ideas include vacations, hobbies, school, camp, friends, autographs, drawings, poems, favorite things, or whatever else you'd like.

Create a cover on the front of one of the folded bags. Glue a piece of paper to it as a background for pictures, photos, or smaller pieces of paper that can frame poems, sayings, or autographs. Or decorate the cover with smaller strips of paper, pictures, stickers, words, or other decorations.

Keep decorating pages of your book, or leave them blank for autographs.

Each bag will have two open ends, and you can glue them shut or use them as pockets to hold more pictures, homemade cards, or other treasures. You can glue small strips of ribbons inside the open bag parts (and then glue the bag together) or to the edges of either the scrapbook pages or the pages that will be tucked into your pockets.

When you have enough pages for your book and have decorated to your satisfaction, line the pages up in order and punch two or three holes in each one at even lengths apart.

Secure the book through the holes with binder rings or pieces of ribbon that are tied in bows.

Collect autographs or share books with your friends.

Homemade Craft Supplies

There are lots of craft materials that we are conditioned to buying in stores that we could just as easily have fun making ourselves. Most likely, the goods will go farther, save money, and be more natural than store-bought ones, too. In addition, making something you would ordinarily buy just stirs the imagination, along with a sense of accomplishment. I've seen this simple act really shake things up and add a layer of wonder to everyday objects and activities. Once you've made your own paper, don't be surprised if you ask yourselves, "What else can we do?"

✳ Muffin-Tin Crayons

Most families have broken crayon pieces all around the house—and in cars, purses, and backpacks; under couch cushions and rugs; and in forgotten supply boxes. Why not recycle them into new, multicolored crayons? As a bonus, these make great party favors.

You'll need:

- Variety of broken crayon pieces, with the paper wrappers taken off
- Minimuffin tin
- Paper muffin or cupcake liners, optional
- Cooking spray, optional
- Toothpicks
- Dish towel

Preheat oven to 275°.

Line the muffin tin with paper liners. (You can also melt the crayons right in the tin, if you're not also using it for food. If you are, you may want to spray the cups with cooking spray.)

Put a mix of crayons into each muffin cup. Pile them in—they don't have to fit neatly.

Bake for about 10 minutes, until just melted.

Remove from oven.

Swirl with a toothpick if the colors haven't completely mixed.

Let the crayons cool.

When completely cool, invert the muffin tin over the dish towel and gently shake out the crayons.

Remove any paper liners.

Note: You can also make these in standard-sized muffin tins. Cooking time will be approximately doubled.

✳ Glitter

You can actually make your own glitter quite quickly and for a fraction of what it costs to buy it! Homemade glitter lacks some of the sparkle of store-bought glitter, but it's great fun to make and use, and the variety of colors that you can create is nearly endless.

You'll need:

- 1/4 cup salt
- Food coloring, liquid or paste, assorted colors
- Bowl
- Wax paper
- Fork

Pour salt in a bowl and add a few drops of food coloring to it.

Mix the food coloring into the salt thoroughly with the fork, until the color is fairly uniform. Some white salt will still add a nice contrast.

Spread the mixture out on a piece of wax paper.

Let dry for about ten minutes.

Store in airtight containers.

☀ Finger Paint

Finger painting has long been a classic craft for young children. When Anna was small, we had many finger-painting sessions, indoors and especially outside. Her finger paintings were her first pieces of artwork, and we proudly hung some in her room and gave others to teachers as gifts. When she was older, finger painting was a great way to make original cards and wrapping paper. This is a very simple and fun recipe that will have you finger painting in minutes.

You'll need:

- 1/3 cup cornstarch
- 2 tablespoons white sugar
- Saucepan
- 2 cups water
- 1/4 cup clear dishwashing liquid
- Food coloring, liquid or paste, assorted colors
- Finger painting or regular paper
- Newspapers, to cover work surface

Combine cornstarch and sugar in a small saucepan.

Slowly add water to mixture.

Cook over low heat for five to ten minutes, stirring until the mixture is smooth and gel-like.

Remove the pan from the stove and let the mixture cool.

Stir in dishwashing liquid.

Pour the paint into jars or bowls, add food coloring, and stir the coloring in until you have the paint colors you want.

Spread newspaper fairly thickly on the ground or on your work surface. Lay the paper out, and begin your finger-painting creation. Let dry.

Store the paint in airtight containers. Recycled jam or baby food jars work well.

✳ Homemade Paper

It's fun to practice the five-thousand-year-old art of papermaking, which was started in Egypt and perfected in China, using plant fibers and the method below. Try creating with recycled items and then using your freshly made paper for drawing or old-fashioned letter writing.

You'll need:

- Blender, egg beater, and bowl, or individual bottles or cups with lids
- Large flat pan
- Hot water
- Piece of screen, approximately the size of the paper you want to make
- Piece of fabric, the same size as the screen, or newspaper, or a dish towel
- Strips and shreds of recycled paper, wrapping paper, tissue paper, magazine pages, or napkins
- Glitter, colored threads, leaves or pressed flowers, optional
- Rolling pin, optional
- Plain paper, optional

Place shredded paper and hot water in the blender, bowl, or cups, using 1 cup of hot water for every 1/4 cup of paper.

Blend or beat the paper, or shake the cups, until the paper is the consistency of thick soup. (This is harder to achieve when using cups.)

Pour the paper mixture into the pan, adding glitter, colored threads, leaves, or pressed flowers, if desired.

Place the screen in the pan, under the paper, trying to catch as much paper as you can, in an even layer, onto the screen.

Lift the screen out of the pan and let excess water drain out.

Place the fabric or dish towel over the paper, still on the screen, and blot with your hands or a rolling pin.

Let the paper dry on the screen for approximately six hours. Carefully flip the paper onto a dish towel, piece of fabric, plain paper, or newspaper and continue to dry.

4

Slow Kitchen

Kitchen time is an ideal family time, especially when it involves stirring, concocting, kneading, or creating one of these fun projects that you can also enjoy later, for yourselves or for gifts. My family has done a lot of bonding in the kitchen, more often over nonfood items than edible ones, although we are known to make food too. During one period, we found ourselves so enamored with making jam that we began to enter county and state fair contests. Another time found us creating a thriving mother-daughter business with our home-crafted natural soaps. Other lazy afternoons and evenings found our whole family in the kitchen, making polymer clay beads that we later strung, magic potions to share with friends, and science experiments that challenged and delighted us.

There was food too, of course, that we enjoyed creating, smelling as it cooked, displaying on special plates for tea, and using to fool family and friends on April Fools' Day.

Kitchen Crafts

We are prime proponents of the notion that kitchen fun needn't center exclusively on food. There are lots of wonderful projects that call for similar concocting and creating and result in beautiful and useful objects, along with terrific opportunities for family bonding.

✳ Colorful Polymer Clay Beads

Be warned! You might get extremely hooked on creating with polymer clay. It happened to my entire family and our neighbor Meryl, who joined us for clay-making sessions at our home. Polymer clay is a great deal of fun to work with, and there are endless variations in design and uses. Polymer clay, a plastic compound used like any modeling clay, is baked at a low temperature or air-dried (depending on the manufacturer) to harden it.

You'll need:

- Polymer clay, available at craft stores
- Craft knife
- Skewers
- Cookie sheet
- Baking rack

Basic Cane Beads

Preheat oven to the lowest possible temperature.

Roll out four or more thin logs, of various colors, each approximately 4″–6″ long.

Place the logs on top of and around one another to form one large log.

Gently twist or roll to mix the colors into a design.

Cut to the desired length with the craft knife.

Create a center hole in each bead and string the beads along a skewer.

Gently lay them on the cookie sheet, or across a baking rack, so that they don't sit flat on anything, which could ruin the bead shape.

Bake according to package directions and let cool.

Flower Cane Beads

This is a spectacular design that is easy to create. Follow the directions for basic cane beads, with these changes:

Roll one log for the center of the flower.

Roll five or more thinner logs, which will be the petals of the flower, and place those symmetrically around the larger log.

Roll a series of even smaller logs, which will be the fill-in color or colors around the flower, and place them accordingly.

Gently roll the entire new log, just enough to create a round edge and remove any air pockets. Try not to distort the flower shape.

Continue, following the directions for basic cane beads.

Round Beads

Round beads are very easy to make and look great. Here are a few ways to create them. After following the directions for each method here, use the basic cane bead directions to complete the beads.

- Roll the clay to form a round ball, smaller than you want your finished bead. Attach different-colored clay to the surface and roll again to mix.
- Break off pieces of a log, made with the cane method, and roll them into balls.
- Create a blob by attaching many small balls or pieces of different-colored clay together. Roll the blob into a ball to mix the colors and create a dense unit with no air pockets. Break pieces off of the blob and roll them into round beads.

Slow Tip: In addition to beads, you can make miniature food and other items for fairies or dolls, *Día de los Muertos ofrendas* (see chapter 8), or Christmas tree ornaments.

✳ Melt-and-Pour Soap

Anna had such a good time making melt-and-pour soap that she started her own business when she was ten years old. (I entered the business later.) Introduced at a school craft-show fund-raiser (which is a fantastic idea, as it really involves kids in making creations to sell), her soaps have been in local stores and have been shipped around the world. We find soap making to be easy, economical, and boundlessly creative. When we scent soaps with essential and fragrance oils, the kitchen smells great. Soap making also features the "concocting" factor that many of us look for in crafts.

For a time, we specialized in soaps with small toys embedded inside. They make fun gifts, and the toy is a nice surprise, both to look at and to play with once the soap has melted down.

You'll need:

- Approximately 2 pounds of clear soap base (available in craft and specialty stores, and in organic versions)
- Square or rectangle soap molds
- Skin-safe colors (available in craft stores—do not use food coloring or colors not meant for cosmetics), optional
- Skin-safe essential or fragrance oil and droppers, optional
- Dedicated (not used for food) microwavable glass container, wooden spoon, and knife
- Cutting board (cover with plastic wrap if used for food)
- Microwave or dedicated double boiler
- Small plastic toys that fit in the mold with room to spare
- Rubbing alcohol, paper cup, and toothpicks, optional (be sure everyone knows the alcohol is not water)

Cut the soap base into small chunks and heat in the microwave or double boiler until completely melted, watching to be sure it doesn't boil. Use the measurements on the glass container and the molds to gauge the amount of soap needed and melt slightly more than needed. Color, if desired.

Pour a thin layer into each mold, pricking any bubbles with a dot of rubbing alcohol on a toothpick.

When the layer is hard (approximately 1/2 hour) gently place the toy on it, facedown.

Melt the soap base again. This might seem wasteful, but if you have colored it, it will be difficult to match colors between batches. When it has melted, scent if desired, according to directions, or approximately six drops of scent per fluid ounce, though this can vary widely.

Gently pour the base into the molds, securing the toy with a toothpick, if necessary. Remove any bubbles and let sit for at least four hours, ideally longer, before gently removing from the mold.

For other kitchen craft projects, see Muffin-Tin Crayons in chapter 3, Dye Eggs with Plant Dye in chapter 7, and Teacup Candles in chapter 3.

Slow Snippet: For the couple years that we seriously sold our soaps at craft shows, our kitchen smelled like roses, lavender, balsam, and birthday cake. We girls liked it, but sometimes Michael found it hard to just eat a piece of toast without exotic smells wafting over.

Kitchen Science

It doesn't take a budding scientist to see the kitchen as one big lab. Anna has a love of creating and transforming in the kitchen, which she displayed early, when she mixed kitchen ingredients to make "potions" and other items. Most everything created in the kitchen involves a large helping of chemistry and perhaps a dollop of physics. Equal parts wonder and fun, these kitchen science projects are great for science fairs, as well as hands-on experimentation and exploration.

✳ Color Race

How do flowers and plants get their water? This fun, colorful experiment will show you.

You'll need:

- Approximately 6 cut flowers, preferably white carnations and/or approximately 6 stalks of celery
- Food coloring
- Small knife
- Several glasses of water

Add about eight drops of food coloring to each glass of water.

Place flower stems or celery stalks into the glasses and leave them there overnight.

Watch to see if any color appears to run up the stem or stalk faster than another color.

Check in every few hours to see how much the stems and flowers, or celery stalks, are colored. It can take up to twenty-four hours for the color to reach the flower. You may want to cut the celery stalks, to better observe the cross-sections.

See if you can tell which color ran up the stem or stalk the quickest, and which colored the flower or stalk the most.

What Makes It Work?

Water is constantly moving up the stems of plants. The food coloring makes the water visible. With the celery, the water can be observed in patterns that indicate its movement up the plant's ducts. The processes? During transpiration, water evaporates from the plant's leaves and petals. Then, during cohesion, the plant pulls more water up the stem to replace it, almost as if through a straw.

✳ Rising Raisins

Have fun learning about the properties of gas.

> **You'll need:**
>
> - Box of raisins
> - Clear plastic cups or glasses
> - 1 large bottle of clear carbonated soda and/or mixture of 3 tablespoons vinegar, 1 teaspoon baking soda, and water filled to half of a cup or glass

Pour some carbonated soda or the soda mixture into a clear cup or glass. If you use the baking soda mixture, pour over a sink because it may spill over the top of the glass. Do not stir.

Drop raisins into the cup or glass one at a time and observe.

What Makes It Work?

The raisins may sink at first. Soon they will rise to the surface, then sink, then rise again for an hour or more. Soda contains carbon dioxide, a gas, which occurs as little bubbles. At first the raisin sinks because it has a higher density than the soda. After a while, bubbles of gas attach themselves to the raisin. Because the gas has a lower density than the soda, the bubbles float up to the top. When enough bubbles attach to a raisin, they carry the raisin up to the top with them. At the top, the bubbles pop, and the raisin sinks back down to the bottom, where more bubbles attach to it, and the cycle begins again. Soda goes flat when its gas bubbles have escaped into the air. See what happens when you drop a raisin into a glass of flat soda. Try this with different sodas or mixtures, or with a different object, such as dried macaroni.

✸ Colorful Sugar

Evaporation is illustrated in this colorful experiment.

You'll need:

- 2 tablespoons sugar
- 10 tablespoons water
- Food coloring
- 2–4 shallow dishes
- Foil

Line the dishes with foil.

In a separate container, stir sugar into the water until it disappears.

Pour two spoonfuls of the mixture into each dish.

Add a few drops of food coloring to each dish.

Leave the dishes in a warm place for a few days.

What Makes It Work?

The water evaporates, leaving colored sugar crystals. The molecules in the water have moved into the air and spread apart. The remaining sugar can be broken up and used either in art projects or for eating.

Chef Time

We all know we're not supposed to play with our food, but the following projects are especially fun, rewarding, and easy, both to make and to eat. And if some of the processes involved feel very much like playing, so much the better to have a great time in the kitchen, learn a few skills, and perhaps foster a lifelong love of cooking and good nutrition.

Most kids really enjoy helping in the kitchen, and you probably won't have to coax them to do so. Even if you're the main cook, a young sous chef will probably enjoy helping with age-appropriate tasks, like cracking eggs, washing fruit, and placing toppings on pizza and sprinkles on cookies, not to mention that tactile mainstay, rolling and kneading dough.

✳ Soft Pretzels

My family has had the joy of folding and baking pretzels in the 150-year-old Sturgis Pretzel Factory in Lititz, Pennsylvania, the oldest commercial pretzel bakery in the United States. There's nothing quite like rolling and then shaping the pretzel dough into its classic shape, and seeing it placed into giant brick ovens on large wooden boards, all in the stone basement of a building that dates back more than two hundred years. Pretzels themselves go back to sixth-century Italy, say the folks at Sturgis, where monks molded them into the shapes of children's praying arms.

Baking pretzels at home offers the same delights—the pleasure of working with dough, the wonderful way it smells when it's cooking, and of course, that classic soft-pretzel taste.

You'll need:

- 1 package (1/4 ounce) active dry yeast
- 1 1/2 cups warm water (110°–115°)
- 1 tablespoon sugar
- 2 teaspoons salt
- 4 cups all-purpose flour
- 8 cups water
- 1/2 cup baking soda
- Coarse salt or mixture of equal parts cinnamon and sugar

- 2 bowls, 1 greased with a pat of butter
- Towel
- Saucepan
- Paper towels and plate
- Baking sheets
- Cooling racks

In a large bowl, dissolve yeast in warm water.

Add the sugar, salt, and two cups flour and beat until smooth. Stir in remaining flour to form a stiff dough.

Turn onto a floured surface and knead about five minutes until smooth.

Place in a greased bowl, turning once to grease top.

Cover with a towel and let rise in a warm place about an hour, until doubled.

Punch dough down and divide into twelve portions. Roll each into thin rope (approximately 12″) and loop both halves up and back around to the middle to twist into a pretzel shape. Apply a little pressure to make the ends stick.

Preheat oven to 425°.

In a large saucepan, bring water and baking soda to a boil. Place pretzels into boiling water, one at a time, flipping once, for fifteen seconds on each side.

Remove with a slotted spoon and drain on paper towels.

Place on greased baking sheets.

Brush with water and sprinkle with salt or cinnamon sugar.

Bake for twelve to fourteen minutes or until golden brown. Cool on racks.

Yield: 12 pretzels

> ***Slow Snippet:*** From the time she was very young, Anna has been a natural pretzel baker, looping and shaping her pretzels in one motion like a pro. Try it!

✳ Homemade Butter

It's easy and fun to make your own butter, which is really just agitated cream. While Asian nomads churned butter in goatskin bags, our grandmothers and great-grandmothers used wooden barrels or hand-cranked jars. No need to find or buy your own churn—homemade butter can easily be made with some simple equipment and a lot of shaking, which kids usually heartily enjoy. My family has had the pleasure of making butter on the farm where we get our milk. Although the process takes a little patience, it is easy to replicate anywhere. No matter where you make it, there's nothing quite like fresh butter.

You'll need:

- 1 quart heavy cream
- Half-pint jam jar per person
- Colander
- Small bowl
- Salt, optional

Fill the jar about half full of cream and close tightly.

Shake about twenty to thirty minutes. (Yes, that's right!) You will probably get tired and think nothing is happening, but soon the cream will begin to thicken. You will then notice the solids begin to separate from the liquids inside the jar, and less liquid will be visible against the jar's glass sides. When the liquids and solids are completely separate, and the butter is in one mass, gently pour the contents into a colander and let the liquids drain out, or capture the buttermilk in a jar for use later.

Put the butter in a small bowl and mix in a pinch of salt at a time, to taste.

Enjoy your fresh-churned butter, preferably on fresh bread. The butter will harden once refrigerated.

❋ Walter Wheatbunny Sandwiches

It's good for kids to have one sandwich under their belts that they can make by themselves—or nearly by themselves. It helps if it's as yummy as this sandwich, which was the house sandwich at one of the eateries at the University of California, Los Angeles, when my husband and I went (and met) there. From what I can gather, it is still on the menu.

You'll need:

- 2 slices of bread
- Peanut or other nut butter
- Honey
- A banana, sliced

Assemble your sandwich.

Slow Tip: Make the sandwich open face, with banana-slice eyes and nose and a smile made from Cheerios.

❋ Dessert Pizza

Pizza is already wonderful in its normal, tomatoey state. But dessert pizza? That puts the category over the top. Anna loved to make dessert pizza with me when she was just starting to help in the kitchen. It proved an unexpected treat to bring to preschool events, and its unusual nature may have contributed to a blue ribbon or two at our county fair. Of course, you could put any sweet toppings you like on a dessert pizza. This is just one variation.

You'll need:

- Cookie sheet, pizza pan, or pizza stone
- 1 pound of pizza dough, homemade or store bought (We make this with regular pizza dough. Substitute sweetened dough, if desired.)
- 1 1/2 cups minimarshmallows
- 2 cups semisweet chocolate chips (approximately 12 ounces)

Preheat oven and prepare pizza dough according to recipe or package directions.

Bake pizza dough until it is just beginning to brown, and remove from oven.

Leave oven at 350°–400°.

Sprinkle the pizza with the marshmallows and the chocolate chips and return it to the oven.

Cook for three to five minutes, until the marshmallows are lightly browned.

Remove pizza from oven and let cool.

Cut into wedges to serve.

✳ Groovy Color Cookies

These wonderful cookies, which can also be made with your favorite butter-cookie recipe, offer a fun project that results in different—and highly colorful—cookies every time. We've made these in designs that resemble pinwheels, with blocks of color;

designs that appear closer to tie-dye; and designs that resemble those of polymer clay beads. Use professional paste colors, if possible (available at specialty stores), for especially vibrant colors. This recipe was adapted from *Williams-Sonoma Kids Cookies*.

You'll need:

- 1 cup (2 sticks) butter, softened
- 1 cup confectioners' sugar
- 2 teaspoons vanilla extract
- 2 cups flour
- Food coloring
- Mixing cups
- Mixing bowl and beater
- Forks, knife
- Cookie sheets

Preheat oven to 350°.

In large mixing bowl, mix together butter, confectioners' sugar, and vanilla until creamy.

Add flour and beat to form smooth dough.

Divide dough into three or four parts, one for each color you want, and add food coloring to each, mixing until the colors are well blended.

Roll each colored section into a log shape. Place the logs on top of and around one another to form one large log.

Begin to roll or twist the log gently, so the colors mix and swirl but still stay distinct. Cut a sample slice from the log to see whether you're happy with the pattern.

Cut slices about 1/4" thick. If the dough is too soft, refrigerate for twenty minutes.

Place slices on ungreased cookie sheets and bake for approximately ten minutes.

Yield: Approximately 44 cookies.

Looking for more ways for kids to get involved in the kitchen? See chapter 10.

Tea Time

Fairies, teddy bears, leprechauns, and gnomes may be tiny (and pretend), but they still have to eat. Many children adore the ritual and whimsy of both pretend and real tea parties, and we've had many wonderful gatherings with a tea-party theme. Teas can be combined with other occasions, such as Valentine's Day, winter holidays, birthdays, May Day, or Mother's Day, and other activities, such as playing games or making valentines, May Day crowns, or fairy or flower crafts. Tea parties are a great way to involve multiple families or generations or to make an everyday gathering more special.

You may want to collect teacups, saucers, and plates in advance (the more mismatched the better!) They can often be found inexpensively at secondhand stores, flea markets, and garage sales. Disposable cups can also be found at party stores (or see instructions for Jeweled Cups in this chapter). You may want to have guests bring a special teddy bear or doll or invite them to dress up for taking tea in hats and gloves. The table, too, might be set with a favorite or antique tablecloth or doilies.

The following whimsical treats can be served at tea parties or other magical gatherings.

✳ Teddy-Bear Tea Sandwiches

Tea sandwiches come in an endless variety to suit many tastes. Here are some to try at your Teddy Bear or other tea.

You'll need:

- Thinly sliced white bread

- Sharp knife or cookie cutters
- Sandwich ingredients (see below)

Cut the crusts off the bread and cut each slice into two triangles, or cut into large shapes, such as flowers, using a cookie cutter. (If using a cookie cutter, note that some sandwiches are better assembled before cutting.)

Spread one bread slice with filling and top with the second slice of bread.

Sandwich fillings to try:

- Peanut butter and jelly
- Cream cheese and jelly
- Cream cheese and cucumber slices
- Peanut or apple butter and honey or Nutella
- Tuna, egg, or chicken salad
- Cheese and butter
- Lunch meat and cheese or mayonnaise

Slow Tip: Serve open-face sandwiches (or minibagels) by spreading them with cream cheese or other spread and decorating with sprinkles.

Slow Tip: Seeking something different? Substitute animal or other crackers, or cucumber rounds for the bread to make especially tiny sandwiches.

✳ Miniature Fairy Burgers

Fairies and other miniature creatures can't be expected to eat our giant food. They need food that suits their unique size. These burgers are among the tantalizing ways to satisfy hungry fairies who have come to tea.

You'll need:

- Box of Nilla Wafers or similar wafer cookies
- Bag of small peppermint patties, such as York
- Shredded coconut
- Green food coloring
- Red or yellow Fruit by the Foot
- Sesame seeds, optional
- Corn syrup, optional
- Toothpicks, optional
- Wax paper, optional
- Mixing bowl
- 1 cup water
- Paper towels

Dissolve a drop of green food coloring into a cup of water.

Place 1/4 cup of shredded coconut into a mixing bowl and pour the colored water over it. Mix the coconut to coat it with color and then let it sit a few minutes to make sure the color is absorbed. Pat dry with a paper towel. That is the lettuce for your burger.

Roll out the Fruit by the Foot and cut small squares of red or yellow to represent tomato slices and cheese.

If you wish your wafer "buns" to have sesame seeds on them, place the desired number of wafers on a flat surface, covered with wax paper. Dip a toothpick into the corn syrup and dot the wafers with drops of the syrup. Carefully place a sesame seed on each syrup drop. Let them sit for a couple of minutes to dry.

Assemble the "burger" by starting with a wafer for the bottom bun and then adding a peppermint patty, the fruit square(s), the coconut, and, finally, the top bun.

Nibble with tiny bites, just like the fairies do.

✳ Jell-O Rainbow

This is an extremely fun way to use gelatin. The result is appropriately colorful and pleasing, not to mention surprising for those who see it for the first time.

You'll need:

- 1 small package each of red, orange, yellow, green, blue, and purple gelatin
- Hot water for each package, per package directions
- Approximately 2 cups Cool Whip, if you want a white layer between colors
- Mixing bowls
- Many small containers or one large flat one, such as an 8" × 8" pan
- Nonstick spray

Dissolve gelatin in boiling water (do not add cold water). Spray large flat pan or separate bowls (as flat as possible) with nonstick spray.

Place each color gelatin in a separate bowl or place 2/3 of your first color in the flat pan as a layer. Chill, trying to keep the gelatin flat.

If making one large pan, wait until gelatin is set to add a next layer of color, in rainbow-color order, listed above. Repeat with all colors. If you want white between your color layers, then mix 1/3 cup Cool Whip into your remaining 1/3 cup gelatin and add that layer to the previous layer, letting it set before moving on.

If making many small pans, once gelatin is set, cut each color into uniform squares or rectangles. Place shapes on platters or plates in rainbow-color order, listed above.

If making one large mold, wait until the final layer has set and carefully cut the gelatin so that it reveals the rainbow through each layer.

✳ Magic Potion

A bit of food coloring can transform many ordinary beverages into magic potions. Choose a color like fairy-blue or leprechaun-green and stir it into apple juice, sparkling water, lemonade, soda, punch, or tea.

> **Slow Snippet:** Tea flavors some kids might enjoy include chamomile, vanilla hazelnut, orange, and berry. Have some honey, milk, and sugar available to mix into the tea.

✳ Jeweled Cups

We've made these easy, yet special, cups for teas, birthdays, and other occasions. They're an alternative to teacups and can help make gatherings feel especially magical and festive. You can use plastic cups, available at party and grocery stores.

You'll need:

- Small or regular-size plastic cups
- School or craft glue
- Sequins or small rhinestones with flat bottoms
- Dish towels

Lay a couple of towels on a flat surface and place a few cups on them. Bunch the towels around the cups to prevent them from rolling.

Place a few dots of glue on the top surface of a cup and place a sequin or rhinestone on each.

When the glue is dry, turn the cup a quarter turn and repeat the gluing. Repeat this two more times, until the cup is fully decorated.

Let dry at least twenty-four hours before using. Wash gently to reuse.

Slow Snippet: High tea began in England during the Industrial Revolution and is named for the high tables at which hungry workers ate meats and cheeses with their tea. Not a finger sandwich in sight.

Preserved Food

Canning has made a big comeback in recent years. For good reason—it's a fun, easy, and economical family or group activity that even offers some kitchen science, as you watch the mixture transform from liquid to gel. Canning is productive too, and you can't help but feel good when you see the bumper crop of jars filled with jewel-colored jam or other goodies that you'll be able to give as gifts or eat all year long.

Anna started making jam with me the summer she was three years old. We had a favorite blueberry farm, about an hour from our house, and we began to travel there each summer during the extremely short (about two-week) blueberry season, to collect ripe berries and sit at a small counter to enjoy the freshest blueberry ice cream imaginable. Versions of this recipe can be made with many fruits. Consult pectin packaging or canning books or sites for recipe proportions.

✳ Triple-Berry Jam

You can make excellent jam from most fruits and berries. Because Michael is from Pennsylvania blueberry country, I absorbed his love of blueberry jam, which can be phenomenal and offers a strong taste of sunny summer in the depths of midwinter when you spread just a little on toast. Raspberry jam is wonderful to use in holiday cookies and tarts. Peaches and apricots are also fun to work with and make excellent jams and chutneys. The jam we turn to most often, though, is the rich, complicated, and flavorful triple-berry jam.

You'll need:

- Canning jars, half-pint size preferable (available in supermarkets and hardware and drugstores—you shouldn't use old household jars, as they might be scratched)
- New canning lids and new or used bands
- Wide-mouth funnel and jar lifter (available at many hardware and drugstores)
- Ladle and tongs
- Pot holders, dish towels or cloths, and sponge
- Mixing bowls
- Wooden spoons
- Heavy-bottomed pot for cooking
- Very large pot or canner that includes an inch of water above the jars and plenty of room for the water to boil, and a jar rack or cake-cooling rack
- 5 cups strawberries, raspberries, and blackberries (3 pints strawberries, 1 1/2 pints raspberries, and 1 pint blackberries) at peak ripeness, chopped (with knife or food processor, see below)
- 7 cups sugar
- 1 box dry pectin

Wash the jars, bands, and lids in soapy water.

Place the bands and lids in a saucepan and simmer for five minutes, without boiling. Turn off heat and leave them in the hot water until ready to use.

Place rack into the pot and place jars on the rack (to prevent them from breaking in the pot). Fill the pot with water to an inch above the jars. Bring the water to a boil and keep the jars in a rolling-boil bath for ten minutes. After that, they sit until ready to be used.

Chop the berries by hand or in a food processor. If using a processor, pulse the berries in small batches so you end up with fruit bits rather than a puree.

Measure sugar into mixing bowl.

Add berries and pectin to the heavy-bottomed pot and mix. Bring to a full rolling boil over high heat, stirring constantly.

Quickly add sugar and continue to stir. Return to a full rolling boil. Then boil, stirring, for one minute.

Remove from the heat and skim off any foam with a ladle.

Remove the jars from their bath with tongs and a pot holder, and place them upright on a dish towel. Ladle the jam mixture into the jars, leaving 1/4" of air, or headspace. Wipe the rims and threads with a wet cloth. Top with lids and screw on the bands.

Place the jam-filled jars back into the canning pot, and boil again for ten minutes to process, or additionally sterilize, them. With certain vegetables and meats, the sterilization process is especially crucial to prevent food poisoning. Although the trend has moved away from the necessity of processing most fruit jams, and just leaving them standing when filled, I still like to boil them a second time, the old-fashioned way.

Let filled and processed jars stand for approximately twenty-four hours at room temperature. Do not retighten the bands. You know you have a good seal when you push on the lid and it doesn't pop back. If the seal is not good, the jam can be stored in the refrigerator for three weeks. Otherwise, it can be stored in a cool, dark place for up to two years.

Label with the date and type of jam, particularly if you plan to make more.

Yield: Approximately 5 half pints.

Note: It's important to understand and follow safety

guidelines for food canning. The U.S. Department of Agriculture offers a set of guidelines that is widely available on the Internet. See the Resources section to learn more.

Slow Snippet: If you enjoy canning as much as we do, you may also find yourself on the county and even state fair circuit, having fun entering canning and food competitions. After all, canning began when Napoleon offered an award for Best Food Preservation, so his armies could stay on the move.

Low-Sugar Jam

Looking to reduce the amount of sugar in your jam? Skip the pectin, reduce sugar by 1/3, and boil the jam for ten to fifteen minutes or until it reaches the jell point. Or use a low-methoxyl pectin, such as Pomona's (available at natural food stores) and follow package directions for recipes.

❋ Jam Jar Topper

Jars of homemade jam make great gifts that recipients know are from your kitchen and your heart. Decorate the jars by tying on custom gift cards with ribbons. Or make a simple jar topper, which finishes a jar of jam in an especially old-fashioned and pleasing way.

You'll need:

- Fabric pieces (fat quarters used for quilting work well)
- Pinking shears or scissors
- Rubber band

- Ribbon (enough for the circumference of the lid, plus approximately 8″)
- Glue, optional

Cut a circle of fabric, approximately 3/4″ larger all around than the jar band.

If you'd like, place a dot of glue on the top of the lid, and place the fabric onto it.

Secure the fabric with a rubber band.

Tie the ribbon around the rubber band to cover, and tie it into a bow.

Attach a gift card or jar label, if desired.

Apple butter is another of my family's favorite preserved foods. See the recipe in chapter 7.

April Fools' Food

Mealtimes provide an especially fun and easy opportunity to turn the tables on family and friends and have some fun with food pranks, items that look like familiar foods, but taste like something else. As a bonus, many of these will be a treat to eat even after the joke's over. We still laugh over the silly and easy April Fools' treats I've served over the years, which prove just as memorable as the April Fools' pranks my parents used to play on me. All these food pranks are quick and easy to pull off, with

BACKWARD MEAL

Even if you don't have time to make or buy special food for April Fools' Day, you can still play a prank on your dining companions by serving a meal backward, starting with dessert. Or you can have a whole backward-meal day and serve dinner in the morning and breakfast at night.

ingredients available at most grocery stores. See what happens when you serve the following items to your family.

Slow Snippet: Even though our current calendar has been in use since 46 BC, some Europeans were still celebrating their new year in April, instead of January, as late as the 1500s. These "April Fools" are the inspiration for today's jokes.

✴ Fishy Fish Sticks

You'll need:

- Log-shaped candy bars, such as Twix, Mounds, or Kit Kat, or wafer cookies (cut into fish-stick size, if necessary)
- Shredded or toasted coconut, or crushed graham crackers
- Peanut or other nut butter or corn syrup
- Wax paper
- Cookie sheet, optional

If using coconut, toast it by placing the shredded pieces on a baking sheet and baking at 350° for two to four minutes, or until it is light brown with some white shreds remaining. Allow to cool.

Spread coconut or graham cracker crumbs on a sheet of wax paper.

Roll the candy or cookies in the peanut butter or corn syrup until they are lightly coated, and then roll the coated candy or cookies in the coconut or cracker crumbs.

✳ Not-So-Fried Egg

> *You'll need:*
>
> - Lemon or vanilla pudding or yogurt, or a canned peach half
> - Marshmallow cream spread (such as Fluff) or sundae topping
> - Piece of toast, optional

Spoon a generous amount of marshmallow spread on a plate or a piece of toast. When it spreads, finesse it with a spoon into an egg-white shape.

Place a small, neat spoonful of pudding or yogurt, or the canned peach half, on top of it so that it looks like a fried egg.

✳ Smile and Say "Grilled Cheese"

> *You'll need:*
>
> - 1 pound cake
> - Buttercream or white frosting
> - Red and yellow food coloring
> - Cookie sheet

Cut the pound cake into slices to resemble bread.

Preheat oven to 300° and toast the slices on a cookie sheet just until golden brown. You can also use a toaster oven.

When cooled, stack two slices for each sandwich and cut each stack in half diagonally.

Mix drops of the red and yellow food coloring into the frosting, stopping when the frosting appears the color of American cheese.

Carefully spread a generous amount of frosting onto the

bottom slice, then gently press the top slice over it. The frosting should ooze a bit over the sides of the "bread," so that the dessert resembles a melted cheese sandwich.

✳ A Stiff Drink

You'll need:

- A package of flavored gelatin

Dissolve the gelatin according to box directions.

Pour the gelatin into drinking glasses and place a plastic straw in each.

Refrigerate until firm, then watch when someone tries to drink their "drink."

5

Slow Garden

When I was a child, I loved to garden with my dad. During the week, he was busy with work, but the weekends were set aside for gardening. I had my own flower and vegetable bed and chose to plant marigolds, which were cheery and easy to grow. Years later, Anna also chose marigolds for her planting area. I also took to experimenting with plant propagation and seed harvesting, like Dad, and lots of my school science projects involved plants. (They really did grow faster when I played classical music for them!) Though our yield would never put any local farmers out of business—some tomatoes and cukes here and there—it was apparent that the joy of being outside, doing something fun together, was what mattered.

Anna and I have enjoyed many fun gardening projects together. When she was tiny, she'd help choose seeds, water, plant, harvest, and tell me "who" was wet and who was dry. Over the years, she tended her marigolds and other favorites, like soft lamb's ear and catnip, which we made into toys for our cats. We made fairy habitats and leprechaun lures, painted flowerpots, and attracted butterflies and birds. And this was all on a deck, in planter boxes, or in a small plot in our local community garden, which proves that you don't need a lot of space to experience the joy of growing things from the ground. You also don't necessarily need a lot of sun, although it's a bonus. Our garden is often in the shade, and as a result, we are especially excellent growers of peas.

I've seen firsthand how gardening helps parents and children spend time together outdoors, take pride in growing their own food, learn about our ecosystem, and connect to one another and to others who have lived on the land before us. Although that may sound like a tall order, it isn't. Even if you only have space for containers or if you've never been much of a gardener yourself, there are simple ways to get everyone growing together.

Ready Your Plot

There are a few basic ingredients that every garden needs, whether it consists of containers on a balcony or sprawling acreage. Getting a good start will help ensure the success and enjoyment of any planting project.

✳ Select Your Site

A site with six to eight hours of full sun per day is ideal. If you don't have that, plant shade crops. If you don't have adequate flat space, explore patios, pass-throughs, or decks. We've grown corn, pumpkins, sunflowers, and more on a deck. Don't forget to think vertically—we often have peas and other vines growing up trellises. If your site is traveled by munching animals, such as deer, construct a fence around it.

✳ Get Comfortable

There are lots of items available to make gardening more comfortable. I suggest knee pads, a sun hat to protect your skin, and gardening clogs or old shoes you don't mind getting dirty. Many people like gardening gloves, and there are a range of them on the market. I find them irresistible to buy, with their cute vintage patterns, but I almost always end up taking them off and getting my hands really dirty—the better to feel the plants, the dirt, and what I'm doing.

☀ Prepare the Soil

Use a pitchfork to loosen the ground, preferably down to about 8″. Clear the surface with a heavy-duty rake. Break up dirt clods and pull weeds—these can go into a compost, if you're composting. You can buy packaged soil for a nice, even top layer that will have some nutrients in it, especially if your soil is poor. (Ask folks at a local garden-supply store for an opinion.) Add fertilizer before planting. Always water thoroughly before adding fertilizer and have kids wash their hands after handling.

If possible, plan some paths in your garden. They will make it easy to water, weed, and harvest without stepping on plants. Some people cover the paths with tanbark or other material (available at garden-supply stores) to mark them and to discourage plants from taking root there. Make sure you have a good path and a water source for your hose.

Slow Tip: Seeking good shade plants? Try these flowers: baby blue eyes, coneflowers, impatiens, lupine, nasturtiums, and snapdragons. Shade vegetables include beans, beets, broccoli, lettuce, peas, and spinach.

☀ Plant the Seeds or Seedlings

This part is especially fun. Follow packet instructions for seed spacing and conditions. You may want to lay a line of string as a guide and either poke the seeds into the dirt or create a shallow furrow in the dirt using a spade. Some stores carry seed tapes, which you lay down in a straight row. Tapes are great for tiny, hard-to-handle seeds like carrots. Large, easy-to-plant and easy-to-grow seeds include nasturtium and pea. Give each seed or seedling lots of room to spread out and grow. Try to anticipate plant height and put the tallest ones in the back. And don't forget to grow something that you'd like to see or eat!

✳ Fertilize

If you didn't add fertilizer to the bed while preparing the soil, add a little while planting. There are fertilizers on the market that are designed specifically for new growth. And there are many organic fertilizers available, which is optimal if you're growing food. Ask the folks at your local garden center to help you choose one. Many people fertilize again six weeks into the growing process.

If you are gardening in containers, get the biggest containers you have space and money for. Check for adequate drainage holes. If there isn't good drainage, you can add netting or pieces of broken pottery to the bottom of the pot. You may also want to add perlite, which will aerate the soil while helping it retain moisture. Fertilize as you would in a garden plot.

✳ Water Your Seeds or Plants

New seeds and transplants like lots of water. Water gently and deeply, so the water soaks through to the growing roots of the plants. Once your plants are established, you will probably need to water every one or two days when the weather is sunny, and perhaps daily for container plants. If a plant droops during the day or if the soil feels dry more than a couple of inches down, it needs water. Try not to water in bright sunshine because the sun can evaporate the water or cause burn spots on plants.

✳ Keep Up the Good Work

Continue watering and caring for plants as needed. Pull out weeds and cut back any growth that has died or become unattractive.

✳ Harvest What You've Grown

Sometimes I've been so unsure of when to harvest that I've let plants go past the point when they're edible or useful and all the way to seed. Take a chance and cut and enjoy what you've done. More will usually grow back!

Nurture a Budding Gardener

It's not hard to entice most kids to garden. Many enjoy the pleasure of poking seeds into the dirt and watching the miracle of the first green plant shoots appearing above ground. Lots of kids enjoy watering, perhaps especially the ones who manage to get themselves more wet than the plants. Those same kids usually enjoy getting muddy or digging in the dirt for worms. Still other children enjoy tending plants, harvesting them, and cooking with them. Then there are those who like to watch for creatures entering the garden.

There are so many delightful aspects of gardening that it's not hard to find one that will resonate with a particular child. Even so, there are easy and concrete steps you can take to make sure that your child is engaged in your gardening project.

- Keep chores manageable by organizing tasks into small blocks so that everyone can enjoy each one and the scope isn't overwhelming.
- Give children ownership of projects and space. Make a sign that identifies the garden or area as the child's, and help them select the plants they want to grow.
- Choose plants that come up quickly and are easy to plant and grow, such as nasturtiums, peas, sunflowers, and beans.
- Create opportunities for learning by teaching children how to check the soil and water the plants.

- Allow for mistakes and experimentation.
- Plant the same plant in different conditions, or grow something you've never grown, just to see what happens.
- Have children harvest what they've grown and then enjoy cooking, baking, or preserving it.
- Eat a rainbow. Form your harvest into a rainbow of colors before eating.

Slow Tip: Host a family or neighborhood farmers market or garden exchange. Our neighborhood has a weekly crop swap, which creates a fantastic opportunity to share produce and trade some for different and varied items, to find out what others are growing and how, and to simply visit with neighbors. Some kids might enjoy selling their produce. Follow the same tips as you would for a lemonade stand (chapter 1).

Partake in a Great Gardening Project

Sometimes the act of creating a theme places an activity in a special and memorable framework that grants it even more meaning and fun. These projects provide especially delightful ways to enhance everyone's garden experience.

☀ Plant a Pizza Garden

You can grow just about everything needed for a pizza right in your own garden and then harvest and eat all the items baked in a pizza. All you'll need to add is the dough and cheese!

Determine the shape of your pizza garden. Some are round, like a pizza, and others are rectangular or square.

Decide how you'd like to divide your space. Pizza wheels can be divided into four, six, or eight spokelike spaces, which will resemble pizza slices. You can divide up rectangular, square, or other shaped gardens any way you'd like. Consult seed package directions for seed spacing. Tomatoes, especially, need plenty of room. You can mark off areas with string or rocks.

Choose your pizza-garden ingredients and purchase seeds. Most anything that comes on a pizza can be grown in a yard or a large planter box. Some likely candidates include tomatoes, zucchini, eggplants, peppers, spinach, basil, oregano, onions, and garlic.

Water, fertilize, and weed your garden. If you've planted an edible pizza garden, harvest your ingredients and make a real pizza, using homemade dough, instant dough (available in markets), or English muffins for your crust.

Fertilize halfway through the season. Snip off any dead stalks, flowers, or weeds.

Slow Tip: Rather plant flowers? Make a decorative pizza wheel by planting bright red flowers all around to represent tomato sauce, a sprinkling of yellow flowers all around to represent cheese, spots of pink flowers for pepperoni, and some green leafy plants for spinach or peppers.

✳ Plant a Sunflower House

Kids love playhouses, and what better way to create one outside than with bright, cheery, and easy-to-grow sunflowers? If you have a large, sunny space, this is a terrific project that everyone will enjoy. As the sunflowers grow, they'll create the walls for the playhouse.

Determine the size and shape of the house. It could be as cozy as 4' × 6', or larger. Squares and rectangles work well, but feel free to be creative. You may want to leave room for a small table and chairs.

Buy sunflower seeds, preferably ones that produce tall, bright flowers with large heads. Use the instructions on the packet to determine how many seeds to buy per foot, and then purchase extra, as you'll be supplementing the initial planting.

Mark the boundaries of the house using string. Dig a furrow next to the string with a spade. Don't forget to leave space for a door.

Plant the seeds according to package directions, making sure to leave room for the sunflowers to grow and spread out.

Cover gently with a layer of dirt, then water.

Water regularly.

Sow extra seeds between existing plants every few weeks, so that the playhouse will last longer than one planting cycle.

✳ Plant a Barnyard Garden

When Anna was young, she loved lamb's ear plants, with their soft leaves and sweet name. She was so attracted to them when we saw them in other people's yards and in public places that when it came to planting our own garden, we knew it had to include lamb's ears. To this day, we always have some lamb's ears growing. There are lots of other evocatively named plants, and a barnyard garden is among one of the many whimsical theme gardens that children usually respond to.

These are some plants, named for our animal friends, that can be planted in a barnyard garden. In addition to their names, they also offer a unique visual appeal.

- Lamb's ears
- Hens and chicks
- Toad flax
- Bee balm
- Goat's beard
- Gooseberry

You may want to add more cheery, easy-to-grow, farm-friendly flowers, such as zinnias, cosmos, daisies, sunflowers, or marigolds.

✳ Grow Your Initials

Everyone likes something they can claim as their own, especially kids. And there's no reason seeds have to be planted in a straight line. You can plant seeds in shapes like spirals, circles, or the outlines of houses. Or you can plant a child's initials, and watch their joy when the shoots, and then plants, come up.

Choose seeds. Leafy greens work well for this project because they come up quickly and fill out nicely. These include lettuce, chives, radishes, cress, and various grasses.

Lay string in the shapes of the letters you like and dig a shallow furrow beside it.

Plant seeds according to package directions. Most greens have fine seeds, which will be planted in a close, continuous line.

Cover with a thin layer of soil and gently water.

Water regularly.

✳ Have a Seed Race

All races are fun, and there's no exception to a seed race, which allows you to make gardening into a game.

Choose two or more types of seeds.

Plant them at the same time, in the same conditions, near each other in the ground or in similar containers.

Water and watch which one emerges first and grows fastest.

Stake them with a store-bought or homemade yardstick if you want to measure their progress exactly.

✳ Grow Food for a Pet

Just as with harvesting food for humans, it's fun and rewarding for kids to know that their garden is growing food for a pet. Anna loved growing catnip for our two very long-lived cats. Other herbivore companions will be very happy to have a portion of the garden devoted to them. If your pet isn't used to a particular food, introduce it slowly to make sure the food agrees with the pet.

Some great pet plants to grow include the following:

Carrots, dandelions, grasses, nasturtiums, parsley, basil, and mint for rabbits.

Carrots, cucumbers, grasses, and lettuce for hamsters.

Collard greens, dandelion greens, mustard greens, turnip greens, parsley, and red hibiscus for iguanas.

✳ Treat a Cat to Catnip

A little catnip made into a simple toy can provide hours of fun for cats, who enjoy both the leaves and the buds of catnip plants. Many say that the buds are the most enjoyable for them. A little catnip goes a long way—catnip is best as a treat rather than a steady diet.

You'll need:

- Catnip seeds
- Planting area, dirt, fertilizer, water

- Twine
- Fabric, cut into approximately 5″ rounds, or old socks

Plant catnip out of reach of cats, in sun or partial shade, according to package directions, and water well. Catnip does well in containers.

Thin out growing plants, as necessary.

When any stem sports its first pairs of leaves, cut the stem right above the leaves. This will create pairs of new stems. Continue to cut the stems above each new leaf pair.

The plant will begin to produce small buds. Harvest these before they flower, and air-dry them.

Harvest stems and leaves after flowers bloom.

Tie bunches of stems and leaves together with twine and hang upside down in a dry, temperate, windless spot in your home or garage.

When the leaves are dried, remove them from the stems and crumble.

Both leaves and buds can be baked in an oven, to speed up the process. Bake on a cookie sheet, in a single layer, at the lowest setting possible, for approximately an hour, or until buds are dry and leaves crumble.

Place a small amount of catnip buds or crumbled leaves into a fabric round or an old sock. Pinch and tie closed with twine.

Give it to your kitty, or hang it from the back of a chair.

❈ Make a Root Viewer

For many, the roots of a plant can be just as fascinating as the parts we see aboveground. This simple root viewer lets budding botanists view the magical processes that happen below the surface.

> *You'll need:*
>
> - Clear plastic cups, bottles, or jars
> - Seeds and dirt

Fill the containers most of the way with dirt.

Plant the seeds close to one side, one or two per cup.

Put them in the sun and water gently.

Watch as roots form and plants sprout.

✳ Save Seeds

Although we entered this increasingly popular hobby somewhat by accident, seed saving goes back as far as plants themselves. Seeds have been saved, swapped, and transported over the years by growers who treasured certain vegetable and flower varieties enough to want to keep them from going extinct. Many of today's heirloom plants benefited from seed saving, which also helps the Earth's biodiversity. Hybrid plants can be created in labs, but only nonhybrid, or open-pollinated, plants can be created through seed saving. This is because the seed comes directly from the plant and is identical to the original seed planted.

One summer we had a cascade of lovely nasturtiums

CREATE AN AREA FOR TEA PARTIES

Tea parties can be especially whimsical in the garden, which is perhaps their natural setting. They can also simply serve as a great way to get kids outside. Any clearing can host a party. A tree stump can serve as a table or chairs. A sunflower house or other area can hold the party. Invite flower fairies and other imaginary creatures (see chapter 3), and make tea sandwiches (see chapter 4).

tumbling over the deck boxes, with their bright colors and peppery scents. When we went to weed them, we noticed that many had gone to seed or completely dropped their recognizable seeds on the ground. We gathered the seeds excitedly and saved them to replant the next year.

Choose high-quality plants, flowers, fruits, and vegetables from which to save seeds. They should be in good health and free of disease.

Try to harvest seeds when the seed pods have dried on the plant. Place a paper bag over the seed heads to catch seeds, or gently shake them from the plant.

Make sure the seeds are completely dry. You may want to dry them on a small piece of chicken wire or window screen. (See the potpourri instructions on page 194.)

Remove any chaff from the seeds and store in a paper envelope, marked with the date the seed was saved. Seeds are best used within a year of saving. Place the envelope in an airtight container and store in a cool, dry place.

Looking for easy seeds to save? Try bean, chicory, endive, hollyhock, lettuce, nasturtium, pea, sweet pea, or zinnia.

✳ Make a Simple Composter

Composting is an ancient practice that dates back to Mesopotamia more than four thousand years ago. Early American settlers composted using fish. Composting remains a wonderful, hands-on way to involve children in gardening and to teach them about the ecosystem, as well as reuse. They'll learn that, like the produce they grow, fresh, ripe dirt doesn't have to be bought in bags. Rather, it is formed from the decomposition of natural materials, aided by a wide variety of bugs, worms, and microorganisms, like helpful bacteria and fungi. It can then be used as high-quality natural soil and fertilizer. Your family may also notice that an increase in composting means a decrease in trash.

There's no need to buy an expensive compost bin, as you can easily make your own. Either way, the principles of basic composting are the same.

You'll need:

- Plastic garbage pail or 5-gallon bucket with lid
- Drill
- Brown matter: dried leaves, twigs, plant debris, shredded newspaper, sawdust, or straw
- Green matter: grass clippings, green leaves, vegetable trimmings, fruit scraps, or coffee grounds
- Potting soil, optional
- Bungee cord
- Garden fork

If using a trash can, drill holes in four or so rows around its perimeter and a few on the bottom. Drill holes in the bucket, if possible. This allows air to enter the composter, which helps the microbes in the compost do their work, while at the same time keeping odors down.

Add brown matter equal to about 1/3 of the can or bucket. Brown matter has a high carbon count and takes longer to break down than green matter.

Add an equal part of green matter. Green matter is high in nitrogen and attracts microbes and insects that help break the ingredients down. Green matter can also be smelly, so you may want to err on the side of having slightly more brown matter. In addition, a layer of straw or sawdust on top can reduce odors.

Do not add dairy, meat, or animal waste.

If you'd like, add a bit of potting soil to the top of the ingredients. This is more important in the smaller bucket composter, as it will help kick-start the process. It is important to have some air at the top of the pile.

Add just enough water to moisten the ingredients.

Close the lid and secure with a bungee cord.

Place in a warm spot.

Making sure that the lid is on, roll the can or bucket once or twice a week to mix the ingredients. With the bucket, you can also open the lid and thoroughly mix the ingredients with the garden fork. Don't mix more often, as the compost needs to settle between mixings.

Your compost may take three months or longer to be garden ready.

❋ Make a Rain Gauge

My family and I have always been fascinated with weather. It's wondrous and constantly changing, and records for heat, cold, wind, snowpack, and rainfall are always being broken. Because it's measured in inches, rain is something that's easy and concrete for amateur meteorologists to measure, and doing so can create an interesting and memorable project.

> ***Slow Snippet:*** Ancient Greeks used rain gauges to determine taxes on farmers: the more rain, the more produce, the higher the tax.

You'll need:

- Large clear glass jar or plastic bottle
- Ruler, tape, and waterproof marker
- Rock, optional

Place the bottle or jar on a flat surface and place a line of tape going up it.

With one person holding the ruler, carefully mark 1/2″ increments on the tape with the marker.

Set the rain gauge outside where it will catch rain (or snow). Weight with rocks if necessary.

Observe how much rain falls into the gauge. You may want to observe at the same time each day and make a weekly or monthly rain chart. Either empty the gauge between uses or collect rain cumulatively. Try to guess how much new rain has fallen before looking at the measurement.

Slow Tip: Use the water you collect in your rain gauge to water plants.

Create Garden Art

Artists and craftspeople have long been inspired by the garden. Just getting outside with art and craft materials can open a world of wonder and observation. Gardens, in all their color and variety, offer great subjects, as well as a place to clear the artist's head. In addition, they often provide a place where one can get messier than inside a house. Bring tempera or finger paints and paper outside, or have fun with a project that will lend beauty and fun to your garden.

☀ Coffee-Filter Butterflies

This simple project is great for young crafters. You can display the finished butterflies or hang them from the ceiling with fishing line.

You'll need:

- Pipe cleaners, cut in half
- Round paper coffee filters
- Watercolors or food coloring

- Paintbrushes
- Cup of water for brushes
- Newspapers, to cover work surface

Flatten the coffee filter and place on a plate or layers of newspaper.

Paint with water colors or food coloring and let dry.

Fold the filter accordion style, approximately 1/2" thick. (See Tie-Dye Bandannas in chapter 3 for accordion instructions.)

Twist the pipe cleaner piece around the filter in its center.

Fan the butterfly wings out, as necessary.

✳ Painted Flowerpot

Painted flowerpots are a super-simple, inexpensive project. The finished pot can add tremendous color and interest to your garden or be planted with a pretty plant to make a wonderful gift. This project is as limitless as your creativity.

You'll need:

- Clay pot, any size
- Poster, tempera, or acrylic paint
- Paintbrushes
- Cup of water for brushes
- Pencils
- Newspaper to protect the craft area
- Dirt and plant, optional

Wash and dry the pot.

Paint your design. You may wish to outline first in pencil.

Let each layer dry before completing another.

Let the pot dry completely.

Plant as desired.

Slow Tip: Add flat buttons to your design. Simply glue them on, before or after painting. Or decorate with seed packets. Cut out the front of the packet and glue or decoupage it to the clay pot. (Decoupage medium and brushes are available at craft stores.)

Slow Tip: Collect rocks and paint them with garden shapes like ladybugs, bees, and mushrooms.

✳ Beaded Spiderweb

This is an enchanting project that mirrors the intricate work of busy spiders while providing a whimsical and colorful garden object when finished.

You'll need:

- 3 bamboo skewers per web
- Scissors or wire cutters
- Ruler
- Thin wire
- Beads of your choosing (make sure the beads and wire are a compatible size)

Clip the pointed tips from the skewers.

Put the skewers in a bundle.

Cut a 12″ piece of wire and wrap half of it tightly around the center of the bundle.

Spread the skewers out until they all point outward like an asterisk, crossing in the middle.

Continue to wrap the wire to secure the new shape.

Cut a piece of wire approximately 18″.

Wrap one end of the wire around one of the skewers twice, about 1″ from the center.

String beads along the length of the wire, and then wrap the wire twice around the next skewer. Continue until you are back to the first skewer. Wrap the wire to secure it.

Cut the next pieces of wire 24″, 30″, and 36″ long, and string and bead them around the skewers, as above.

Place or hang your spiderweb in your garden.

Slow Tip: You can string beads tightly along the lengths of wire, or you can leave room for the wire to show through.

Slow Tip: Try beading flowers, leaves, butterflies, ladybugs, or other garden features.

✳ Wind Chimes

Nearly everyone delights in wind chimes, which tinkle musically in a breeze and signify long, lazy afternoons.

You'll need:

- Household or other items that make noise when the wind runs through them or when they gently hit one another, such as silverware, varying lengths of copper or metal pipe, metal cans and measuring cups, and wooden spoons
- Heavy-duty fishing line
- Circular or straight piece of scrap wood, or a branch
- Drill, optional

Drill one hole per object in the piece of scrap wood. You can also tie objects to the wood or branch without drilling, or simply use the branch of a tree.

Drill one hole on the top of each object, where it will hang from, optional.

Plan your wind chime. You will want some objects to be within touching distance, so they will make noise.

Run the fishing line through the hole in each object and attach it to the wood or branch, knotting the line to secure it.

Add as many items to the wind chime as you'd like.

Hang your chime where it can catch a breeze.

Welcome Wildlife

Small creatures like birds and butterflies are always fun to watch. There are lots of ways to encourage them to visit the garden and linger a while throughout the year, many of which provide fun and fascinating projects while benefiting the local habitat and the garden. It can be especially rewarding to know that you're helping animals find food and, perhaps, shelter and that you're participating in helping the greater ecosystem of the Earth. You don't need a large yard to have a habitat garden. Apartment balconies, window ledges, school gardens, and decks can all host local animals.

Habitat Gardening Basics

Supply Food

Any creature in the wild is going to be looking for food. Your garden can be an eatery if it provides plants, nectar, pollen, seeds, and other goodies that the animals in your area would like. Native plants from your area are the best food source. (Visit a local nursery or other resource to learn about these.) Supplement with feeders or other plants.

Provide Water

Animals need water to drink and bathe. If there isn't already water in your garden, you may want to add a water source, like a birdbath or even a small, shallow pan.

Create Shelter and Places
for Animals to Raise Their Young

Creatures need shelter from the elements and from predators. They also need safe places to lay eggs or raise their young. Shelter can be created with native plants, hollow trees, piles of brush, or cheery birdhouses. Certain native plants can also provide good egg-laying habitats.

Keep the Garden Pesticide-Free

Chemical pesticides and fertilizers aren't good for the creatures (or small gardeners). Aim to keep the garden natural and to maintain it. Native plants tend to be low maintenance, as well as desired by local creatures. There are also beneficial bugs that can help keep undesired pests out of the garden, as well as natural soaps. Inquire about these at a local nursery.

✳ Attract Butterflies to the Garden

Beautiful butterflies are actually lower maintenance than they might appear. They provide a great deal of joy and wonder, and they really don't need much to grace our gardens. You can attract butterflies to any size garden.

Butterflies need two kinds of plants: nectar plants whose flowers offer sweet liquid to feed the butterflies, and host plants on which to lay their eggs and to provide food for caterpillars.

For nectar, choose flowering plants that are native to your area. Your local nursery will be helpful in choosing these. The Lady Bird Johnson Wildflower Center and the Pollinator

Partnership offer very detailed guides to the best butterfly-attracting plants for your area. (See the Resources section.)

Choose colorful plants that attract butterflies, with bright red, pink, purple, yellow, and orange flowers. They are particularly drawn to flat or clustered flowers.

Plant in a sunny spot that is sheltered from wind, and provide plant variety. Also provide a sunny resting spot for butterflies, such as a flat rock or balcony ledge.

Plant long-blooming or continuous-blooming plants, so that there are often flowers for the butterflies.

Include host plants that provide a place for butterflies to lay their eggs and yield food for emerging caterpillars. Butterfly species depend on specific host plants. For example, monarchs will lay eggs only on milkweed. Your local nursery is a resource, as is the chart available at the Butterfly Website (butterflywebsite.com/butterflygardening.cfm). Plant butterfly host plants a short distance from the nectar plants. Because they will be chewed on, you may want to place them in the back of a garden.

Provide water, either in a butterfly and bird feeder or in a pie tin or shallow pan. Add sand to the pan, if possible, as butterflies like to congregate in sand and mud.

Slow Snippet: North American monarch butterflies fly an amazing two-way migration each year, up to three thousand miles each way, to and from their warm winter hibernating sites in California and Mexico. Somehow they find their way to the same sites each fall, even though the ones who migrate are the great-great-grandchildren of the butterflies that returned the previous spring.

✳ Make a Bird Feeder

Birds are a great deal of fun to welcome to the garden. Ever since Anna was small, we've always had a bird feeder up and enjoyed watching the various birds and listening for their songs. As with butterflies, we keep a chart (available at nurseries or bookstores or on the Internet) handy so we can identify our visitors. It can be fun to experiment with different kinds of seeds, as well as feeders, to see which birds each attracts.

Pinecone Bird Feeder

This is a very simple feeder that you can make and hang most anywhere to attract local birds.

You'll need:

- Pinecone
- 2′–3′ of string
- 1/2 cup vegetable shortening, peanut or other nut butter, suet, or lard
- 1/4 cup cornmeal or oatmeal
- 2 1/2 cups mixture of birdseed (e.g., sunflower and millet; check your local nursery for suggestions), chopped nuts, and dried fruit
- Mixing bowl
- Plate, shallow dish, or pie tin
- Spoon or butter knife

Tie the string around one end of the pinecone.

In mixing bowl, combine peanut butter or other spread with meal.

Spread that mixture over the pinecone with the knife or spoon.

Pour the birdseed and feed ingredients onto the plate.

Roll the pinecone in the seeds.

Hang from a tree branch or window eave.

Slow Tip: Don't have pinecones? Use a toilet-paper tube for the feeder base and punch a hole in one end to hang it.

Milk-Carton Bird Feeder

This bird feeder is modeled after store-bought feeders, but because it uses recycled and available materials, it can be created for a fraction of the price. Have fun painting and decorating the feeder any way you'd like.

You'll need:

- Milk carton, washed and dried
- Popsicle or craft sticks
- Wooden dowel, approximately 8" long, or a skewer
- Craft glue
- Scissors
- Paint and brushes or seed packets or magazine pictures and decoupage medium
- Sandpaper and primer, if needed
- Sealer (decoupage medium or other), optional
- Birdseed
- String or wire

Cut doorway- or archway-shaped openings on two opposite sides of the milk carton. The top of the cutout should be about halfway from the bottom of the milk carton, and the bottom of the cutout should be about 1/4 of the way from the bottom of the milk carton. Leave 1″ or more on the sides of the carton. The opening should be big enough to pour seed into.

Paint the feeder any way you'd like, or cut the fronts of seed packets or other pictures and attach with decoupage medium. If you're using a plastic-covered carton, you may need to sand first and use a coat of primer paint. Seal with craft sealer, if desired.

Glue craft sticks to the top of the carton to create a roof, and paint the sticks, if desired.

Poke parallel holes below each opening and run a dowel through the holes to create a perch for the birds.

Scoop birdseeds into the feeder. Cut a hole and add a loop of string or wire on top. Hang the bird feeder from the loop.

See Birds of a Feather in chapter 2, for some typical and lyrical bird songs.

✳ Make a Hummingbird Habitat

It's hard not to be fascinated by tiny, busy, quick hummingbirds, whose wings beat so fast (up to eighty times per second) that they appear to move in a blur.

They can fly between twenty-five and thirty miles an hour and six hundred miles nonstop. They don't even stop to drink and bathe; they do that while in flight. Of course, they need a lot of fuel for all that activity, the equivalent of 155,000 daily calories for a human!

Besides being powerhouses, hummingbirds are terrific pollinators of other flowers, so they are good for the garden and the Earth. Important components of the hummingbird diet are sugar, from flower nectar, tree sap, and food from backyard feeders.

Provide Water in the Habitat

Hummingbirds like to bathe in shallow water and find typical birdbaths too deep. Put a little water in a shallow pan or pie tin.

If you want to hang the tin, cut three holes into the sides and hang with rope.

Attract Hummingbirds with Flowers

Unlike some other animals, hummingbirds have no sense of smell and rely solely on sight. They like bright colors—red feeders and brightly colored red, orange, pink, and purple flowers. They also like trumpet-shaped flowers, with long tubes that they can stick their beaks into. Some good choices for hummingbirds include azaleas, bee balm, columbines, fuchsias, hibiscus, hollyhocks, trumpet honeysuckles, impatiens, morning glories, petunias, and phlox.

Choose and Care for a Hummingbird Feeder

Feeders are another simple way to entice hummingbirds into your garden. Hummingbirds are drawn to red, so start with a small feeder with some red on it, or hang red ribbons or other items from the feeder.

Hang the feeder from a tree branch, an eave, a garden stake, a pole, or another location in relative shade and close to the flowers. You may want to have two feeders, as hummingbirds are territorial, and some may not visit the first one if another is present. Hang where you can easily observe the action.

Clean the feeder at least once a week, more often in hot weather, to prevent fermentation of the nectar.

Homemade Hummingbird Nectar

You will need nectar for your feeder. You can buy hummingbird nectar in stores, but it's very easy, rewarding, and economical to make your own.

> **You'll need:**
>
> - 1 cup (or part) water
> - 1/4 cup (or part) sugar

Bring the water to a boil.

Add the sugar and boil for two minutes.

Allow to cool and pour into a hummingbird feeder.

Do not use honey or artificial sweeteners. They are bad for hummingbirds. Nectar can be kept in the refrigerator for two weeks.

The National Wildlife Federation is a great resource for lots of other habitat gardening projects. (See the Resources section.)

Dry Flowers and Herbs

Well-off medieval families had still rooms, which housed potions and cures, as well as bunches of dried flowers for sachets and potpourris. Each family had a still room book, full of secret recipes that were passed down through generations of women. Today, flowers can be dried in garages, pantries, kitchens, sheds, and studios. We almost always have flowers hanging somewhere. Even my wedding bouquet is dried and displayed in a beautiful hanging container in our guest bathroom, where it has been for seventeen years.

✳ Air-Dried Flowers and Garden Items

> **You'll need:**
>
> - Small square of chicken wire or window screen
> - 4 pieces of wood, 8″ or any size, as desired, or a box

- Hammer and nails, or glue
- Freshly picked flower petals, leaves, or seeds

If using wood, create a frame out of the wood pieces and nail or glue to secure them.

Cut the screen to fit and place on top of the frame or over the opening of the box. Nail or glue it in place.

Collect flowers and petals when they are just past full bloom and still attractive.

Place flowers, leaves, buds, or seeds onto the screen, leaving air around each item.

Place the screen in a dry place with good air circulation for approximately one week or until the flowers have dried.

✳ Hang-Dried Flowers and Herbs

You'll need:

- Scissors and string or rubber bands
- Hammer and nails or hooks
- Fresh bunch of flowers or herbs

Cut and gather a bunch of flowers or herbs.

Remove some leaves if they are exceptionally dense, and arrange them if you want to keep them in a bunch when dried.

Fasten the ends of the stems with string or rubber bands.

Decide where you want to hang the flowers. Hammer a nail or hook in a dry place with good air circulation and no direct sunlight.

Suspend the bunch from the nail or hook. Allow to dry for one week or more.

Leave the flowers in a bunch or remove individual petals.

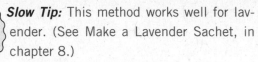

Slow Tip: This method works well for lavender. (See Make a Lavender Sachet, in chapter 8.)

Slow Tip: Oven drying, though fine for catnip, is usually too hot for flowers.

✳ Potpourri

This is one of our favorite garden projects. It involves many things we enjoy, including scent, creation, and nature. There is an endless variety of combinations to make potpourri, and it's such a joy to make your own from scratch. The resulting sachets can be used to scent drawers, closets, and rooms. They also make great gifts. Enjoy potpourri in an open bowl, for display, as well as for scenting a room.

You'll need:

- Mix of dried herbs and flower petals
- Nonmetallic bowl
- Jars with lids
- Orrisroot powder (available at craft and specialty stores)
- Essential oil and dropper, optional
- Muslin or other drawstring bags, or netting circles and ribbon
- Bowls for display

Smell the flowers in your garden before drying to discern which you might like in a potpourri. Popular potpourri flowers and herbs include calendulas, chamomile, lavender, lemon verbena, mint, roses, and rosemary. Orange peel is also a nice addition.

Dry the flowers and herbs, using either the air-dry or the hang-dry method.

Mix a blend of flowers and herbs in a nonmetallic bowl until you arrive at a combination you like. Add a teaspoon of orris-root per cup of potpourri mix and stir well to blend. If you'd like, add a few drops of essential oil, in a similar or complimentary scent to the flowers you are using. Write down your formula so you can make it again.

If making sachets, scoop small amounts of the mix into drawstring bags or onto netting circles and secure with ribbon.

If displaying, arrange in an open bowl.

If you're not using it right away, cure your potpourri by storing it in lidded jars, in a dry, dark place, for two weeks or more.

Slow Snippet: Flowers were once used in a language that goes back to ancient China and even predates written language. Roses, which we associate with love, stood for virtue in the Far East, silence in Egypt, and festivity in ancient Rome. England's Queen Victoria occasionally spoke in flower language in the mid-1800s, when flower dictionaries flourished. The 2011 royal wedding of Kate Middleton to Prince William featured a bouquet based on flower language:

Lily of the valley—Return of happiness

Sweet William—Gallantry

Hyacinth—Constancy of love

Ivy—Fidelity

Myrtle—Married love

6

Slow Nature

Many of us want our children to have high-quality experiences in nature. Indeed nature-deficit disorder has been named a condition of the twenty-first century, and nature play has been linked with improved imagination, cooperation, wonder, and health. Nature also provides a terrific setting in which to have new and different experiences that can greatly enhance family memories and bonds.

I've seen firsthand, with my family and with groups of children, the way people open up in nature and experience more sharing, discovery, and play. My family and I often get into deep discussions in nature, when we're not observing or playing games. Something about being out under a vast sky in the constantly changing natural world leads to different insights, connections, and experiences than those we may have indoors—insights about the greater world and also about ourselves.

Although we often want more time in nature, for our children, and perhaps ourselves, we sometimes don't know where to begin or what to do once we get there. Even if we do have an idea and a map, it can be difficult to know just how to combat the boredom that some kids complain about in nature and to compete with the stimulation of electronic entertainment.

Here are some easy ideas for getting kids out in nature, for enjoying the time while they're there, and perhaps for encouraging their own lifetime love and stewardship of the outdoors and its opportunities for wonder and beauty.

Observe Nature

There are so many fun things to make, do, observe, and learn in nature, whether in deep woods, at a sea shore, in a city park, or in your own backyard. These simple and rewarding activities will help children slow down enough to observe and experience nature's small wonders and have fun while they're doing so. As a bonus, many of these activities require minimal or no equipment.

❋ Name Walk

As lovely as nature is, the instruction to observe it can be overwhelming, especially for kids. Just as birdwatchers focus on birds, other opportunities to focus on specific elements of nature can help children tune into their surroundings.

> *You'll need:*
>
> • Paper and pencils, optional

Before beginning your walk, instruct everyone to look for things that start with the same first letter as their names.

Lead kids on a route or trail or around a park and encourage them to look in the sky, on the ground, and in trees. Be prepared to walk slowly and perhaps not cover much distance, to allow for deep observation.

Slow Tip: Try other observation walks by having everyone look for the same type of thing, such as flowers, leaves, birds, rocks, small items, smooth items, or certain colors. See how many varieties the group can find within one category.

Participants call out what they see or write their findings down to share with the group later.

✳ Listen, Do You Hear?

This is an activity I remember from elementary school, when, on long sunny afternoons, our class would go out to a grassy hillock in front of the school and lie down, shut our eyes, and simply, quietly, listen to the sounds around us. This easy activity is a great way to get everyone to be still and to observe more than they might if they were walking, seeing, and doing other activities with multiple senses. It provides both relaxation and heightened awareness as people enjoy the variety of sounds in nature.

Find a comfortable spot in the grass and lie down.

Participants settle in, shut their eyes, and get used to the sounds around them.

 Slow Tip: Try having people count how many different sounds they hear in a set time period.

✳ Cloud Race

Watching the sky and clouds can be somewhat of a luxury in our busy lives. Formed from evaporated water that rose through the air and condensed, clouds are lovely, miraculous, ever-changing, and not to be missed.

Lie down in the grass.

Players or teams each choose a cloud and root for it to go faster than the others across the sky.

Slow Snippet: Clouds aren't really white, but appear white because they are dense and reflect sunlight back to us. Because sunlight does not shine through rain clouds, they appear gray.

☀ Poetry Walk

We took a lot of poetry walks when Anna was young. Often they were in the neighborhood to a special spot near our house that is ripe with ferns and shade trees and has a small creek running through it in the winter. Something about the act of recording your observations—with a camera or journal—causes you to look around in a different way.

You'll need:

- Journal or notebook and a pen

Take your journal on a walk in nature and stop every so often to record your thoughts. Don't worry about writing your thoughts in poetic form. Just write what you notice.

Slow Tip: Try a vertical poem. Choose a word that represents your feelings and observations on the walk. Write that word vertically. Each letter of the word will then be the first letter of a sentence in your poem.

If you or your child are struggling to record thoughts, try asking open-ended prompts, such as, "What does the hawk's flight remind you of?" or "What do those rustling leaves feel (or smell, look, or sound) like?" You might be surprised at some of the connections that you and your child will make, the leaps of poetry and interesting phrases that can be conjured once you are quiet in nature.

✳ Nature Bracelets

I've done this very easy activity with groups of all ages. It encourages people to look all around them.

> **You'll need:**
>
> • Masking tape, 1″ or wider, enough to go around each child's wrist

Tear off a piece of masking tape, slightly longer than the child's wrist.

Place it around the wrist with the sticky side out.

Go for a walk or hunt and look for small items in nature that can be stuck to the masking tape, such as leaves, twigs, seeds, acorns, and pods. In general, things that have already fallen on the ground are safe to pick. If in doubt, leave something.

Fill the bracelet by sticking the items onto it and wear it proudly.

Play Nature Games

Games are a surefire way to engage members of a group and ensure that they have fun and create memories in nature. The following games can also be great tools to enhance children's understanding of the outdoors and its inhabitants.

Some of these and the observation games have become school and scout classics, some of which were adapted from Joseph Cornell's wonderful book *Sharing Nature with Children*, which contains many more.

☀ Predation

This game helps kids learn about our ecosystem and food chains, and the various roles different animals play in nature.

> **You'll need:**
>
> - Small items to represent food, such as smaller rocks, leaves, or game pieces
> - Blindfolds, optional
> - Rocks, string, or hula hoop, optional

Introduce the predator-prey relationship: Predators depend on the prey in their environment for food, and use smell, sight, hearing, stealth, speed, camouflage, and poison to capture and eat the prey. The prey tries to avoid being eaten by using some of the same techniques. Most predators and prey have evolved together as part of the same food chain. Prey animals might themselves prey on other animals or on plants. Try to get kids to think of different predators and prey, perhaps some that live in your area, such as owls and mice, bear and fish, or fox and rabbits.

Divide the group into predators and prey animals, with a ratio of about two to one prey animals to predators. The players may be blindfolded, so they depend on their hearing. (If so, use a smaller area or designate a circle with rocks, string, or hula hoops and have kids tap others if they veer away.) Place food items around the area for the prey animals to eat. Predators roam the area searching

GEOCACHING: A WORLD-WIDE TREASURE HUNT

Got a GPS device? Try geocaching, an outdoor treasure hunt game played by people around the world. Visit www.geocaching.com to get involved.

for prey, whom they tag to represent eating the prey. Prey animals try to get food without being tagged. The game ends when all the prey animals are tagged or all the food eaten.

✳ Web of Life

This is another powerful game that teaches kids about the interconnectedness of living things. We encountered it on a school field trip to a vibrant marsh and have never forgotten it.

You'll need:

- Ball of string, yarn, or twine

Players form a circle. The leader asks them to name a plant or animal that lives in the area. When someone names a plant or animal, he or she is handed the end of the ball of string. The leader then asks the group to name a living thing that depends on that first living thing for its food or shelter. When someone names another plant or animal, the string is unraveled and handed to that person. The game continues this way until everyone is holding the same piece of string. It can be very dramatic for everyone to realize that they are webbed together. Choose one of the players to illustrate what happens when there is change, such as when a tree burns down or an animal is eaten. Have that person pull his or her piece of string to see its effect on all the others.

Slow Tip: If people get stuck on what to say next, help them go backward or forward in the food and shelter chain. The bird eats a frog, the frog eats an ant, the ant crawls under a tree, the tree provides oxygen for the deer, and so on.

✳ Kim's Game

This well-known scout game has entertained many generations and is easy to organize and play, indoors or out.

> *You'll need:*
>
> - 20 small items, such as acorns, shells, twigs, rocks, pinecones, or seeds
> - Pencil and paper for each person
> - Towel or something to cover items

Decide whether you are playing in teams or individually.

Uncover items for two minutes.

Cover items again. Teams or players remember and name as many objects as they can.

Each player earns one point for each correct article named.

Slow Tip: Seeking a different way to play? Try Duplication. Uncover items for two minutes. Players go out in nature to find duplicates of the items.

✳ Scavenger Hunt

Everyone loves scavenger hunts. It's great fun to be on the lookout for things during this classic nature activity that can be as unique or open ended as the leader or group desires. Hunts can turn a simple walk into an adventure or a game. They can cause us to look around in nature a little more closely than we may have.

You'll need:

- Pencils and paper

HOW DO YOU USE A COMPASS?

Orienteering by compass is a basic skill made no less (and perhaps more) necessary in the era of GPS and other orienteering aids. In addition to being useful, it's fun and confers a sense of accomplishment.

The red arrow on a compass always points north (in the Northern Hemisphere). Hold the compass at waist level and line up so that the directional arrow, at the base of the compass, also points north. Keeping the compass at your waist, turn your body. Watch the compass rotate. Line up the red arrow so it points north again. Note where the directional arrow is facing. It should be ____ degrees (the closest number on the compass) ____ direction (N, E, S, W, or something in between), such as 45 degrees NE. Practice a bit before trying the scavenger hunt or orienteering for direction.

Create a list in advance or have players contribute to one list of ten to twenty things they might find in their game's setting. Examples include an oak tree, a pond, a duck, a dandelion, a wildflower, a nest, a feather, or a hollow log.

You or the hunters could also list more subjective items (which is especially good for team play), such as something rough, something orange, something unexpected, something heart-shaped, and so on.

If you create the list, keep in mind the difficulty of the items and the ages of the group.

Teams or players go off to seek the items on the list and cross each off when they see it.

Each player earns one point for each item found. The person or team with the most points wins.

✳ Compass Hunt

This is a fun game that also teaches compass use and orienteering skills. Although compass hunts take a little preplanning, they provide an exceptionally worthwhile experience.

You'll need:

- Compasses for each person or team
- Paper and pencil
- Prewritten clues
- Hammer and nails or string, optional.

Visit the area you will use for the hunt in advance of the game.

Using a compass, mark off a certain number of paces in a certain number of degrees and direction. Write the number of paces, the number of the degree, and the direction so you can later create a written clue. Mark off a different number of paces in a different number of degrees and direction. Record what you did and go back and leave a written clue in your last spot (nailed or strung to a tree or placed under a rock) that will tell players how many paces to walk, and in which direction.

Continue pacing off distances and directions and scattering clues. You may wish to have something special at the end point of the last clue.

On game day, teach compass skills.

Hand out or announce the first clue and have teams or players set off, on the basis of the clue.

Make Nature Crafts

My family has found it very gratifying to work with and create things outdoors, using natural materials for inspiration.

✳ Leaf Prints

Leaf prints make a great keepsake that captures the unique patterns on the undersides of leaves. You can print on T-shirts or other items of clothing to create wearable art, or you can make leaf-print cards or other paper items.

You'll need:

- Acrylic paint
- Paper or fabric to print on
- Newspapers, to cover work surface
- Small pans or bowls for the paint, optional
- Small brayer, cardboard, tape, and wax paper, optional

If you will print on a T-shirt or other fabric, spread the fabric out and tape it to the back of the cardboard to sturdy it.

Hunt for leaves that have interesting shapes, textures, or designs.

Lay the leaves out, facedown, on the fabric or paper to get an idea of your design.

Place one leaf, facedown, on the newspaper.

Paint it thoroughly, making sure that paint covers every surface cranny.

Carefully lift the leaf, and place it, paint side down, onto your item.

Press down gently, with your hands, being careful not to shift the position of the leaf, or place a piece of wax paper over the leaf and roll it gently, using a brayer. Make sure that you've pressed on each part of the leaf.

Gently lift the leaf back up so that the paint relief remains.

Repeat with the other leaves in the design.

Let the finished piece dry flat.

✳ Flower Press

Pressed flowers and other botanicals are beautiful reminders of your time in nature and can be used to create many lovely objects, such as paper (see chapter 3), placemats (see chapter 7), or smaller items like bookmarks.

You can press flowers in thick books, like phone directories, or make a traditional flower press, which works better than a phone book because it presses items to flatten and dry them, while also allowing some air to circulate. This press also has the benefit of being portable, so you can use it as you collect your flowers. We've used ours many times.

You'll need:

- 2 squares of particle board or wood, about 5″ × 5″ and 1/2″ thick.
- 2 same-size squares each of newspaper, plain paper, and cardboard
- Drill and lanyard lacing or string, or adjustable C-clamp, or bungee cord

Drill four holes in the wood pieces, each approximately 3/4″ diagonally from each corner. Thread lacing or string between two parallel pairs of holes, leaving enough to tie and untie, as needed.

Seek fresh, dry flowers that you like and think will look pretty when pressed.

Place a piece of cardboard, then a piece of newsprint, then a piece of paper, on top of one of the wood pieces. Place the flower on top of that. If pressing other flowers, make sure that they don't touch.

Cover the flower with another piece of paper, another piece of newsprint, and another piece of cardboard, in that order.

Place the second piece of wood on top and secure with the lacings, C-clamp, or bungee cord.

Check the flowers in a couple of days. If the newsprint is damp but the flower is not fully pressed, replace it and press again.

✳ Sand Candles

These unique candles are fun to make for yourself or for gifts. Because the finished candles have a layer of sand on their surfaces, they're also great reminders of the place in which they were made.

You'll need:

- 4 or more ounces paraffin, soy, or bees wax per vessel, or as needed to nearly fill each
- Pretreated candle wicks with metal tabs at the bottom and at least 2" more than needed at the top
- Wax color chips, optional
- Essential oil or fragrance oil and dropper, optional
- Double boiler, or equivalent
- Old pan for double boiler, optional
- Dedicated craft/candy thermometer
- Dedicated wooden craft spoon
- Small craft scoop or toothpicks
  (many of these items are available at craft and specialty stores)
- Newspapers, to cover work surface
- Small item, such as a vase, cup, votive holder, milk carton, or shell, which will form the candle's shape
- Sand
- Bucket or dishpan, optional

Decide whether you will pour your candle wax in a sandy location or fill a bucket or dishpan with sand to work elsewhere.

Wet the sand enough so that it holds together, and compact it.

Press your small item into the sand to form a shape, and lift it back out carefully. The shape left in the sand will be the shape of your candle.

You can also form a shape directly in the sand, making sure to create a flat bottom.

If the shape collapses, wet and compact it again and press the container in again.

Break or chop wax into small chunks, place in the old pan, and heat.

Continue to watch the melting wax, stirring occasionally and adding more wax if needed. (Wax should never be left unattended. It's also a good idea for candle and soap makers to have dedicated tools, if possible, so that soap and wax don't get onto food utensils.)

When the wax has completely melted (this can take up to twenty minutes, depending on the type and size of the wax pieces), use the candy thermometer to ensure that it has reached 225°.

Stir in one color chip at a time until the desired color is achieved, or leave natural. Remove from heat.

Note: Because sand candles require especially hot wax, use extreme caution in heating and pouring.

Also, do not add fragrance to this extremely hot wax. You can add it on the second pour.

Pour wax into the opening in the sand.

Allow the wax to absorb into the sand (approximately one hour), which will create an outer layer of sand on the candle. Heat more wax—this time in a double boiler, to a temperature of 180°. Add fragrance now, if desired, and add a second pour, which will fill out the shape of the candle.

Gently lower the wick into the candle.

Cover with cardboard or a plate that is larger than the candle, if you are concerned about sand floating into it.

Let the wax dry overnight.

Carefully lift the candle out of the sand.

✳ Pinecone Folk

Pinecones are wonderfully adaptable and can be used in a variety of crafts. We've collected and used them to create natural fall centerpieces, as well as these creative pinecone people and families. When you add acorn heads and other tiny details, they become especially unique and delightful.

You'll need:

- Variety of pinecones
- Acorns with caps intact, for heads
- Glitter, pipe cleaners, twigs, small pieces of yarn, popsicle sticks, toothpicks, fabric, felt or lace scraps, beads, markers, paint, paper, and other decorative items
- Hot glue or craft glue

Glue the acorn head onto the pinecone body and let dry slightly.

Decorate as desired:

Glue twig or pipe cleaner arms, approximately 2″ each, to the pinecone.

Draw or paint a face on the acorn, or glue on beads for eyes and a nose.

Decorate the pinecone with a glitter, beaded, or lace "dress."

Make a hat out of a cone of paper.

Wrap a piece of yarn around the neck area for a scarf.

Attach felt shoes to the bottom of the pinecone and felt mittens to the pinecone person's arms.

Glue two popsicle sticks to the bottom of the pinecone for skis, making sure the pinecone can stand upright.

Cut two small disks of felt and pierce each with a toothpick. Glue the toothpick ski poles, with the felt toward the bottom, to the pipe cleaner arms.

✸ Simple Twig Loom

Twig looms help teach the basics of weaving while occupying hands in this charming, old-fashioned craft. Making a twig loom and weaving on one are peaceful, contemplative, and engaging activities.

> *You'll need:*
>
> - 2 twigs, approximately 4"–6" long each, or one twig that has branches in a *Y* shape
> - Ball of yarn
> - Assorted yarn pieces and natural items

Place the twigs approximately 4"–6" apart.

Tie one end of the yarn to one of the twigs or to the narrowest part of the *Y*.

Bring the yarn across to the other twig, wrap it around once, and bring it back to the first twig.

Continue stretching and wrapping the yarn around the two twigs, until there are strands of it going all the way up, with just a little bit of space between each strand.

Knot the last end of the piece of yarn. You have created the weave's warp, as if on a loom.

Take another strand of yarn of any length and begin to weave it through the warp, alternately going under and over the strands. You can go back and forth with the same piece of yarn (which is the weft), or weave various different pieces in.

You can also weave or tuck in grasses, flowers, or other items from nature.

Leave the yarn ends loose or knot them.

Gaze at the Night Sky

Some of my family's most relaxed and memorable moments have occurred while gazing at the stars together. You can't help but be infused with a sense of wonder, awe, history, and mystery while contemplating the cosmos. It's natural to share those feelings with those around us, as we use the stars to try to look back through distance and time.

The night sky offers terrific year-round entertainment: dramatic meteor showers, constellations, and the glorious moon in its many phases.

✳ Take In a Meteor Shower

My family and I love to observe meteors, or shooting stars, which can produce dramatic and memorable shows. I still remember one especially wonderful August, when we went to the top of our nearest mountain to see the Perseid meteor shower.

GET TO KNOW THE CONSTELLATIONS

With eighty-eight constellations (groups of stars) and numerous individual stars, the night sky can seem overwhelming. Begin to get to know it by locating a few key constellations, like the Big Dipper, and orienting toward those. After all, the idea of grouping stars into constellations was created to help the ancients better understand the night sky.

Buy a star chart (portable if possible) or get acquainted with the major constellations in your area and season. Bring a small flashlight for viewing the star chart. Enjoy the stars, many of which traveled billions of years through the Earth's atmosphere to reach us.

Lying in the grass in the dark, we could hear choruses of "oohs" and "aahs" coming from all around the mountain, as people caught sight of the meteors blazing through the night sky.

Luckily, you don't need to wait for a meteor shower to explore the night sky. There are other wonders to observe in the many constellations that offer different sightings each time you look at them. Although the naked eye is the best viewer, and you don't need special equipment, binoculars can be helpful for viewing the moon.

Slow Snippet: A meteor is dust and ice from a comet or asteroid that glows when it enters the Earth's atmosphere from outer space.

Choose a cloudless night when the moon is new or nearly new.

Get as far away as possible from any light sources, such as city lights, streetlights, and household lights, and try to get an unobstructed view of the sky.

If you live in the Northern Hemisphere, an unobstructed view of the southern horizon is ideal. For Southern Hemisphere dwellers, try to see the northern horizon.

Consult websites for exact dates of meteor showers. Although the Perseids in August, and the Leonids and Geminids in November and December, are often the most dramatic, meteor showers occur throughout the year. Most meteor showers are best between midnight and dawn.

Let your eyes adjust to the darkness and be patient. It could be a long time before you see anything.

Slow Tip: Hot chocolate is a good accompaniment to cold-weather sky watching.

Slow Snippet: A blue moon is the second
full moon in a month.

✳ Keep a Moon Diary

The changing moon is another source of fascination for people
of all ages. When the moon is full, our family takes "moon
baths," by resting outside or inside near a window to enjoy the
bright moonlight. When the moon is a new sliver, we call it a
"baby's fingernail moon," because that's what Anna called the
new moon when she was young and reminded of a nail clip-
ping. Taking note of the moon's phases and rhythms, as it moves
through its cycle, is a great way to feel the rhythms of our lives
and of nature. It can help smaller children understand how long
a month is. Of course, everyone has fun searching for the "Man
in the Moon." Look outside during the next full moon to try to
find it.

You'll need:

- Blank calendar or pencil and paper
- A view of the moon

Look at the moon each night after it has risen and record its
phase, in writing or drawing, as it makes its monthly rotation
around the Earth. The amount of moon we see is really the
amount of sunlight that is reflected on it during each phase.
New moons are between the Earth and the sun, so that the sun
almost entirely shines on the part of the moon we don't see.
Full moons are on the side of the Earth opposite the sun, so
that sunlight shines on them in full. The moon always follows
this pattern:

- New
- Waxing crescent
- First quarter
- Waxing gibbous
- Full
- Waning gibbous
- Third quarter
- Waning crescent
- New

Slow Snippet: Native Americans named the full moons according to the activities that took place under them, such as harvesting and the first shoots of corn.

Enjoy Timeless Pursuits

There was a time when most people, especially those in rural areas, knew how to catch fireflies or skip stones. The following time-honored activities hearken back to a simpler time and can provide hours of fun and bonding in nature.

✳ Skip a Stone

Learning to skip stones takes a lot of practice and perseverance, but it's an impressive skill once you master it.

Find a calm body of water.

Find a smooth, flat, lightweight stone. The flatness will allow it to skip; the lightness will allow it to be tossed a long way.

Balance near the water and fling the stone with the wrist, as you would a Frisbee.

Try to have the stone enter the water at a 20° angle. If the angle is smaller, the stone will bounce but lose energy. If the angle is bigger, the stone will sink.

Keep practicing!

✸ Whistle with a Blade of Grass

This is fun to do when sitting in the grass with friends or family, or even by yourself.

Find the widest blade of grass you can. It should also be long and relatively thick.

Hold your thumbs upright, so they face toward you and touch at the knuckles and tips.

Place the grass between your thumbs, holding it so that the piece of grass is taut and there is a little air on each side of it.

Purse your lips so that a small but strong bit of air comes out of their center and blow into the opening where the grass is.

✸ Make a Daisy Chain

This is a charming activity to do while relaxing in a grassy meadow or field. If you'd like, make your chain into a necklace or crown.

You'll need:

- Small daisylike flowers (pick only from grassy fields, where they are in profusion, as it may not be okay to pick flowers in some protected areas.)
- Pin (your fingernail will work as well)

Carefully prick a pin or fingernail into the daisy's stem, approximately 1/3 of the way down from the flower.

Gently thread a second daisy stem through the hole, taking care not to break it. The second flower head now rests atop the first stem.

Continue to add daisies to the chain, until you have achieved a length you like. Attach the ends, if desired.

✳ Catch Fireflies

They're called fireflies, lightening bugs, glowworms, and moon bugs. They wink at us with their intermittent glow in darkening skies on humid nights. For many, seeing and catching them is the ultimate summer nature experience.

You'll need:

- Flashlight
- Net
- Clear, lidded jar, with a few holes punched into the lid, using a hammer and nail — if you don't have a lid, use plastic wrap, punched with small holes and secured with a rubber band
- Leaves or a moistened paper towel, placed at the bottom of the jar

Find a humid environment—the best are fields or forests with bodies of water nearby, although fireflies are also found in parks and backyards. Though fireflies live all over the world, they are rare in the western United States.

Turn off all surrounding lights, if possible. Let your eyes adjust to the dark.

If you don't see fireflies, turn a flashlight on and off in a flashing motion to attract one.

When you spot a firefly, place the net over it and gently transfer it into the jar. You may be able to catch it right in the jar. Fireflies are not dangerous to touch, but be careful not to crush them.

Keep your fireflies for a short time, releasing them again the same or the next night, to ensure their survival.

Slow Snippet: Fireflies glow for lots of reasons, mainly to attract mates, as well as to scare off other suitors, which is very important in their short lives.

✳ Go Tide Pooling

The undersea world at the ocean's edge is always fun to explore at low tide, when creatures like barnacles, crabs, periwinkles, and sea stars, which are normally underwater, become revealed in their sandy homes.

The moon's gravity pulls at the oceans every day, and that pull creates high and low tides—usually two of each per day. It's the low tides that make for the best tide pooling, and especially the minus tides, which are written in a number less than zero, and usually occur at least a few times per year on every coast.

Tide pooling is always a special and memorable adventure, as it often happens in early morning and involves going to a unique beach to see fascinating creatures by simply walking around.

You'll need:

- Tide table (available online)
- Field guide or other reference
- Towels and layers of clothes
- Shoes with good traction that can get wet

Consult a good tide table that measures the height of the tide at any given time. Available online and in bookstores, they're written in military time and measure tides in feet. A 2.0 tide means that the water is 2' high.

Get additional information from the table or online about particular beaches in your area. Some offer better tide pools than others.

Plan to visit when the tides are 1.5 or lower. You will see the most creatures when the tide is listed as a minus tide, which is an especially low tide.

Try to time your visit to arrive before the time listed, so you catch the tide going out. Tides generally go out for about two hours, and come back in for an hour and a half, so that's the window of time for the visit. Be sure to look up additional information about the beach you visit to ensure that it is not known for large waves or drastic tide changes that could leave you stranded.

Pick up a field guide to local sea life at a bookstore or library. Some places also sell easy-to-reference cards that you can wear around your neck, which saves you from fumbling with a book while out along the shore.

Walk gently as you explore and look before you walk to avoid stepping on barnacles, mussels, and other creatures.

Take the time to really observe tide-pool life. Lots of small animals, while underfoot and in plain sight, are not immediately apparent to

WHO MIGHT YOU SEE AT A TIDE POOL?

» Limpets and barnacles cling to rocks
» Periwinkles have a snail-shaped shell
» Sculpins are tiny fish that swim in shallow pools
» Sea urchins are prickly
» Starfish (sea stars) are lovely—and aggressive predators
» Crabs might crawl by
» Anemones are really one big mouth

visitors. Crouch down by pools or water to watch the fish and other creatures.

Leave animals and other sea life where they are. Many don't survive once removed from their habitat, even if people think they are placing them back in their spots.

Slow Tip: Not near an ocean? Observe plant and animal life by a lake, bay, river, stream, or other body of water.

✳ Build a Sand Castle or Village

I spent a lot of time at the beach, as a child and then as a parent. The beach and the ocean are endlessly fascinating. There was an age when I was certain if I dug far enough, I'd reach China from Southern California. And of course, there were epic sand-castle building sessions that would go all day, involve many people, and last until the wind or the water made the castles all but a memory.

You don't have to go to a beach to build a sand castle. A sandbox will work just as well.

You'll need:

- Fine-grained sand
- Water source
- Shovel, spade, or scoop
- Bucket
- Molds, optional
- Carving tools or plastic knives, optional
- Flag, optional

If you're at the beach or shore, find a spot a few feet from the water (farther away if the tide is coming in), and dig until you reach water. Place some wet sand into the bucket.

If you're at a sandbox, fill the bucket with water and sand to make wet sand.

Begin to pack the wettest sand, either from the bottom of the hole or from the bucket, into a mound, working quickly so the sand stays wet.

Continue to gently add wet sand to the mound, in handfuls, patting each until it adheres to make one solid shape. The mound should be wide at the bottom and smaller as it rises up.

Shape into a castle, using molds for individual details, or carving parapets, windows, balconies, and other details with carving tools or plastic utensils. Carve shallowly and gently, so you don't disturb the structure.

To build a moat around your castle, dig a circle around its perimeter until you reach water (or fill with water, if at a sandbox).

To build a wall around your castle, get more wet sand and flatten it vertically between two hands (as if clapping). Place it on the sand floor, and continue to guide and shape it into a wall, adding more wet sand. Smooth the new sand to be sure it adheres to the original wall.

Build walls between additional castles and bridges over narrow moats, using the same techniques.

If you'd like, adorn your castles with homemade or other flags, or twigs, shells, and other found objects.

✳ Travel by Snowshoe

Ever since people have inhabited snowy places, they've yearned to trek in the snow on foot. In fact, snowshoes, which originated in Central Asia more than six thousand years ago, are one of mankind's earliest inventions. They work by distributing your weight, allowing you to walk on snow, rather than sink into it.

You don't need to buy snowshoes to have fun in the snow; you can easily make your own.

> *You'll need:*
>
> - 2 large pieces of cardboard
> - Approximately 6' of rope
> - Scissors
> - Marker
> - Snow boots

Cut two identical cardboard pieces that are at least 6″ larger all around than your foot. If you'd like, cut them into the traditional snowshoe shape, which is wider at the top than at the heel, or cut them into shapes resembling giant bear paws.

Place your snow boot onto the cardboard and cut four holes large enough for the rope to go through, one on each side of the top of the boot, and one on each side of the heel.

Cut two 3' lengths of rope. From the underside of the cardboard, thread one piece of rope through each of the top two holes and another piece of rope through each of the bottom two holes.

Tie each of the rope pairs around the snow boot to secure the snowshoe, crisscrossing the rope if necessary.

Have fun trekking in the snow!

Slow Tip: For a sturdier shoe, glue extra layers of cardboard to the original one. Seal with a waterproof sealant, available at craft stores.

Take a Hike

Hiking is an especially easy and gentle way to explore your surroundings and get in touch with nature. Hiking often takes you into beautiful and peaceful places. My family has wonderful memories of special hikes we often take to commemorate birthdays and Mother's and Father's Days (running into lots of other families on the trails!), in addition to just ambling to enjoy a Saturday morning or a sunny afternoon. Hikes don't need to be rugged. A walk on a bike trail, in a park, or around a neighborhood can provide similar adventure, fun, and connection, as you explore together.

We've learned a few things along the way to make hiking go even more smoothly:

- Have a map with you or consult a map at the trailhead.
- Follow marked trails.
- Apply sunscreen and bring extra sunscreen and a hat.
- Wear comfortable shoes and socks.
- Bring snacks and plenty of liquids.
- Have a halfway picnic on long hikes.
- Locate the restroom and have everyone go before the hike.
- Honor children's limits and pace.
- Bring a magnifying glass or binoculars to get close-up looks at wildflowers, birds, butterflies, and other creatures.
- Learn how to identify a rattlesnake.
- Leave animals and large rocks alone.
- Recite "Leaves of three, let it be" and teach children how to identify poison oak and poison ivy by their three lobed leaves.
- Check for ticks at the end of the hike.

7

Slow Seasons

The changing seasons present special opportunities to create lifelong family memories while slowing down and honoring the turning of the year. Celebrating the seasons can lend us perspective and put us in greater touch with the natural world and its rhythms. Throughout history and cultures, seasonal celebrations have also provided opportunities for families and communities to get together, to celebrate one another and their blessings, and to acknowledge inevitable outward and inward change.

My own family honors the changing seasons in a number of ways. We join people around the world in celebrating the precise and dramatic moments, at each solstice and equinox, when one season moves into another, and we mark the unique joy of each season in numerous small ways. Celebrating seasons allows us to participate in weather, time, community, generations, place—a continuum in which we each have a role. Honoring the seasons helps ground us. It naturally slows us down, as we adapt to a schedule that is based more on the turning wheel of the year than on artificial markers. It allows us to get in touch with our slower, more agrarian ancestors and to experience the satisfaction that comes from doing things in their right time.

Of course, for families, and especially for children, seasonal observations and celebrations are, above all, fun. Yes, they have historical significance and temporal meaning. But in addition to that, the valentines made in winter and the maypole danced in spring help provide lifelong memories and give us joyous things to do with those we hold dear.

Celebrate Spring

Springtime conjures growth and new life, play, beauty, flowers, and the return of the sun and longer days. There are many simple ways to honor spring, from erecting maypoles to dyeing eggs.

Celebrations of beautiful spring happen all season, of course, as buds bloom on trees and the tulips, daffodils, and other bulbs planted in the dead of winter show their cheery, colorful heads. Many people feel a little more expansive in spring, as the weather warms and lots of fun and lovely traditions beckon.

☀ Dye Eggs with Plant Dye

While you can get brightly colored eggs with commercial dyes, we've enjoyed great success and lovely, natural colors, using plant dyes to decorate eggs. This project has served as the center of wonderful family and community get-togethers during a festive time of year. We love gathering a group in our kitchen to enjoy a tradition that goes back almost five thousand years—to ancient Persia, and then the Eastern Europeans, who added elaborate decorations for eggs used in sun worship and spring ceremonies. The larger your group, the more unique coloring and decorating ideas you will be exposed to.

You'll need:

- Plant or vegetable material for dyeing, chopped in small pieces (see list that follows)
- Pot and strainer
- Water
- White vinegar
- Mixing bowl
- Jars for storage

- Hard-boiled eggs
- String or craft wax

Place plants in the pot with approximately double their amount in water and two tablespoons of white vinegar.

Bring to a boil, then lower heat and simmer for approximately forty-five minutes.

Strain dye into a bowl, and then transfer to jars if storing.

These are just a few of the many plants that can be used for egg (and fabric) dyes, with suggested amounts per eight ounces of water:

- 4 cups red cabbage (purple to blue)
- 4 cups chopped beets (pink)
- 3 tablespoons turmeric or cumin (gold)
- 8 cups onion skins (yellow)
- 4 cups orange or lemon peels (orange, yellow)
- 4 cups spinach leaves (green)

Place hard-boiled eggs in bowls of dye and leave for fifteen minutes or longer. To create effects on the eggs before dyeing them, tie string around them or cover spots, stripes, or other designs with craft wax, so that the dye won't take in those places, and a design will emerge.

✳ Create Felt Eggs

Eggs are an important symbol of spring around the world. They are a lot of fun to create in many media, and especially satisfying and pretty to make from felt, a fabric that dates back an astonishing nine-thousand-plus years. My family loves making felted projects of all kinds. Wool roving, and the felt that is created from it when its fibers bond and tightly interlock, is great fun to work with and the results are often lovely. There are two ways to make felt eggs.

Needle Felted Eggs

You'll need:

- Wool roving (available at craft and knitting stores)
- Felting needles
- Styrofoam eggs

Wrap a layer of roving around a portion of the egg.

Stab it repeatedly with a felting needle until it has adhered. (Needle felting takes a little practice to get the fibers to take—don't be discouraged.)

Repeat with pieces of roving until the egg is covered.

Needle felt accent pieces, if desired.

Wet Felted Eggs

You'll need:

- Wool roving
- Towels
- Bowl of warm, soapy water
- Raised screen, dish-drying rack, or other drying surface

Roll a piece of roving into a tight, rounded barrel shape.

Dip the felt into the bowl of soapy water to just (not completely) wet it.

Begin to mold the felt into an egg shape with your hands. The wool will begin to wet evenly and the soap will start to lather.

Keep forming, molding, and smoothing the egg. Your hand motions, along with the water and soap, will help the fibers in the roving form into felt.

When it's close to an egg shape, wrap accent threads around it, as desired, and continue to smooth until they are adhered. Needle felt them to secure, if necessary.

Briefly run cold water over the egg to further tighten the fibers.

Let the egg dry for approximately twenty-four hours on a towel, raised screen, or dish-drying rack.

Once the egg is dry, needle felt small bits of roving onto it to form stripes, dots, or other designs, if desired.

Slow Tip: Try needle felting the roving directly onto the Styrofoam egg, if desired. Or make a miniegg and attach to an acorn cap for a sweet felt acorn.

Slow Tip: Felt roving into a shallow bowl to make a nest for the eggs. Work the roving, using the bowl as a guide and removing it when the roving has felted and is close to a nest shape. Adjust further once the bowl is removed.

✳ Make a Maypole

May Day, or Beltane, comes at the exact midpoint of spring and, as such, calls for celebration. Ancient Romans honored the goddess Flora with lively Floralia festivals, and parades with trees. In medieval Europe a tree would be cut down and brought from the woods into the village by a procession at sunrise while horns and flutes played. The tree, a maypole, would be festooned with ribbons, garlands, flowers, wreaths, and other decorations to celebrate Beltane.

I've had the good fortune to take part in a few maypole dances with family and community groups. The tradition remains a special and delightful one that honors the season in a way that takes participants back to a more gentle and pastoral time.

You'll need:

- Tall tree branch or pole and a stand or something similar to anchor it—volleyball, tetherball, flag, umbrella, and wooden poles work; 8'–10' is the optimal height
- Even number of 1 1/2" or wider ribbons, at least one per dancer, in various colors, each 1 1/2 times the length of the pole
- Hammer and nails
- Shovel, optional

Nail one end of each ribbon streamer to the top of the pole.

Anchor the pole into a premade or homemade stand (see Show an Outdoor Movie in chapter 1), or dig a deep hole in the ground and make sure your pole is anchored properly in it.

Your maypole is ready for the dance.

✻ Do a Maypole Dance

May Day, which actually marked the first of summer for many years—with our current summer solstice being midsummer—has long featured feasting and dancing, and often the crowning of a May queen and king. The maypole dance is beautiful and joyous, as the dancers weave ribbons in and out of one another's steps, until the ribbon-covered pole is left with a specific pattern. You may want to instruct dancers and have them practice in advance of the actual maypole dance.

You'll need:

- Decorated maypole
- Dancers
- Live or recorded music

Participants each hold a ribbon around the pole.

Every other person should face clockwise, with the others facing counterclockwise. (Have young children count off one-two, one-two, to determine which way to face.)

Dancers alternate—first going in toward the pole and under the ribbon of the person coming toward them, and then going out away from the pole, raising their ribbon over the person coming toward them. To start, tell the ones to go in and under and the twos to go out and over.

Chant or dance to music. Continue until the pole is completely wrapped with ribbons.

Maypole Chant

In and out, in and out,
Weave the ribbons tight;
'Round the maypole we will dance,
To the left and to the right.

✳ Make and Wear a Floral Wreath

Floral wreaths are a grand and ancient celebration of spring, and everyone feels lovely when they wear one.

You'll need:

- Assortment of real or artificial flowers

- A coat hanger or other wire and wire cutter if needed
- Floral tape or dark-colored masking tape
- Ribbons, optional

Make a circle out of a coat hanger or other wire and make sure it fits the intended head. Wrap the ends of the wire tightly around the main circle to secure it.

Tape each flower on by the stem and wind the tape around the base a few times. Vary the types of flowers to create a design, or plan larger ones in the front and smaller in back, if desired.

Wind ribbons around the crown and tie more onto the crown at intervals. To do so, cut and double a length of ribbon, so that each side is as long as you want it to hang. Make a loop at the top. Place the loop against the wire with 1"–2" to spare at the top, and pull the two ends through the loop to secure the ribbon. Knot the ends, if desired, to prevent from fraying.

Slow Tip: Wreaths and crowns can be made in any season. Try a winter wreath with evergreens and holly.

✳ Create a Paper-Plate Garden Hat

We made this simple, sweet craft when Anna was little, and she wore it to honor spring.

You'll need:

- Paper plate
- Construction paper
- Scissors and pencil

- School glue
- Glitter, optional

Cut a large hole in the center of the paper plate so that a thick rim remains.

Cut various flower and leaf shapes out of the construction paper. Glue them to the plate (hat brim) for a one-of-a-kind creation. Add glitter, if desired.

✳ Make a May Basket

May baskets are another tradition from a bygone time. They summon an era when children filled baskets or other containers (even simple paper cones) with freshly picked flowers and left them on neighbors' doorknobs or doorsteps as a first-of-May surprise. Because May Day often falls on a school day, we varied the tradition by bringing a basket of flowers to school and giving individual flowers to Anna's teachers. Some people fill May baskets with candy. Seeking an opportunity for reuse? Make a May basket from a strawberry or other produce container.

You'll need:

- Basket of any type
- Fresh or paper flowers or candy
- Ribbon
- Paper and hole punch, optional

Wind ribbon around the basket handle or weave it through the slats, or decorate a sheet of paper and tape into a cone shape.

Tie ribbons to the handle ends in bows or in a loop to hang

the basket on a doorknob. Punch holes in a paper cone for ribbon to go through.

Fill with flowers or candy.

✳ Make Paper Flowers

Brightly colored tissue- or crepe-paper flowers make a cheery gift or decoration for May Day, Mother's Day, or any time in spring and are a great way to fill a May basket. These are so easy to make, don't be surprised if you end up creating a whole bouquet.

> ### You'll need:
>
> - Sheets of tissue paper or crepe paper, in a variety of colors
> - Pipe cleaners
> - Wooden dowel or cardboard tube from a dry-cleaning hanger
> - Floral tape or green paint

Wrap floral tape around the dowel or tube, or paint it green and let dry.

Layer five or six sheets of paper.

Fold the pile accordion style (the long way, if there is one), approximately 3/4″ thick. (See Tie-Dyed Bandannas in chapter 3 for accordion instructions.)

Wrap a pipe cleaner around the center of the papers, leaving two equal ends.

Gently separate the layers of paper and fluff them until they are fairly evenly distributed, to form petals.

Attach the flower to the stem with pipe cleaners.

Slow Snippet: "Spring has returned. The Earth is like a child that knows poems."
—Rainer Maria Rilke

Live Summer

For many, summer's longer days and lighter schedules have a naturally positive and slowing effect. Summer is a time to take vacations, to get outdoors, to eat fresh-grown food, and to spend quality time with family and friends. Summer can be carefree, playful, sunny, and expansive. It also calls for simplicity, and there are lots of simple ways to honor summer and create memories that will last throughout the year.

For my family, summer means visiting our county fair, making jam from fresh fruit, spending hours in the water, playing games outside until dark, having picnics, embarking on longer craft projects, and being with friends in the sunshine, at the beach or in a park

We traditionally mark the longest day, the summer solstice, at a community-wide event on the beach. We enjoy a bonfire, nature storytelling and campfire songs, and a ritual walk around the fire, holding stalks of sweet flowers and herbs, and then throwing them into the fire, both to greet the new season and to let go of things that no longer serve us. It's a very memorable way to take time and soak in the long, joyful day with our neighbors the way people have done for thousands of years.

GO ON A WILDFLOWER HUNT

During spring in many places, colorful wildflowers return each year. Pick up a field guide to spot your favorites or turn a hike into a wildflower hunt by searching for different colors, specific flowers, tall or short flowers, or flowers with a certain number of petals.

☀ Bake Summer Solstice Cupcakes

Throughout the Northern Hemisphere, the solstice is marked by midsummer festivals, especially in Scandinavia, where people celebrate with maypoles that honor nature's bounty and bonfires that recall the heat and warmth of the sun.

An easy way to celebrate the summer solstice, whether your gathering is a large one or a cozy one, is to bake summer solstice cupcakes, in which the sunny cupcakes hold within them tiny bits of dark night. These are adapted from the wonderful book *Circle Round: Raising Children in Goddess Traditions*, by Starhawk, Diane Baker, and Anne Hill.

You'll need:

- Your favorite yellow-cake recipe
- 1 cup chocolate chips
- Cupcake tin and paper cupcake liners, or flour and butter
- Mixing bowl and beater or spoon
- Frosting, optional

Prepare tins and follow directions to make yellow cake.

When the batter is completed, gently stir in chocolate chips.

These tasty cakes don't need frosting, but you can add it, in a solid color or cheery sun or flower design.

✳ Do a Solstice Spiral Dance

We did this sweet activity, which can be done for the summer or winter solstice, the longest or shortest day of the year, at Anna's preschool. It's a simple ritual to mark the changing season and the turning of the Earth.

Gather in a circle and hold hands.

Sing or chant simple songs to honor the Earth and the changing season while moving slowly in a circle. Have a leader break one handhold and lead the group in increasingly smaller circles within the larger one to form a spiral.

Wearing Our Long Tail Feathers

The boundaries of the Earth,
The planet of our birth,
The sacred Mother Earth.

We circle around,
We circle around,
We circle around the universe,
Wearing our long tail feathers
As we fly.

Witchi Tai Tai

O witchi tai tai, witchi tai o,
O witchi tai tai, witchi tai o,
May we all be like eagles, flying so high,
Circling the universe, on wings of pure light.

Earth My Body

This is a good chant to start or end the circle. Make sure to really yell on *spirit*.

Earth my body,
Water my blood,
Air my breath,
And fire my spirit!

✳ Wish on the First Stone Fruit

Some time ago my friend Tom told me about his tradition of making a wish as he bit into the first peach of the season. I've never heard or seen anything about this custom since, but

I made a point of adopting it nonetheless. It's such a happy moment when our trees bear fruit, our seasonal farmers markets start up again, and our grocery stores offer local berries and the stone fruits of summer—peaches, apricots, nectarines, cherries, plums, and the hybrid pluots and plumcots—in season and at in-season prices. Perhaps even more so because they are so delicious and their season can seem so short.

It's an extremely happy moment, then, when one takes the first juicy bite of delicious summer stone fruit. Stopping to truly savor it and to make a wish as you bite is one small way of hitting life's "pause" button, of marking a passage in time and appreciating one of the tiny moments that weave together to make family life memorable and pleasurable.

✳ Make an Old-Fashioned Fruit Dessert

When Anna was in second grade, her class studied a unit on food. When the teacher asked the class for things that can be made with fruit, Anna's hand shot up and she answered, "Pies, tarts, crisps, cobblers, and jam." She was well on her way to being a connoisseur of all the wonderful desserts that can be made with fresh summer fruit. Crisps are my favorite. You may want to try them all to find yours. Consult your favorite cookbook or Internet site for recipes. I often use *Jim Fobel's Old-Fashioned Baking Book*.

A Glossary of Fruit Desserts

Betty—fruit baked between layers of sweetened crackers or bread crumbs, resembles a pudding

Buckle—fruit baked in cake batter and topped with crumb topping, resembles a coffee cake

Cobbler—fruit baked in biscuitlike batter

Crisp—fruit baked under sweet, crunchy topping

Crumble—fruit baked under soft streusel topping

Grunt—fruit topped with biscuit dough and baked on a stovetop

Pie—fruit baked on top of, and perhaps beneath, a pastry shell

Slump—fruit topped with biscuit dough and baked in an oven

Tart—fruit in a shallow pastry shell with no top

✳ Make Homemade Vanilla Ice Cream

While ice cream is available year round, its cold, creamy goodness seems best in summer, when the freshest ice cream of any flavor brings to mind beach boardwalks and ice-cream trucks, family vacations, and fairs.

You can make fresh homemade ice cream without an ice cream maker in a couple of different and delightful ways. This one, which Anna's Girl Scout troop made as part of a science badge requirement, is probably the easiest and most fun for kids.

You'll need:

- 1 cup milk
- 1/2 cup sugar
- 1/4 teaspoon salt
- 1 cup half-and-half or 3 egg yolks, beaten
- 1 tablespoon vanilla extract
- 2 cups chilled whipping cream
- Small pan or double boiler
- Bowl
- 1 pound coffee can and lid or other can and lid, cleaned
- 3 pound coffee can and lid or other can and lid, cleaned
- Duct tape

- 10 cups ice
- 1 1/2 cups rock salt (kosher salt may be substituted)

Heat the milk in the pan or double boiler, over low-medium heat. Do not boil.

Remove from heat and add sugar and salt, stirring until blended.

Add half-and-half or egg yolks, vanilla, and whipping cream, stirring well again.

Pour into a bowl and cool.

Once it is cooled, pour the ice-cream mixture into the smaller coffee can. Cover and seal well with duct tape.

Place the smaller can inside the larger can and fill the space in between the two cans with half the ice and half the salt, alternating between layers of ice and sprinkles of salt.

Once the larger can is full of ice and salt, place its lid on and seal well with duct tape.

Roll, kick, and shake the can for fifteen minutes or more.

Open the cans. Dump out the ice water. Stir the ice cream to mix, as the sides should have begun to freeze.

Reseal the small can. Put it back into the larger can, surround with the remaining ice and salt, reseal it, and resume shaking, rolling, and kicking.

Open the ice-cream can and enjoy or freeze for up to a week.

Yield: 1 pint ice cream, approximately 8 scoops.

Experiment with ice-cream flavors! For chocolate ice cream, substitute chocolate milk for regular. Mix in fresh berries or other fruit, crumbled cookies, or small caramel pieces.

Slow Snippet: How does it work? Salt makes ice freeze at lower than usual temperatures, which allows the ice cream to quickly freeze and cool.

> ***Slow Snippet:*** The first ice cream was actually snow, topped with fruit and honey.

✳ Shop at a Farmers Market

Farmers markets are a delight for the senses and a wonderful way to buy fresh seasonal vegetables, fruit, flowers, and other treats. Strolling through a market can be a magical experience for a child and can offer a chance to meet local growers. Many markets also offer activities for kids, such as pony rides, jump houses, and face painting.

Try the following to maximize your market experience:

- Leave plenty of time to leisurely explore the market, talk to vendors, and try new foods.
- Try to arrive early in the day, to enjoy the best selection and quality of goods. Select carefully or have a cooler handy to keep foods cold, if you're not going home right away.
- Alternately, shop late in the day for bargains on perishables.
- Dress for the weather. Wear sunscreen or sunhats, and comfortable shoes. Bring a fanny pack for ease of handling money while shopping. Bring shopping bags. Consider bringing a stroller for additional storage.
- Consider buying new ingredients for cooking or baking. Many farmers are happy to educate and to provide cooking tips. Involve your child in some of the menu planning.
- Honor your child's (and your) limits.
- Return again to enjoy seeing your favorite foods or farmers.

✳ Visit a County Fair

County fairs are a staple of summer across the United States. We like to visit ours and our neighboring counties' each year. Most are inexpensive and offer unique, down-home family activities, in addition to carnival rides and games, animal attractions, classic fair food, craft exhibits, and more. Our favorite fair activities include sheep shearing contests, pig races, jam and food judging, midway games, and of course, the Ferris wheel, which we like to ride at dusk to get a good view of the entire fair below.

Embrace Fall

The turning of the year is often most distinctly felt in fall. It's a season of harvesting, gathering, heading back to school, longer nights, dramatic nature; of Halloween, celebrating blessings, letting go, and transitioning to the quieter days of winter. It's also a rich time to enjoy some very distinct craft and cooking projects that honor the harvest and the season.

Fall also always inspires my family to ramp up our outdoor decorating and keep doing so until spring. Perhaps this is because the warmer months provide their own decorations in the forms of nature, or because winter's traditional candles and lights allow us to brighten and cheer the longer nights. It could just be that we unabashedly love everything about fall, with its crisp days and changing leaves, Halloween and harvest rituals, and all the accompanying decorations, from pumpkins to scarecrows, hay bales to ghosts, yellow mums to wheelbarrows full of gourds.

☀ Stuff a Scarecrow

Scarecrows are classic fall decorations that are great fun for kids to make and to see. They can be as individual as you'd like. We've put homemade scarecrows out for years (and keep the supplies in the garage for reuse). Scarecrows have long been a staple of many cultures. Just be glad we're not in medieval Britain, where live children were employed in the fields as bird scarers to throw stones at marauding birds.

You'll need:

- Burlap sack, pillowcase, or 1/2 yard of fabric
- Rope
- 1 or 2 3'–4' dowels or other sturdy sticks
- Markers, buttons, or felt squares, and glue
- Pencil
- Scissors
- Sweatshirt or long-sleeved shirt and pants, the more used the better
- Hat, optional
- Work gloves, optional
- Straw or hay
- Pillow stuffing, available at craft and fabric stores

Stuff the sack, pillowcase, or fabric with foam stuffing until it is a round shape, for the head, and tie it at the neck with the rope.

Sew button eyes and a nose onto the face, cut out and glue felt features, or draw features with markers. If drawing, you may want to outline with a pencil first.

Place a dowel up into the head until it is secure. Lash the second dowel cross-wise to the first for arms, if desired. To do this, loop your rope around the cross a few times in an X pattern, until the two sticks are secure.

If the pants have belt loops, string the rope through them. Dress your scarecrow, tucking the shirt in and drawing the pants waist tight with rope. If the dowel is long, place it down one pants leg.

Stuff the clothes with small batches of straw or hay. It takes a little patience to stuff the scarecrow and get the shape and proportions right.

A little stuffing will stick out. Tie rope around any place where too much is escaping.

Add a hat and gloves, if desired.

Slow Tip: For many, bright, jolly pumpkins are the items that most symbolize Halloween and fall. Instead of carving your pumpkins, consider painting them! My family has done this for years. Even the youngest children can take part. The paintings are vivid and the pumpkins last for about a month outdoors, as opposed to a few days. Outline the shapes you want with a pencil or crayon, and paint in the desired areas.

✳ Make Spooky Ghosts

Scary and not-so-scary ghosts are another standard decoration at Halloween. Halloween marks the exact midpoint of fall and, like May Day (spring's midpoint), has its roots in ancient festivals. The precursor to Halloween is the Celtic festival, Samhain (pronounced "sah-win"). At Samhain, villagers two thousand years ago took stock of their postharvest supplies in preparation for winter. The ancient Celts also believed that on October 31, the boundaries between the living and the dead became blurred, and they feared that evil spirits would damage people and crops. They wore costumes and made bonfires. When the Romans conquered the Celts, they created their own festival, called Feralia, to commemorate the dead. A second festival honored Pomona, the Roman goddess of fruit and trees, and is perhaps the impetus for the tradition of bobbing for apples. Today, many cultures honor their ancestors on November 1 and 2, *Día de los Muertos*, or Day of the Dead (see chapter 8).

You'll need:

- Old sheet or approximately 1 yard of white fabric
- 3'–4' dowel or other sturdy stick

- Twine
- Markers or felt squares and craft glue
- Pencil
- Scissors
- Pillow stuffing, available at craft and fabric stores
- Lace, hats, fabric ties, and other decorations, optional

Place a ball of foam stuffing in the inside center of the fabric. Form into a round shape, for the head, and tie it at the neck with the twine, so that the rest of the fabric flows down.

Cut out and glue felt features, such as large black eyes, or draw features with markers. If drawing, you may want to outline with a pencil first.

Place the dowel up into the head until it is secure.

Personalize your ghost or ghosts by adding other used or homemade items. Make a large bow tie by folding a felt square in half and gathering and tying it about its center before looping it around the ghost's neck with twine. Or add a top hat to one ghost and a veil of black lace to the other to create a scary bride and groom!

Slow Tip: Use plastic milk jugs or Styrofoam balls, and smaller squares of fabric, to make minighosts. Sew a loop to the top of each ghost's head and run fishing line through all the loops for a decoration that can be hung from trees.

✳ Create Pasta Skeletons

Pasta comes in such a variety of shapes that it makes great art material. Pasta skeletons are another easy and satisfying fall project that younger children can accomplish. They also make you think a bit about the bones in your body.

> *You'll need:*
>
> - Black construction paper
> - Dried pasta in different shapes
> - School glue

Thinking about bones, and perhaps even looking at a picture of a skeleton, lay out various pasta shapes on the black paper until satisfied with the design.

Glue down the pasta pieces and allow to dry.

✴ Roast Pumpkin Seeds

If you carve pumpkins, you will have handfuls of seeds. Pumpkin seeds are delicious and nutritious, and they make the house smell like fall when they roast.

> *You'll need:*
>
> - Pumpkin seeds
> - Cookie sheet
> - Olive or other oil
> - Salt or 1 teaspoon cinnamon, 1/2 teaspoon allspice, 1/4 teaspoon cloves, 1/4 teaspoon ginger

Preheat oven to 275°.

Rinse pumpkin seeds and remove any pulp.

Dry on paper towels.

Brush a cookie sheet with oil.

Place seeds on the cookie sheet in a single layer and sprinkle with salt or cinnamon, ginger, clove, and allspice mix.

Bake for approximately twenty minutes or until roasted, checking and stirring them after ten minutes.

✳ Make Colonial Apple Butter

In a world of wonderful jams and butters, apple butter might just be the ultimate slow food. Comprising just a few natural ingredients, and no sugar, the best apple butter cooks most of the day over a low flame, so that the resulting mixture is wonderfully dense and aromatic and has a rich caramel taste.

In colonial homes, it was not uncommon to hold an apple paring, in which friends and neighbors came to help peel the crop of apples for winter's dried apples, applesauce, and apple butter. The ingredients for apple butter were put into large brass kettles, which were then hung in big open fireplaces. The finished apple butter was stored in barrels in the basement.

You'll need:

- 8 cups apples (a cup is approximately 2 small apples)
- 2 1/2 cups apple cider
- 1 tablespoon honey
- 1 teaspoon cinnamon
- 1/2 teaspoon cloves
- Wide-mouth funnel, ladle, and 2 or more canning jars and lids

Wash, peel, and chop the apples into small pieces.

Place the apples into a large pot and cover with the cider.

Bring mixture to a boil, then reduce heat to a low simmer.

Add remaining ingredients and stir to combine.

Simmer on low heat, uncovered, for six or more hours, or until the mixture cooks down to a paste. You may opt for occasional periods of slightly higher heat if you find that your mixture remains too watery or if you want to caramelize some of the apples at the bottom of the pot.

Using a wide-mouth funnel, ladle the mixture into jars that have been prepared for canning. (I boil them for ten minutes in a boiling water canner to sterilize.)

Seal the jars and boil them again, for ten minutes. Let them sit for a day. (If you follow strict canning guidelines, you can store your apple butter for the future. If you do not, then you'll want to eat the apple butter within a couple of weeks and store it in the refrigerator; see chapter 4 for more information on canning.)

Preserves and butters of all kinds make wonderful gifts and spreads, especially one like this, in which there is barely anything to get in the way of the terrific, fresh fall apple taste. Try apple butter on toast or crackers, with cheese, poultry, or even other fruit.

Yield: 2 jars of apple butter. The recipe can be doubled or tripled.

✳ Make a Fall Leaf Placemat

I never fail to be stunned by the magical sight of trees turning their dramatic colors in the fall. This easy and rewarding project allows you to capture their beauty in placemats that you can enjoy for years, as we do ours. Even small children can be involved by gathering leaves and helping with the design.

Slow Snippet: "Never jump into a pile of leaves with a wet sucker." —Linus van Pelt, *It's the Great Pumpkin, Charlie Brown*

You'll need:

- Iron-on flexible vinyl, available by the roll in fabric stores
- Medium-weight white cotton fabric, about 3/4 yard per placemat
- Your favorite fall leaves

- Phone directory or other heavy book, or flower press (see chapter 6).
- Iron and ironing board

Gather some wonderful, colorful leaves that have fallen.

Place the leaves in a phone directory or other thick book to flatten them. Put them toward the back of the book, so there will be enough pages over them to press them. Make sure you leave space between the leaves and space between the leaves and the book's fold. Leaves will be flat in a couple of days.

Cut fabric rectangles, 2″ larger all around than you want your final placemat to be. I cut my fabric into 13″ x 20″ pieces, to make 11″ × 18″ placemats. For the exact shape, I traced the outline of an existing placemat, which had rounded edges. Turn the fabric pieces over and make occasional guide marks 2″ around from the outside edges, lightly with a pencil.

Turn the fabric right side up again and play with the placement of the leaves. When you are happy with the way they look, you will be ready to iron the vinyl down. Don't forget to leave more than a 2″ space all around your design.

Heat the iron. Peel the backing off the vinyl and place it sticky side down onto the leaves. Smooth the vinyl with your hands, then iron it onto the fabric, following package directions.

When the fabric is cool, turn it over and cut according to your guidelines. For further sturdiness, you can iron vinyl onto the back of the placemat as well.

Slow Tip: Use leftover leaves to create a natural holiday table centerpiece. Each fall and winter we combine fallen leaves and branches, acorns, chestnuts, gourds, mini-pumpkins, and even fruit for pretty and festive decorations that are both casual and celebratory.

✳ Make Corn-Husk Dolls

Corn is an enduring symbol of the harvest for much of the world. Native Americans and Mexicans have made corn-husk dolls for thousands of years, both for play and for ceremonies. We always enjoy making them with family and larger groups. According to similar Iroquois and Seneca legends, traditional corn-husk dolls do not have a face, as the Corn Sister, in comparison with Bean Sister and Squash Sister, became so vain that, as punishment, she was forced to lose her face.

You'll need:

- Approximately 12 corn husks per doll
- Bowl of water
- String, twine, or raffia
- Scissors

Soak corn husks in warm water briefly, then blot.

Bundle four corn husks together and tie with string approximately 1″ from the top.

Turn the bundle inside out, so that the string is now in the inside, and shape the top of the husks into a head.

Cut a husk in half lengthwise and place it over the doll's shoulders, like a shawl, crisscrossing in front of the chest, to create shoulders and form.

Tie another piece of string halfway down the body to form a waist.

Cut a husk in thirds and braid the pieces together, tying off the ends with string. Place between the front and back of the upper body to form arms.

Separate the corn husks below the waist into pants and tie at ends, or tie two to three additional corn husks lengthwise to the waist, wider end on the bottom, to form a skirt.

Slow Tip: Soak the husks in food coloring, coffee, or natural dyes (see Dye Eggs with Plant Dye in chapter 7) before using to create various colors.

✳ Make Beaded Corn Ears

I made these with my daughter's Brownie Girl Scout troop when the girls were young. Everyone enjoyed sitting around a table and creating them. They also enjoyed the finished products, each one a slightly different interpretation of corn.

> *You'll need:*
>
> - Approximately 30 pony beads (9 mm or larger) in varied corn colors, like yellow, brown, orange, ivory, and black
> - 1 yard raffia or twine
> - Scissors
> - Pin back and glue, if desired.

Cut raffia or twine in two 18″ pieces.

Slide both pieces through one bead, so that the bead is right in the middle of each piece, and separate the four strands.

String seven beads onto each strand. The original bead will now be at the bottom of the "ear" of corn.

Slide one bead through the four strands at the top to pull them together.

Tie remaining raffia or twine into a bow.

Glue a pin back to the husk, if desired.

✳ Create a Family Gratitude Tree for Thanksgiving

Feeling and expressing gratitude is a hallmark of close families, not to mention happy people. Slowing down enough to realize and count our blessings also provides a measure of calm and solace. The habit of gratitude—for loved ones, special things, and the world's beauty and bounty—is a tremendous gift we can pass on to our children. Although giving thanks is an important quality to engender all year, Thanksgiving can help focus our thoughts and feelings. And a special project can help us access and express them. This tree can be done by a family, individual, or group.

You'll need:

- Poster board
- Construction paper
- Markers, colored pencils, paint, pens, or other drawing implements
- Scissors
- School glue

Think about what you are grateful for.

On the poster board, draw or paint a tree of any style, with a trunk and branches.

Make a leaf template out of paper that is large enough to hold writing.

Cut many identical paper leaves or other pieces from the template.

Write down something you are grateful for on each leaf.

Glue the leaves onto the branches.

> ***Slow Tip:*** Celebrate the Harvest! Around the world, people celebrate their harvests. Ghanaians and Nigerians have yam festivals. The Chinese eat moon cakes. Celebrate the harvest during fall or Thanksgiving by enjoying and expressing gratitude for your food.

Welcome Winter

Winter conjures images of family, snow, tradition, introspection, mealtimes, celebration, and the warmth of fire glow and loved ones, if not the sun. The extroverted ancient Romans celebrated the winter solstice for a full and rowdy week called Saturnalia. For us, winter is a season of going inward and enjoying quiet activities, like game night with family during longer nights, as well as a season of gathering, giving, and exhilarating sports.

We often mark the longest night, the winter solstice, at a community event in our local national park. We partake in bonfires, nature storytelling, wreath making, shadow puppets, and carols, and the evening's highlight, a walk through redwood groves on paths lit by glowing luminaria candles. Experiencing the heightened awareness and wonder of walking in the darkened woods with our neighbors slows us down and brings us joy. One year in the woods, we came upon carolers in costumes. Another year, we witnessed an elaborate dance performed by men dressed as reindeer, complete with antlers, which they knocked together as part of the dance.

☀ Make Paper or Doily Snowflakes

In a season in which you may spend more time indoors, it's wonderful to have crafts to make as well as to decorate our homes. These snowflakes grace our windows each winter.

> *You'll need:*
>
> - Doilies, or paper in circle or square shapes
> - Scissors
> - Ribbon, optional

Fold a doily or paper circle in half, then in half again, and then in half again, resulting in eight wedge-shaped layers, or fold a square piece of paper in half to form a triangle shape, then in half again. Then fold both halves of the triangle in toward the middle, so that there is one pointy top, with the pieces overlapping, and two pointy ends sticking down. Trim the bottom to cut the pointy ends off.

Cut out small shapes along the folds or ends, such as triangles, half circles, or swirling edges.

Unfold the paper and enjoy your snowflake. You may wish to string many snowflakes together on a piece of ribbon to create a garland decoration.

☀ Celebrate the Winter Solstice

The winter solstice provides a special opportunity to slow down during the hectic holiday season. Take a walk or have a family game night on the year's longest night. Celebrate the sun's return by making or eating sun-colored foods, such as oranges and frosted yellow cupcakes. Place gold-covered toys or chocolate coins in bags and surprise children with them at night or during the morning after the solstice. Take a walk at sunrise to greet the return of longer days.

Slow Snippet: In Scandinavia, some families place all their shoes together at the winter solstice, in the hope of living in harmony throughout the year.

✳ Decorate a Gingerbread or Milk-Carton House

It's the rare person whose imagination isn't captured by the delight in creating a gingerbread house. There's the architecture aspect, as the house's pieces are baked and fitted—and caulked with icing—together in a variety of ways. There's the decorating, which is done with bright candies and decorations that recall familiar items. And there's the very whimsical, one-of-a-kind structure that results. Ever since Anna was small, we have always made fun holiday houses in winter. Some years they are more elaborate than others, becoming whole developments. Some years, we bake the gingerbread ourselves; many cookbooks have terrific recipes and templates for the thousand-year-old European delicacy. Other years we buy houses and get right to the decorating. When Anna was very small, we recycled old milk cartons and decorated those. However you begin, this is a creative and wondrous project that will always result in some surprises. It also makes a great activity for a party or gathering.

You'll need:

- Homemade or purchased gingerbread house, or milk cartons, empty and cleaned

- Large piece of cardboard
- Aluminum foil
- Large bowl of cake frosting, canned or homemade
- Spatula or knives
- Candy decorations (see suggestions below), in bowls

Cover the cardboard in foil, tucking the bottom corners under as if wrapping a gift.

Spread the whole piece of cardboard generously with frosting.

If the house is large, place it on the foil before frosting. If using smaller carton houses, frost each and place them on the foil.

Decorate the house and surrounding area, using the ideas below or your own. The frosting will harden quickly and the decorations will be stuck on. You can eat the house or leave it as a decoration.

- **Brown sugar**—dirt
- **Candy canes**—gates or decorations
- **Candy corn**—decorations
- **Chocolate kisses**—bells or decorations
- **Chocolate nonpareils**—shingles or decorations
- **Chocolate soldiers**—decorations
- **Confectioners' sugar**—snow
- **Frosting**—icicles
- **Fruit loops**—decorations
- **Graham crackers**—shingles
- **Graham crackers, halved, atop two miniature candy canes**—sleds
- **Gumdrops, cut in half**—edging or decorations
- **Gumdrops, small pieces rolled flat with rolling pin**—stained glass for windows
- **Gummy bears**—decorations

- **Jelly beans**—edging or decorations
- **Licorice, small pieces**—edging or bricks
- **Licorice ropes**—road
- **M&Ms**—ornaments or decorations
- **Marshmallows**—snowballs or snow people
- **Mints**—decorations
- **Necco wafers, whole or broken**—shingles, walkways, or decorations
- **Nilla wafers, crushed or whole**—walkways
- **Orange half on toothpicks**—barbecue
- **Pretzel sticks**—fences and logs
- **Ritz crackers**—walkways, shingles, or siding
- **Shredded-wheat cereal**—thatched roofs
- **Tootsie roll minis**—logs
- **Upside-down ice-cream cones, frosted and dipped in green sprinkles**—trees

Slow Tip: Make a spring cottage or a haunted house to celebrate other seasons.

✳ Build a Snow Globe

Everyone loves magical snow globes and the way they capture the imagination. It's actually not hard (and a lot of fun!) to make one yourself.

You'll need:

- Empty clean jars and lids (baby-food jars work well)
- Glitter or small sequins
- Small figurines, ornaments, plastic toys, or cake decorations
- Silicon or other waterproof glue

- Mineral oil, baby oil, or water
- Food coloring, optional

Glue the figurine to the inside of the lid and let sit for twenty-four hours.

Place a small amount of glitter or sequins into the jar (approximately 1/2 teaspoon per baby-food jar).

Carefully fill the jar with mineral oil or water and food coloring, if desired. (Oils allow the glitter or sequins to float nicely.)

Place the lid onto the jar (with the figurine pointed down) and gently screw to close.

Dry the lid. You may wish to surround the lid with glue and let dry again.

Turn the globe over and watch the snow fall.

✳ Make a Pomander Ball

Pomander balls look and smell delightful and, for many, their scent signifies winter and winter holidays. Making them also allows families to gather around a hearth or kitchen table and take a break from any holiday madness.

The tradition of pomanders dates from the Middle Ages, when sweet scents were thought to ward off the plague and other illnesses and cover up the smells of poor hygiene. The word *pomander* translates to "apple of amber," and the original pomanders were wooden or metal housings filled with ambergris and spices that people wore on chains around their necks. In seventeenth-century Europe, pomanders made with oranges became a Christmas and New Year's tradition. Oranges have also come to signify prosperity in the new year in many cultures.

> You'll need:
>
> - Orange .
> - Cloves
> - Toothpicks
> - Ribbon
> - Scissors
> - Paper clip, optional

Decide on a design and begin to carefully poke cloves into the orange, using a toothpick to make holes, if desired. Just the head of the clove should stick out. Some clove heads will break, but that's all right.

The orange should be more covered than not, as that will allow the pomander to stay intact. Vertical stripes are a popular design.

Tie a ribbon around the orange and a bow at the top. (Many people tie the ribbon starting downward, then crisscross it and bring the ribbon up again, so that there are four ribbon lengths on the orange.) Add another loop or paper clip, to hang in a window or on a tree.

The pomander will dry slightly as it ages.

✳ Create a Gift-Box Pin

These festive little pins make great teacher gifts or favors. They also fit the bill when you need gifts for multiple people.

> You'll need:
>
> - Small pieces of Styrofoam, cut in cubes or rectangles
> - Wrapping paper
> - School or craft glue

- Ribbon or string
- Pin backs

Wrap a square of Styrofoam in wrapping paper, as if wrapping a gift.

Glue wrapping paper into place and tie with ribbon.

Glue the pin back onto the back of the package and let dry for twenty-four hours.

✳ Make Candy-Cane Bath Salts

Bath salts are great fun to make, receive, and use, especially when they're decorated with a festive, seasonal twist.

You'll need:

- 2 cups Epsom salts
- 1/2 cup sea salt (if unavailable, use kosher salt)
- Peppermint essential or fragrance oil (available at health-food, beauty, and other stores)
- Red cosmetic-grade coloring (available in craft and specialty stores)
- 2 mixing bowls
- Jars and ribbon

Place 1 cup Epsom salts and 1/4 cup sea salt in a bowl and mix to combine.

Repeat in the other bowl.

Add a few drops peppermint oil to each, until you are happy with the scent and mix to combine.

Add red coloring to one of the bowls and mix to combine.

Repeatedly add layers of white and red salt in the jars until they are filled.

Tie with ribbon.

Add a jar topper, if desired (see chapter 4).

Get Outdoors in Winter

If winter's freezing weather has you thinking you can't play outside, think again. There are plenty of wonderful opportunities for outdoor winter fun.

Create Ice Art

Simple fun can be had by creating ice sculptures, or ice art. Gather a variety of empty containers with large openings, such as milk cartons, juice boxes, and disposable cups and bowls. Collect rain or water in your containers and color with food coloring, if desired. Leave the containers of water outside to freeze. Carefully remove your containers to reveal your ice sculptures.

Dress Up Your Snow Angels

Lots of people make snow angels by lying in the snow and spreading arms and legs to create the angels' wings and garments. But have you ever thought of giving your snow angels a fashion makeover? Fill plastic squirt bottles with water and add a few drops of food coloring to each. Head outside, make snow angels, and then paint clothes or faces on them with the colored water.

Construct a Snow Fort

Forts are fun hideouts, no matter what they're made of. Construct one with snow, if you've got it. Collect snow, by hand or shovel, and roll into fairly large balls. You can also use sand buckets or baking pans to create snow bricks. Place the balls or bricks tightly together to form the base of the fort (usually three sides), packing loose snow around them to further strengthen them. Continue to pile additional layers of balls on the preceding ones, packing more snow around them. When the fort reaches the desired height, cover with a roof of branches or evergreen boughs.

Make a Snowman Kit

The next snowfall, you'll be ready to go out and play if you keep a snowman kit handy. Collect and store together coal pieces, rocks, or buttons for eyes, and woolens such as a knit cap, scarf, and mittens. Have carrots handy in the fridge. Take your kit outside and create your snowman, adding branches, twigs, evergreen boughs, and other items.

❋ Make Paper Lanterns

I made these as a child and, of course, passed the activity on to my daughter. Paper lanterns make a great party decoration and are a fun activity to do at holiday time and to celebrate the Chinese New Year, which is based on the lunar calendar and occurs as winter is winding down.

You'll need:

- Construction paper
- Scissors
- Tape
- Glitter or other decorations, as desired.

Fold a piece of paper in half lengthwise.

Beginning at the fold, cut out approximately four long, skinny triangles, point side up, that go halfway up the folded section of paper.

Unfold the paper and curl together so that the two shortest ends of the paper meet and the cuts run vertically—the cuts should each result in a diamond shape.

Tape the paper closed with the fold facing out. This should resemble a lantern that can be decorated with glitter, stickers, or other decorations, and then hung for display.

✳ Create Old-Fashioned Valentines

Approximately 25 percent of all cards sent in the United States each year are valentines. And why not? In addition to proclaiming love, valentines can be lovely, bright, traditional, and varied. As such, they make a wonderful craft for children, who can easily decorate large paper hearts with simple things found in grocery and craft stores, in nature, and around your house.

> ***Slow Snippet:*** Long before the creation of Valentine's Day, the Romans celebrated mid-winter with a fertility festival.

Slow Tip: Collect valentine items over time and store them when not in use.

When it's time to make valentines, we often combine the occasion with a tea (see chapter 4) and have Anna's friends and their parents over to celebrate and create. We also visit her preschool each year to make valentines with younger children, who are always extremely loving when designating their valentines to parents, siblings, and their friends across the table.

You'll need:

- Construction paper in various colors
- At least 1 good heart-shaped template, made of cardboard, that you can trace around to make valentine hearts (Make one or find one in a craft store)

- Scissors, regular and/or pinking edged
- School glue and glue stick
- Paper doilies that are slightly larger than the heart shape
- Small bowls for decorations

To decorate your valentine hearts, choose from the following:

- Smaller doilies, whole or cut
- Store-bought valentines, whole or cut
- Stickers (valentine or floral themes, or other)
- Small pom-poms
- Ribbon pieces
- Small paper cups for candies or baked goods (available at specialty or grocery stores)
- Paper, foam, and felt hearts
- Feathers
- Buttons
- Beads
- Tissue-paper shreds
- Crinkle-cut paper
- Pipe cleaners
- Party napkins, whole or cut
- Fabric scraps
- Crepe-paper pieces
- Glitter
- Markers, to write messages

 Slow Tip: Younger children especially like very tactile items like pom-poms, feathers, and candy cups.

8

Slow Celebrations

Celebrations of both everyday and special occasions add rhythm and texture to family and community life. They allow people to gather for happy occasions and honor and celebrate a range of life passages, even some that may be challenging. They also allow individuals and families to punctuate time and mark transitions, both publicly and internally.

Many of us yearn to have more meaning and richness in our lives. Some of us want to have the kinds of traditions and family memories that echo our own experiences, if we have been lucky, or provide our children with those things we may have missed. Others of us may seek a deepened sense of community, which can be lacking in today's fast-paced and relatively solitary culture. Celebrations offer occasions for others to gather in witness of our event, to lend it power and blessings that help separate it from the everyday.

Celebrations needn't be lavish or costly. Many events, rituals, and objects are inexpensive and simple while meaningful and fun.

Crafts and Rituals for Special Times

Slowing down to mark rites of passage allows us to feel, appreciate, and honor the times in life when changes occur. It can be extremely rewarding and memorable to create small tokens or rituals that can help celebrate and even ease some common childhood transitions.

✳ Make a Tooth Fairy Pouch

The loss of baby teeth is a distinct rite of passage. It can be an exciting time for children and parents, as well as an occasion to acknowledge change and the passage of time. The loss of the first baby teeth also signifies an end to early childhood and its heightened state of wonder and awareness, child development experts say. Perhaps this is why most cultures around the world employ legends and rituals around the losing of teeth, and tooth fairies who visit in the night, bringing tokens or blessings to ward off the sting of change.

Slow Snippet: In parts of Asia and Africa, children throw baby teeth onto the roofs of their houses while singing a good-luck song. In many European and Latin cultures, teeth are taken from under pillows, not by fairies, but by mice.

We greatly enjoyed creating a homemade pouch to hold Anna's teeth under her pillow each time she waited for the tooth fairy. We still have Anna's tooth fairy pouch, a very unique concoction of bright felt scraps and rickrack that went under her pillow for many years.

You'll need:

- 2 pieces of fabric or felt, 3" × 4" or any size of your choosing
- Fabric or felt scraps
- Approximately 18" of ribbon or rickrack for tying
- Scraps of ribbon, rickrack, or other flat decorating items
- Needle and thread
- Scissors
- Pencil

- Straight pins
- Cardboard, optional

Fold the fabric in half and draw the shape of the pouch onto the front, or onto a cardboard template. The pouch can be square; U-shaped, with rounded edges; or any shape you'd like.

Cut the pieces and decorate one or both sides by sewing scrap pieces of fabric or ribbon onto them.

Place the pouch pieces, outsides together, and pin in a couple of places to secure.

Sew a seam, by hand or machine, around the perimeter of the pouch, leaving an allowance of 1/4″ and leaving the top of the pouch open. Turn right side out.

Attach the 18″ length of ribbon at its center to the center of the back piece. That will be the tie that cinches the pouch.

If you'd like, make a drawstring by turning the pouch inside out and folding and sewing the top down about 1/4″. Leave a small opening in the fold to run a piece of ribbon through it. Or, if desired, sew a line of stitches around the top of the pouch at approximately 1/8″ down to prevent fraying.

Place the pouch under the pillow to hold baby teeth to be collected during the night by the tooth fairy.

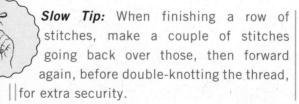

Slow Tip: When finishing a row of stitches, make a couple of stitches going back over those, then forward again, before double-knotting the thread, for extra security.

✳ "Donate" Baby Items to New Baby Animals

Transitions during young childhood can be confusing for children, who may have uncomfortable and unarticulated feelings about growing older and leaving behind familiar objects of security. We adults may also regard these changes with mixed feelings. Rituals can help everyone ease some transitions.

When Anna was two years old, we recognized that she was clearly ready to leave her pacifier behind. She no longer relied on it for comfort and seemed to use it as more of a prop. At the suggestion of Maureen Pinto, a lovely teacher at her preschool, and with a little fortunate timing from the seasons, we embarked on a small ritual to give the pacifiers away.

Just before her half birthday in May, we announced that the "new baby deer" that had been born in the spring and seen in our neighborhood needed her pacifiers. The idea of baby animals needing the items more than she did seemed to resonate with Anna. On the appointed day, we decorated a paper bag, filled it with the pacifiers, and went out on our land to place it on the ground for the deer. A few hours later, Michael and I snuck back to retrieve the bag, in case Anna went back to see if the deer had taken it.

> **Slow Tip:** Baby bottles and even diapers can also be left out for animals. None nearby? Package items for the "new babies" and take them to a collection agency or your pediatrician's office, if appropriate. There may even be a new baby in your own family—trust your instincts as to whether this approach would work in that case.

After nearly two and a half years of nightly use, Anna slept fine the first night without her pacifier and never even asked for one again. We think that the power of a small ritual helped mark the change in a positive way and helped her to move to the next phase.

✳ Make a Lavender Sachet for a Child Who's Having Trouble Sleeping

Lovely smelling lavender has been prized around the globe for thousands of years, for the soothing quality of its distinct scent. The ancient Egyptians used it in cosmetics. The ancient Greeks and Romans employed it for perfume and for healing practically everything, from stomach and kidney ailments to dropsy, jaundice, migraines, and insect bites. Today, lavender remains a popular home scent, if not quite a cure-all. It's grown around the world, from Provence, France, to Japan and Australia. Its gentle and soothing qualities for babies and others are well known. We often hung a sachet of lavender from Anna's crib or placed a pouch of lavender under her pillow, to help her fall asleep and rest calmly through the night.

You'll need:

- Small muslin or other slightly porous drawstring bag or 5″ circles of netting (available at craft and fabric stores)
- Ribbon
- Lavender buds, fresh or dried

Place the lavender into the bags or netting.

Tie the netting with the ribbon.

Attach ribbon to the bag or pouch for hanging, if necessary.

Hang from the crib railing or other location.

Replace every few months, or when lavender loses its scent. Lavender sachets also make great gifts. For other sachet and dried-flower crafts, see chapter 5.

 Slow Tip: Lavender is easy to grow, even in a small or container garden, with decent sun, moderate water, and an alkaline soil with good drainage.

✳ Plant a Tree to Mark a Season or Occasion

Planting a tree is a simple and powerful act of faith and stewardship, and there are many occasions in life that are enriched by doing so. Even a small yard or balcony may accommodate a dwarf or potted tree. Alternately, there may be a neighborhood or public space available for the planting.

Many school, scout, community, environmental, and other groups have adopted the tradition of planting trees near the beginning of spring, on Arbor Day, which varies by state from February through April, or on Earth Day, which is traditionally April 22. Another seasonal variation? Plant living Christmas trees into the ground in January to see them grow to a nice size by the next December. My elementary school did this—it was my own mother's idea—and the trees grew into huge, healthy evergreens.

Still other people may wish to plant trees to honor a birth, life, or graduation, or to bless a new home. Some people plant trees in the same area year after year. When Anna was young, we enjoyed planting trees each year at Tu B'Shevat, the Jewish holiday celebrating the new year of the trees, and we have watched them grow over the years. There is additional power to the ongoing ritual if you plant at the same time each year.

You'll need:

- Tree seedling, available at nurseries
- Shovel
- Wet ground or water source
- Mulch, optional

Find a spot that has the right requirements for your tree, including enough light and enough space to grow, both above and underground. It should have some moisture from rain or be otherwise easy to dig.

Dig a hole large enough to plant the seedling. If there are roots present, make a small mound of dirt.

Gently place the seedling into the hole (and on the dirt mound, if applicable), removing any materials that are not biodegradable.

Re-cover the hole with dirt. Water if needed. Place mulch around the tree if weed control is necessary.

Continue to water as necessary until the tree is established.

✳ Blessings and Poems for Trees

When it's time to plant your tree, gather together and recite a blessing or poem encouraging a long life for the tree—there are many religious and other blessings available. You may also want to pass a chalice of water and have each person who receives it share a wish, thought, or memory. Once the chalice has gone around, the water can be used to nourish the tree.

Simple Blessing for the Planting of a Tree

We plant this tree to honor (name of person or occasion). May this tree's roots go deep, its trunk grow strong, its branches spread wide, and its leaves and fruit provide nourishment, beauty, and shade. May it always remind us of this special moment.

Growth of a Tree

I'm a little maple, oh so small,
In years ahead, I'll grow so tall!
With a lot of water, sun, and air,
I will soon be way up there!

Deep inside the soil my roots are found,
Drinking the water underground.
Water from the roots my trunk receives,
Then my trunk starts making leaves.

As I start to climb in altitude,
Leaves on my branches will make food.
Soon my trunk and branches will grow wide,
And I'll grow more bark outside!

I will be a maple very tall,
Losing my leaves when it is fall.
But when it is spring, new leaves will show.
How do trees grow? Now you know!

—Meish Goldish, author and poet

Slow Snippet: In old Jewish homes, a cedar tree was planted for each baby boy and a cypress tree for each girl. When two people married, branches from their trees were used to create their chuppah, or wedding canopy.

✳ Perform a Ritual Cleansing for a New Home or a New Year

Many cultures employ rituals and blessings for cleansing a space of negative spirits, or energy, and clearing the way for prosperity and blessings to enter. Some cultures employ similar rituals at the new year. The Roman god Janus is the god of both doorways and beginnings, each a threshold in its way.

Traditional Hmong people thoroughly clean their houses and place the dirt outside near a loop of rope, which children jump in and out of to confuse the dirt spirits. House cleansings may also take their cues from Native Americans, who burned sage to drive out negative energy and purify a space, and from ancient and Neolithic China, where feng shui was employed to orient dwellings and environments for optimum harmony and life force six thousand or more years ago, using early astronomy as a guide.

You'll need:

- Percussion or other instruments, such as drums, bells, and horns, or pots and pans and wooden spoons, or noisemakers
- Sage, cedar, sweetgrass, or rosemary
- Water to boil or matches, optional

Gather family, friends, and neighbors, as desired.

Have everyone set his or her intention, either by speaking or writing what they'd like to bring into the new home or year and what they'd like to leave behind, or what they wish for the new year or the home dwellers.

Open all the doors and windows to let air and new energy in and old energy out.

With a new broom, sweep old energy out of the house, from back to front and out the front door.

Walk clockwise around the perimeter of the house or each room, sounding the instruments or clapping hands and stomping, to drive away old energy.

Employ herbs to cleanse your space. Smudge the house or rooms by lighting and gently waving a bundle or stick of sage, to drive old energy out, and/or do the same with sweetgrass or cedar to bring good energy in. Some people also hang sprigs of fresh rosemary on doorknobs or on the front door. You can also boil rosemary in a pot on the stove, so its smell permeates the house, or fill spray bottles with it, once cooled, and spray throughout the house.

If you'd like, say a blessing as you pass through rooms.

Simple House Blessing

May this home be blessed,
Sacred and pure,
Love and joy
Come in through the door.

Blessings That Invoke the Elements

Many blessings, stemming from various cultures, invoke the four compass directions or their corresponding elements.

Earth to ground us,
Clean breath of air,
Energy of fire,
Water that flows,
Bless this home.

With the purifying power of water,
With the clean breath of air,
With the passionate heat of fire,
With the grounding energy of earth,
We cleanse this space.

✳ Make Noisemakers to Welcome the New Year

Noise and revelry have survived from ancient times as an attempt to ring out the evil spirits of the old year and ease what many viewed as a vulnerable transition between years. Ancient Chinese people used loud firecrackers to drive away evil spirits, while medieval Germans hissed in the streets. Eighteenth-century Scots were draped in cowhides and chased by villagers who yelled, "Raise the noise louder," and beat them with sticks. I have my own childhood memories of staying up until midnight and clanging pots and pans on our porch, something I now do with my family.

You can easily make and use your own noisemakers, a project most kids enjoy, in addition to staying up late and marking the turn of the year.

Tube Kazoo

I have childhood memories of making this timeless noise-maker, along with a harmonica out of a wax-paper-covered comb, proving that things made with the simplest materials are often very enduring.

You'll need:

- 1 empty toilet-paper or paper-towel roll per kazoo
- Small squares of wax paper, approximately 4″ × 4″
- Rubber band
- Pencil
- Crayons, markers, paint, fabric, tissue paper, glue, glitter, sequins, or other decorative items of your choice

---

Decorate the tube, as desired.

Cover one end with the wax paper square and secure with a rubber band.

Punch holes in the wax paper with a pencil.

Slow Tip: If midnight is too late for little ones, celebrate the new year's arrival in a region or country with an earlier time zone.

Paper-Plate Maraca

We have fun making these at New Year's and throughout the year. They're great to use for family music nights.

> *You'll need:*
>
> - 2 paper plates
> - Crayons, markers, paint, fabric, tissue or construction paper, ribbons, glue, glitter, sequins, foil, or other decorative items of your choice
> - 1/8 cup large dried beans
> - Stapler
> - Craft or popsicle stick
> - Tape

Decorate the underside of the paper plates, as desired.

Tape a craft stick to the inside rim of one plate's undecorated side, for a handle.

If you'd like, glue ribbons or strips of paper or fabric to the plate's underside, to create decorative streamers.

Place the two plates together, decorated sides out.

Staple around the edges of the plates to secure them together, leaving an opening to drop the dried beans in.

Continue stapling to shut.

Slow Tip: Pots, pans, wooden spoons, and other kitchen items also make excellent noisemakers.

✳ Make New Year's Resolutions

Making resolutions can be a powerful act. Doing so encourages us to slow down, take stock of the year, and think about what we'd like to change or create in the coming year. Before Anna was born, Michael and I started a tradition of writing our resolutions on paper and then burning them in the fireplace, a ritual we have continued to do as a family. Young children can write something they wish to take with them in the new year and something they wish to leave behind. The urge to start over is an enduring one—New Year's resolutions go back four thousand years to the ancient Babylonians, who also made sure to return borrowed farm equipment before their new year at the spring equinox.

Slow Snippet: Think the New Year was always in January? Not so. Ancient Egyptians celebrated it in August, when the Nile flooded to water their crops. It has been celebrated in May (the Mayan agricultural high point), at the fall harvest (Jews), on the winter solstice (Incans and Chinese), and on the spring equinox (ancient Romans and Babylonians).

✳ Honor Coming of Age with a Circle of Elders

Adolescence is, of course, a powerful time of change, yet because of the dynamics that surround it, which can include a heightened need for independence and privacy, we do not usually take the opportunity to honor and guide this part of life's passage.

This is compounded by the fact that, unless we are part of a religious, ethnic, or regional group that employs a coming-of-age ritual, such as a Hindu sacred thread ceremony, a Lakota vision quest, or a Jewish bar or bat mitzvah, the child often passes into adolescence in an unheralded way.

A simple remedy for this is to have a circle of elders who welcome the young person into adulthood. This recognizes the individual with community gathering and witnessing, in a way that can also be casual and personal.

In advance, tell participants the purpose of the gathering. Ask them to bring a piece of advice; a memory from their own adolescence; or a memory, thought, blessing, or wish for or about the person.

Also in advance, designate a leader for the circle. Ask the young person to think about something he or she would like to leave behind and something he or she would like to take along into the future. (This can remain private.)

Create a warm space with a circle of chairs or pillows and simple food for after the ceremony, if desired.

Smudge the room (see Perform a Ritual Cleansing earlier in this chapter), burn incense, or ring a bell and have a moment of silence to focus everyone on the present moment and the intent of the ceremony.

If you'd like, invoke the four elements with a blessing from the ritual cleansing, substituting the words "bless this circle" or "cast this circle," where appropriate. Smaller children can run around the circle clockwise to help set it.

The leader tells everyone why they are there and shares or invites others to share what they've brought. You may want to make time for dialogue, sharing, and stories in an informal way, which is often what happens at wedding and baby showers.

If you'd like, say a blessing, such as:

May your day be filled with blessings
Like the sun that lights the sky,
And may you always have the courage
To spread your wings and fly!

If you'd like, reopen the circle with the blessing used earlier, adjusted to "open this circle."

Slow Tip: For those seeking a more formal ritual, there are many religious, pagan, and cultural ceremonies available on the Internet.

✳ Make Marbled-Paper Journals During Life Transitions

For many, life transitions create a heightened need to express feelings, wishes, and desires in a private or nonverbal way. Crafting with a young person can provide an outlet for sharing quiet and respectful time and space, as well as an opportunity for their creative expression. Some children and pre-teens may enjoy the solace of shoulder-to-shoulder, pressure-is-off activity with a parent.

Marbling paper is a wonderful craft practiced in many parts of the world, from Japan, where it was done one thousand years ago with plant dyes, to Europe, where bookbinders make elaborate papers today. It results in unique monoprints, as it's impossible to make the same design twice.

You'll need:

- Dishpan, or other large, shallow pan

- Thick card stock or paper
- Dishwashing liquid
- Tempera or other thin or thinned paint
- Skewers or straws
- Newspapers, to cover work surface

Fill the bottom of the pan generously with dishwashing liquid.

Place a few drops of paint into the pan. They should float on the surface.

Add other colors of paint, if desired, and gently swirl the paint with the skewer or straw. Experiment by forming dots, swirls, feathery patterns, or other random shapes. One pattern can be made by laying the paint in parallel lines and then running a straw through the lines at perpendicular angles.

Hold a piece of paper with two hands and lower into the mix (this might be easier if you lower the center first, then the sides), then remove quickly, so the paint doesn't smear. This will probably take some practice.

Place the marbled paper on many layers of newspaper to dry.

Homemade Journal

You can make a journal and cover it with your marbled paper, or with wrapping paper or fabric. We learned this technique from our neighbor, Eva.

You'll need:

- Thick cardboard, 6″ × 9″ or other size (at least 1/2″ smaller all around than your piece of paper or fabric)
- Marbled or other paper, or fabric
- Glue, any
- Craft knife or box cutter
- Scissors

Make two folds in the cardboard, so that there is a book cover and back of equal size, and a spine. For example, you can fold a 6″ × 9″ piece of cardboard into a 4″ × 6″ book with a 1″ spine.

. Carefully run the craft or other knife down each fold, making a light indent to score it, which allows the cover to fold cleanly.

Place the cardboard onto the back of the marbled paper (or other material).

Fold the paper over half of the cardboard to cover it, folding the corners into a triangle shape, as if wrapping a present.

Begin to glue the paper down on the inside of the cardboard.

Bend the cardboard into the book shape before proceeding to secure the paper over the other half, so that your paper will fit properly.

Finish gluing all the paper over the cardboard book form.

If you'd like, finish your book with endpapers: Cut two squares of paper, 1/2″–1″ smaller than the cover and back size. Glue them to the inside covers, so that they cover the ends of the wrapping paper or fabric.

✷ Create a Magazine Collage

Making collages from magazine and other images is another powerful way to discover and express feelings and desires. This activity can be especially useful for groups, as it gets everyone crafting together right away, or for people who are intimidated to draw their own designs.

You'll need:

- Magazines with lots of visuals
- Scissors
- Glue stick

- Piece of cardboard, poster board, card stock, or a blank cardboard journal (see the Homemade Journal instructions)
- Decoupage medium, such as Mod Podge, or sealer, optional (available at craft stores), and paintbrush

Peruse magazines and decide on a theme, colors, and design for your collage.

Cut out pictures and begin to place them onto your surface, with some edges overlapping. You may want to cut things out in different shapes, or in strips, which you can lay down or weave.

When you're confident with a portion of the bottom layer of your design, glue it down.

Continue to glue pieces of the collage down. When you're done, seal the top with decoupage medium or other sealer, as desired.

✳ Make a Wish Jar for Times of Transition

The act of writing down a wish, goal, or something you want to leave behind, can give that thought a great deal of power. Placing the writing in a special jar can help seal your intentions and act as a reminder of them. Even the process of creating the jar can help you access your dreams and goals.

If you're moving into a new home or starting a new school, you may want to write your wishes on the strips of paper. If you're transitioning into a new phase or birth or calendar year, you may want to write down things you wish to take with you, as well as leave behind. Wish jars can also be used to hold the blessings and thoughts of guests at weddings, showers, or birthday parties. They can be as simple or elaborately decorated as you'd like.

You'll need:

- Strips of paper
- Pen
- Jar and lid
- Paint, fabric, ribbon, rickrack, letters cut from magazine pages, or other items, as desired
- Primer, optional
- Box cutter or screwdriver and hammer, and cardboard, optional

Decorate your jar. You may want to prime and paint the jar lid and tie a ribbon or fabric bow around the neck. Or make a jar topper (see chapter 4).

If you want to make a slit in the lid for papers, place the lid over a piece of cardboard and carefully cut with the box cutter, or hammer a screwdriver into it, in a straight line. You can also just open the jar to insert wishes.

Put the papers into the jar and place it somewhere special.

To make a pouch instead of a jar, see Make a Tooth Fairy Pouch earlier in this chapter.

✳ Make a Dream Catcher

Dream catchers can be a powerful and beautiful tool for helping someone through a period of stress. Traditionally made by tribal grandmothers for newborn babies, dream catchers resemble the webs of spiders. In the early 1900s, Ojibwa people in Minnesota, Wisconsin, and Ontario, Canada, hung objects that represented spiderwebs on the hoops of children's cradle boards. Called dream catchers, they were said to catch evil, just as a spider's web would. They were made of willow hoops and woven with cords of plant-dyed nettle (and later yarn), and they often had small holes in their centers to let the good thoughts come through. Enjoy making your own and using it to induce sound sleep.

You'll need:

- Twigs, grapevine, or other soft wood, soaked, or wire, hoop, or paper plate to make a circle, approximately 5" in diameter (traditional dream catchers were 3"–5" across)
- Approximately 4' of twine or yarn, in varied colors, more if desired
- Beads
- Feathers, optional
- Hole punch, if using a plate
- Scissors

Form a circle from the desired material. If using wire or twigs, overlap a bit where the pieces meet and wrap wire around it a few times to secure it.

If you'd like, wrap yarn around the surface of the circle.

If using a paper plate, cut the center out so that a 2" rim is left all around. Punch holes around the plate rim, approximately one per inch.

Tie one end of twine or yarn to the hoop or plate. Place a bead or two on it and bring it to another part of the hoop, or a hole in the plate.

Run the yarn around the hoop or through the hole and then bring it to another area on the hoop of your choosing, adding beads, if desired. Continue lacing the yarn.

Dream catchers vary in pattern, so feel free to create any pattern you like with yarn or twine. Knot the yarn, as needed, if starting another color.

When you are satisfied with the design, make a yarn loop at the top of the dream catcher to hang it.

Cut three pieces of yarn, approximately 5" each, and attach

them in a row to the bottom of the dream catcher (knotting around the hoop or through the hole). Add a bead or two and/ or a feather to the end of each and knot to secure.

Hang your dream catcher from or near a bed.

✳ Make a Chair Throne to Celebrate a Birthday or Achievement

Our family has always placed a great importance on birthdays. After all, that's the day to celebrate a person's actual birth, their very existence on the planet. By celebrating a person on their birthday, we revel in the richness they contribute to our family and community life. We also mark the milestone by celebrating the birthday person's life, achievements, and aspirations. By celebrating birthdays, everyone in the family is given a chance to shine on his or her individual day.

In addition to the celebration, birthdays can provide families with a time to recount a child's birth story. Everyone's birth story is unique, and it can bring joy to families to reminisce about the actual day of birth. Is there something funny or poignant you can share about your or your child's unique birth story?

We always mark the precise day and time on Anna's actual birthday, and that moment has special power for us. Because Anna was born at 11:19 on a Saturday morning, we even often stop what we're doing at 11:19 on Saturdays throughout the year. (This is a blessing of having a birth time that is easy to commemorate, as opposed to Thursday at 3 a.m.) We just make a simple note of that time—nothing more. We have all come to know that that is an expression of gratitude for Anna and even a little prayer for all the babies coming into the world at that moment.

Children at school or elsewhere on their birthdays can look at the clock and mark the exact time of the year turning. Of course, with more children, and odder or less precise birth times, it could be potentially difficult to mark the birth time. It's simply a nice gesture to remember and note the moment or a token of it when possible. After all, what better birthday gift can there be than the knowledge that those around you are grateful for your existence?

Designating and decorating the birthday chair is another of those small gestures that can help make a child feel special. When Anna was small, I never let a birthday go by without decorating her high chair (and then bigger-girl chair). The chair would be colorful and special, a temporary throne, much the way the party room in the house was transformed for the day.

This project makes a basic slipcover for any chair with a back. It can be as elaborate as you'd like, and you can store it for future birthdays or other family members.

You'll need:

- Felt or other fabric
- Ribbon decorations, like large rickrack or pom-poms
- Contrasting fabric and glitter glue, optional
- Letter stencils (available at craft and office-supply stores)
- Tape, glue, and sewing supplies
- Scissors

Measure the height and width of the chair back.

Cut two pieces of fabric that measure about 3″ wider than the chair back.

Decorate one or both of the pieces, as desired. You may want to cut out a triangle-shaped birthday hat, a four-pointed crown, or a cupcake and candle, which you can sew or glue on and decorate further with glitter glue or pom-poms. Sew on rows of rickrack, decorative ribbon, or a birthday garland to add color and fun.

When you're satisfied with the design, sew the fabric pieces together, right sides facing each other, leaving the bottom of the slipcover open, so it can go over the chair back.

If you'd like, add a row of pom-poms to the top of the slipcover, above the seam.

Slow Tip: Want to keep it simple? Purchase crepe-paper streamers in two colors. Twist pieces of it and decorate the chair, taping the ends to the bottom of the seat. Add a construction-paper decoration to the chair front or back. Twist and tape remaining streamers across windows, doorways, and elsewhere to decorate the party room.

✳ Make a Happy Birthday, Get Well Soon, or Welcome Home Garland

Sweet fabric garlands of triangular flags have become quite popular in recent years, a throwback to the coats of arms of medieval knights and the ships of the British Royal Navy. They can be called banners, garlands, or bunting; the word *bunting* comes from the lightweight wool once used in flag making. Whatever you choose to call yours, they're enjoyable to make, from fabric or paper, and as those early nobles knew, they add a great deal of festivity to any occasion.

You'll need:

- Assortment of fabric pieces (fat quarters work well— each makes one or two flags, depending on flag size) or scrapbooking papers.

- 3 or more yards of 1″ ribbon or folded bias tape, depending on flag size
- Cardboard or construction paper and pencil
- Pinking shears or scissors
- Pins
- Sewing supplies or glue stick
- Stencils, optional
- Fusible web, optional
- Rickrack, optional

Decide on the shape and size of each of your flags. A large triangular flag might be 9 1/2″ long down its center, with sides of approximately 10 3/4″. A smaller flag might be 5″ long, with sides of approximately 6″ each. Flags can also be perfect triangles, rectangles, or squares.

Draw your desired shape on the cardboard and cut out for a template.

Place the pattern over each piece of paper or fabric and cut out the flags, making sure to maximize the space on a large piece of fabric or paper. Cut with pinking shears for a finished, whimsical look. If you'd like, sew a seam or row of rickrack around each fabric edge to finish it.

Place the flags on a table or other surface, in the order you'd like them to go. If you are putting letters on flags, draw or stencil them onto fabric or paper, cut out, and place where desired.

Sew or glue on fabric letters, or appliqué using fusible web (follow package directions). Glue paper letters to attach.

Pin or place completed flags onto the ribbon, making sure to leave a bit of space between each flag, and a large length on each end for hanging. If you're using bias tape with a fold, pin the flags inside the fold.

Sew or glue the flags onto the back of the ribbon, so that a line of ribbon shows in the front, or sew the two halves of the bias tape together.

Crafts and Rituals to Honor Family

Family is extremely important to young children. Celebrating our immediate and extended families allows us to appreciate and pass on family lore while providing children with a fuller sense of who they are and their place in their family and in the global community. Of course, celebrations can also create new family traditions.

✳ Create Unique Books for Family Members

When Anna was four years old, our dear friends Bob and Nicole found out they were expecting. For the shower, I "interviewed" Anna about her advice to the parents-to-be and compiled her hilarious answers in a book. Likewise, I've seen families pass down beautiful recipe books through generations by asking grandparents and parents for their favorite recipes—ones they enjoy making or enjoyed as children. These and similar projects are wonderful ways to preserve and bestow thoughts and information before they are lost.

Passing on family lore in written or photo form is a wonderful and personal gift to the recipient as well as the creator.

Use the marbled-paper journal from this chapter, or the paper-bag scrapbook (chapter 3) as your starting point for the following:

- Write an advice book by children for new parents.
- Compile a cookbook of family recipes.

- Write a poem or wish book for a couple about to be married.
- Make a book to welcome a new sibling.
- Create a scrapbook or photo album to honor grand-parents or commemorate a vacation.

✸ Create an Appreciation "Recipe" for a Special Person

I got this lovely idea from Anna's fourth-grade teacher, D. J. Mitchell. It's very easy and fun to do, and it conveys a special relationship and feelings that may be otherwise hard to articulate. Help your child create a recipe for a "marvelous mom" or a "delightful dad" or a "fabulous friend" or any other combination using an adjective and the person's name or role.

> ### You'll need:
>
> - Piece of construction paper or poster board
> - Markers and crayons or colored pencils
> - Ruler

Think about the attributes of the recipient that make him or her special.

Write a heading on the paper: Recipe for a (fabulous friend or other).

Using a ruler, draw six or more lines on which to write your various ingredients.

Write the "ingredients" for the person, in recipe terms, such as "6 cups kindness," "5 tablespoons love," or whatever else you can think of.

Leave space at the bottom to write out your instructions, also using recipe terms, like *mix*, *add*, *fold*, *blend*, and so on.

Decorate the rest of the paper, as desired.

> **Slow Snippet:** Anna's recipe calls for 20 cups womanness and for the creation to be baked in a woman-shaped pan!

✳ Make an Altar or Art Piece to Honor Ancestors on the Day of the Dead

The Latin American, and especially Mexican, tradition of *Día de los Muertos* (Day of the Dead) is a time to remember and celebrate loved ones who are no longer with us. Far from morbid, the day or days (which can encompass the widely celebrated Catholic All Saints' Day on November 1 and All Souls' Day November 2) have a celebratory quality. In Mexico and other places, people play music, enjoy family, and make and enjoy special breads, pottery, puppets, paper cutouts, dancing skeletons, and candy skulls. Brightly colored marigolds adorn displays, as the flowers' scent is said to attract souls and bring them back.

Although it's near Halloween, its roots are joyous, not ghoulish, and arise from Aztec harvest festivals, during which corn was shared with the dead. *Día de los Muertos* is a colorful and meaningful time to honor those who have come before us and to recognize that, although we can't bring them back, their spirits and essences live on with us.

Anna made an altar, or *ofrenda*, with her second-grade teacher, Susan Falkenrath, to help her be more connected to a grandfather she didn't know and to remember a grandmother who had recently died. We still have the very lighthearted *ofrenda* in a prominent place in our house. (Traditional ones often have more temporary offerings on them, such as real food and flowers.) They serve as a nice way to keep the departed close to us.

You'll need:

- Shoe box or oblong tissue box and one or two increasingly smaller boxes (large enough to work with your photo and frame; traditional *ofrendas* often have three tiers)
- Cardboard or a large, flat box lid
- Construction paper, wrapping paper, or fabric
- Photo of the deceased
- Colorful tissue paper
- Modeling or polymer clay
- Branches or wire
- Scissors or craft knife
- Other items or mementos, as desired
- Paint and brushes, optional
- School or craft glue

Think about the ancestors you are honoring. What were their hobbies and interests? What was their favorite food?

Cover and wrap your boxes in construction paper, wrapping paper, or fabric, so that there are no openings.

Glue the boxes, one above the other, with the smallest one on top.

Use the box lid or cut a rectangle of cardboard, 1"–2" larger than the photo all around.

Glue the photo to the cardboard or lid. If you'd like, paint or paper the cardboard first and/or decorate the frame of the photo with drawn pictures depicting the ancestor's hobbies, or with construction paper cutouts of skulls.

Place the cardboard or lid behind the largest box, if large enough, and glue to secure it, so that it shows above the boxes. If the cardboard is smaller, follow these directions:

Cut 4 pieces of cardboard, 1" × 2". Fold each in half. Glue two to the front and two to the back of the photo cardboard, to make *L*-shaped feet. Glue the bottom of the Ls to the top box, so the photo stands up.

If you'd like, construct an arch out of paper or branches and place it around or in front of the photo, poking the ends into the top box to secure it.

Because it's traditional to offer the deceased their favorite food, in addition to bread, fruit, or candy, have fun making miniature clay food and placing it on the tiers of the altar. Some altars also include soap, so the loved ones can freshen up after their journeys.

Make other clay or paper decorations, as desired, perhaps to represent more of the loved one's interests, to place on any of the tiers. You may want to add real or paper flowers anywhere on the altar (see Make Paper Flowers in chapter 7), or make a string of paper cutouts (*papel picado*) and hang them across the top of the arch or the picture.

✳ Make Paper Cutouts (*Papel Picado*)

Traditional *papel picado* for the Day of the Dead depicts elaborate skeletons, flowers, or other items in nature, and patterns. It is typically made with tissuelike paper and perforated (*picado*) with chisels. A version of it can be done with folding and scissors.

> *You'll need:*
>
> - Squares of tissue paper, in your choice of size and color.
> - Small, sharp scissors and/or a craft knife and cutting board or cardboard
> - Pencil
> - String and glue, optional

If using the chisel method, trace your design onto one of the pieces of tissue paper.

On the cutting board or cardboard, layer two pieces of tissue paper underneath it and carefully follow the drawing with the craft knife.

If you'd like, lift and fold the papers to cut out larger areas with the scissors.

To use the scissors method, fold the tissue paper in half and half again. Draw a design on the top quarter or cut freehand to create spaces and designs in the tissue paper, much like paper snowflakes (see chapter 7).

Glue the papers to string to hang as a banner, on your altar, or elsewhere.

☀ Create a Simple Family Tree

Children often enjoy learning about their ancestors and putting names and possibly places, dates, and faces to their lineage. Creating a family tree doesn't need to be an elaborate project, unless you want to make it so. In our family, Anna was most interested in the stories of her ancestors (and we admittedly had some colorful ones), so she asked family members questions and wrote up abbreviated versions of the stories on 3" × 5" index cards, which went on a poster. Often, the most wonderful aspect of creating a family tree is the connections it allows us to form with others, the time spent, and the stories learned.

You'll need:

- Poster board
- Construction paper
- Markers, colored pencils, paint, pens, or other drawing implements
- Scissors
- Photos, optional
- Elders and curiosity

Decide how many generations you want to represent on your tree and how detailed you want to be for each generation. Younger children may want to make a simpler tree, with only themselves, parents, and grandparents. Older and especially interested children may want an elaborate tree with many generations and family members, such as cousins, spouses, siblings, and blended-family members. Plan your design accordingly.

On the poster board, draw or paint a tree with a trunk and at least three or four rows of branches coming off each side, one level of branch for each generation.

Make a paper leaf template that is large enough to hold writing and/or photos. Some people prefer using an apple template, for a rounder shape.

Cut many identical leaves or other pieces from the template.

Begin to write family members' names and information on the leaves, attaching photos or other information, if desired.

Glue the leaves onto the branches. The child's piece goes on the bottom, with any siblings on the same level branch. Parents, aunts, and uncles are one level up. Grandparents are one level above that. Be sure there's room for increasingly large branches of the tree. If there are a lot of names, then siblings, spouses, and children can share the leaf with the main ancestor. For instance, the child's father's brother (uncle) gets a leaf, and his or her aunt's name is written to the side of the uncle's; cousins' names are written beneath the uncle's.

Alternate Family Trees for Adopted Children

Families with adopted children don't necessarily need to shy away from family trees. Some therapists believe that tracing adopted and/or birth family trees, if the information is available, can be comforting. Seeking an alternative? Consider a caring tree or a loving tree, which offers more flexibility and might be more enriching to create.

You'll need:

- See the family tree supply list

Paint or draw a tree trunk and branches.

Make a heart template, or another of your choice, such as a circle, an apple, a flower, or a leaf. Use the template to cut multiple identical shapes.

On each shape, write the name of someone in your life that you love or care about, or someone who loves or cares about you. Include photos, or write something about the person, if desired. The tree can include neighbors, teachers, extended birth or adopted family members, and anyone else who's important.

Make a cutout to represent you and put it at the base or in the trunk of the tree. Glue the pieces onto the tree.

✸ Make a Personal or Family Crest or Coat of Arms

Since the seventh century in Japan and the twelfth century in Europe, families, individuals, countries, states, schools, knights, clergy, and others have used decorative and distinctive coats of arms, or family crests, to identify themselves or their clans. It's a wonderful tradition that can be adapted in a lighthearted way to proclaim or discover individual or family identities and interests.

You'll need:

- Paper
- Colored pencils, crayons, markers, paints, or other drawing implements

- Ribbons, scrap paper and fabric, glitter, and other decorative items, as desired
- School or craft glue
- Frame, optional

Draw the outline of a shield shape, which resembles a pointed shovel.

Draw lines inside of the shield to divide it into various regions. It is common for crests to have four sections. You may want to give each family member a section.

Inside each section, draw or write the name of one or more things that you enjoy doing or that you like about yourself or your family. If you'd like, leave a space inside the crest, or below it, to write the family name.

Color and decorate the items and the background of the crest. Most crests are elaborate, with lots of decorative items and flourishes.

Frame or display your unique crest.

9

Slow Travel

It may seem counterintuitive, and it might not always be possible, but travel (not to mention actual vacations) can offer wonderful opportunities to slow down as a family and create lifelong memories. Being somewhere new and out of our usual routines can heighten our awareness, and that heightened awareness can lead to more gratitude, observation, and joy. It certainly has for my family.

But what about those times between points A and B? When the family has yet to unpack at the relaxing lake cabin or beachside motel and is enduring a travel day packed with frenzy, discomfort, crowds, whining, and baggage?

There are plenty of things you can do to make the travel itself more fun and meaningful, whether it's through adopting a playful attitude, along with some tools, or trying a new mode of transportation.

Play Travel Games

In addition to many of the games in chapter 2, there are still more time-tested games requiring little or no equipment that are especially great for taking on the road and helping slow travelers truly enjoy the journey.

Simple, portable games also allow you to take along a spirit of play, no matter where you are. In addition to being terrific for travel, most of these work just as well while waiting in a line, taking a walk, or enjoying a family game night at home.

Fun games can also add to the texture of the journey. Because these games might be different from the ones we normally play at home, they can also end up weaving themselves into the fond memories of the trip.

✳ Guessing Games

Who doesn't love a good riddle? Guessing games are longtime boredom busters that let players engage their creativity and keep others on their toes. We played and continue to play guessing games quite often, especially during waiting times or while walking.

Twenty Questions

One player is appointed to keep count of the questions.

Another player thinks of something that falls into the category of animal, mineral, or vegetable and tells the other players which category the object is in.

The players then take turns asking questions that can be answered yes or no. For instance, if the category is vegetable, a player might ask, "Does it grow in a garden?" or "Is it edible?"

If no one has guessed correctly within twenty questions, the same person tries to stump the group again. If someone guesses the answer before twenty questions have been asked, then that person becomes the next player to come up with an animal, vegetable, or mineral.

What Animal Am I?

One player thinks of an animal.

Other players ask questions with yes or no answers to determine what animal the first player is. Players might ask, "Do you live in the ocean?" or "Do you have four legs?"

There is no limit to the number of questions. Players can simply give up when stumped and choose who gets to be the animal next. Otherwise, the player who guessed the animal gets to be the next up. A variant is What Person Am I?, which can be played by guessing from among people whom everyone in the family knows.

The Name Game

One player thinks of a name. That player announces whether it is a boy's name or a girl's name and gives the first letter of the name.

The group then tries to guess the name by calling out all the names they can think of that start with the appropriate letter.

The person who guesses the name first is the next one to choose a name.

Faker, Faker

One player lists three things about him- or herself, two which are true and one that is not.

For instance, "I sang in public when I was four," "I like broccoli," and "I've never been stung by a bee." Other players have to guess which statement is not true. The first person to guess correctly goes next. You can play the game for points or just for fun. Obviously, it's harder to come up with things that close family members won't know. That same aspect makes the game a fun icebreaker for less familiar groups. Young children also get a big kick out of this game.

☀ Observation Games

These wonderful road-trip games add a fun element to looking at the scenery during the journey. The whole experience changes for many when they are actively seeking something. My family has had epic rounds of Semi Search on long stretches of highway, sometimes continuing over days of a trip and including hundreds of semis counted.

What I See from A to Z

This game can engage players in challenging play for a long time.

Players try to find letters in license plates, billboards, road signs, or objects and must call out "I see an *A*," or "I see something that starts with *B*," when they spot a letter.

The first person to complete the alphabet wins.

Want a more challenging game? Limit the search to license plates, or restaurant signs, or another category of object. A variation for younger children is to pick one letter and have everyone look for things with that letter.

Travel Scavenger Hunt (also known as Travel Olympics)

You'll need

- Pencil and paper for each player

Players all contribute ten to twenty things to one list of things that they can see or do while in the car. For example, a list might include passing a cow pasture, seeing a gas station that has the color red in its logo, holding one's breath through a tunnel, spotting two yellow license plates, or passing an RV.

The first person to accomplish everything on the list wins.

Semi Search

If you're traveling on the interstate, you will probably have a lot of trucks for company, and this fun game makes use of that.

Each player chooses a different color. That color will be the color of truck trailer that the player is then searching for.

Players announce when they see a semi on the road in their color, and they get one point for each.

You can appoint a scorekeeper to keep count, or everyone can keep their own score.

The game is played until one person reaches twenty-five points or another agreed-on number.

> **Slow Tip:** Want to seek a more obscure car? Play Punch Buggy and count Volkswagen bugs, awarding points either by finding cars in one's chosen color or by being the first to claim a particular colored bug.

I Spy

This is a game even very young children can play.

One player decides on an object that all players could conceivably see and says, for instance, "I spy with my little eye… something that begins with the letter *A*" or "I spy with my little eye…something that is blue."

Other players take turns trying to guess what the object is.

When players run out of guesses, the first player gives another clue and other players guess again.

The person who guesses the object gets to be the next spy.

✸ Alphabet Games

These perennial participation games are wonderful in a car, on a walk, around a campfire, or just about anywhere.

Going on a Picnic

The first player announces, "I'm going on a picnic and I'm bringing (an object that begins with the letter *A*)."

The second player then says, "I'm going on a picnic and I'm

bringing (what the first player said) and (an object that begins with the letter *B*)."

The next player lists what the first two players have said and adds something that begins with the letter *C*.

As the game progresses, the participants run through the alphabet, and the list of what's included in the picnic gets longer. Players who forget items are out of the game. The last person who can complete a list without any mistakes wins.

I'm Going To...

This variation of Going on a Picnic works for older children.

The first player creates the following sentence using words that start with *A*: "I'm going to (a place, for example, Antarctica) on an (animal, for example, aardvark) to (do an action, for example, applaud)."

The next player repeats that sentence and then adds a second sentence, filling in the blanks with *B* words, such as "I'm going to Bermuda on a butterfly to bathe."

Players continue creating new sentences and adding to the previous sentences, through the alphabet. Players who forget items are out of the game. The last person who can complete a list without any mistakes wins.

Geography

Geography is another classic game for children who know some place names and their spellings.

The first player starts by naming a city, state, country, or continent, such as Arizona.

The next player must name a place whose name begins with the last letter of the previously named place. As the word *Arizona* (like many places!) ends in the letter *A*, the new place must start with an *A*, such as Annapolis.

Because Annapolis ends with an *S*, the next player might say Suriname, and so on.

Players who are stumped are out of the game. The last person remaining wins.

> **Slow Tip:** Decide in advance which geographical features will be counted as place names. Mountains, bodies of water, or other geographical entities might be fair game—or not!

✳ License-Plate Games

A staple of family road trips since, well, the advent of license plates, these games are fun, varied, and even offer a little reading and word practice for younger family members.

License-Plate Scramble

The first player calls out all the letters, in order, that appear on a passing license plate.

All players try to create a word using those letters, in the same order. The first person to do so gets a point. For example, a player might call out, "*C, R, B,*" and he, she, or any other player might come up with *carbohydrate* or *curb*.

Decide if you want to play to a certain number of points, like twenty-five. The first player to reach that total wins.

An alternate? With pencils and paper, see how many words each player can make out of the same letters.

OSLP

This is a classic road-trip game that, like most of these, I played as a kid.

> *You'll need:*
>
> • Pencil and paper, optional

Players search passing cars for out-of-state license plates, or OSLPs (out of the state they are currently traveling in).

When such a plate is spotted, the player yells, "OSLP!" If that player is the first to see a particular plate, he or she scores a point.

Decide whether you want to play to a certain number of points, like ten. The first player to reach that total wins.

An alternate? Players write down the names of the states they spot and play until one player gets to a certain number of states, say, five.

✳ More Games That Require Little or No Equipment

There are still more timeless games that promise a lot of spontaneous fun for minimal effort.

Concentration

I've seen this simple game, which involves reciting words that fit a certain topic, keep groups engaged for hours.

What makes the game of concentration both fun and challenging is that it is played to a chanting and hand-clapping rhythm. Players sit in a circle and begin to perform the following simple series of hand-clapping movements: slap both thighs, clap hands together, snap left fingers, snap right fingers, repeat. They then begin reciting, to the clapping, "Con-cen-tra-tion (pause saying the words while slapping thighs for a beat) elimi-na-tion. Starting with (category)." Here, the first player names a subject category, such as states or kitchen utensils or cartoon characters. The next player, on the finger snaps, has to name an object that fits the category. The player after that does the same, and so on. If a player repeats or can't think of a word, he or she is out. Once you get good at the game, play the more challenging version: repeat all the words that have come before, in order, before adding yours.

Rock, Rock

This is another fun and bonding game, played in a circle, that you can enjoy indoors or out. I've been outdoors with groups and spontaneously picked up a rock for play. If you're indoors, you can use a coin and change the words accordingly.

> ### You'll need:
>
> • Rock or coin

Players sit or stand in a circle, holding their palms out to their sides, facing up. Right palms should be directly over the left palm of the person to the right, continuing around the circle. One player is in the center of the circle. That player momentarily closes his or her eyes while the rock is given to someone in the circle. Each player lifts his or her right hand and moves it across the body to the left neighbor's right hand. The person with the rock in hand does this as well. After a few such motions, the person in the middle opens his or her eyes. The rock moves around the circle, but because everyone is making a passing motion, the person in the middle can't see where it is. As the rock moves around the circle, players chant in rhythm with their hand motions.

Rock, rock, where do you wander?
In one hand and out the other.
Is it fair? Is it fair?
To keep poor (name of player in the middle) sitting (or standing) there?

At the end of the chant, the person in the middle guesses where the rock is. If he or she guesses correctly or doesn't guess after three tries, the person with the rock goes into the middle. If that person has already gone in the middle, you can have the person next to him or her, clockwise, go in.

✳ Make and Play Auto Bingo

Most people love scavenger hunts, which deftly combine observation and game play. Auto bingo uses the traditional bingo-card layout and play to create a portable object-hunting game that can be done while traveling by car or train. Auto-bingo cards are available in toy stores, but with a little advance preparation, you can create your own and can even customize them with things you might see in your area.

You'll need:

- Computer, paper, and printer, or markers, paper, and copier
- Cardboard or clipboards
- School glue or glue stick
- Pencils with erasers

Decide how many squares you will have on each auto-bingo card. Cards for smaller children might have nine squares, in three rows of three. Cards can also have sixteen squares (rows of four by four) or twenty-five squares (rows of five by five).

Think of items that one would see on the road (ideas follow). The number should be about 1/3 more than the number of items per card.

By computer or by hand, draw the largest square you can on your paper and divide that into squares. Save this blank template so that you can print it or copy it repeatedly.

On a copy of the template, declare the middle or another space free. Draw by hand or type the names of your items in the other spaces, making sure that each card has different items in different orders.

Cut out cardboard pieces that are the same size as the papers. Glue each paper to a cardboard backing. If you'd like, skip this step and use clipboards.

POSSIBLE ITEMS FOR AUTO BINGO

Have fun with these! You can be as general, specific, or custom as you'd like.

- » Gas station
- » Grazing cow
- » Horse in field
- » Horse in a trailer
- » Doughnut shop
- » Fast food establishment
- » Rest stop
- » Maple (or other) tree
- » Stoplight
- » Stop sign
- » Mailbox
- » Hotel or motel
- » Bridge
- » Bird
- » Tow truck
- » Train
- » Billboard
- » Police car
- » Ambulance
- » Field of flowers
- » Barn
- » Silo
- » Church
- » Tractor
- » Log truck
- » RV
- » Bus
- » Motorcycle
- » VW Bug
- » Airstream trailer
- » Campground
- » Baseball or football field
- » School
- » Mall
- » Mountain
- » Lake

On the road, play as you would bingo. When players see an item on their cards, they mark that space with a pencil. The first player to see a complete row of items wins. You can also play until the first player sees and marks everything on his or her card. Erase the markings to use cards again.

Pack a Travel Backpack

Having a few items on hand in a simple and lightweight travel backpack can make road trips and traveling just a bit smoother and more fun for everyone. You may want to have a version of this in the car at all times.

Here are a few things we like to have in our travel backpack:

- Active toys for road breaks, such as a jump rope, sidewalk chalk, and jacks
- Quiet activities like coloring or blank books and crayons, Sudoku, Mad Libs, or word searches, for restaurants and similar places
- Playing cards
- Portable, compact crafts like finger weaving
- Portable, long-lasting snacks
- Tissues, wipes, and Band-Aids
- Disposable camera

Slow Tip: Involve kids in trip planning or following the trip's progress on a map. If you're an AAA member, maps are free. Have a child keep a trip journal with spaces for adding photos when you get home.

Travel by Train

Although the train used to be synonymous with travel, traveling by train today may be one of the ultimate slow activities. Train travel can prove a relaxing alternative to planes, buses, or cars. Trains often pass towns and scenery that other transportation misses. Many offer family-friendly activities on board, like games, play areas, movies, and guides to the local sights. Some take you to fun destinations. And for those who succumb to the lure of the railroads, it doesn't much matter where you end up, as long as you travel by train.

My family travels by train every chance we get because we love the pace and the feeling of watching the world go by out the window and the glimpses of an ever-changing landscape of natural wonders and man-made sights. Lots of kids are fascinated with the workings of a train—the conductor, engine, cars, and routes. On long-distance trains, school-age kids often make friends with their peers, who are traveling for a variety of reasons—we've met father-son pairs touring the country's ballparks, foreign travelers seeing the United States, and children of train personnel, among others. For many of us, train travel offers a novel adventure, whether the trip takes a few days or a couple of hours.

How to make the most of your train trip:

- Involve kids in planning a route that offers scenic beauty along the way, special features on the train, or a fun destination at the end, perhaps a park, railroad museum, or other unique place. Try to get your ticket early—some routes book far in advance.
- If possible, book a standard sleeper compartment or a family sleeping car for overnight trips. Sleepers offer pull-out or pull-down beds and a bit of privacy. Family sleeping cars are good for larger groups, though I have found that

sometimes, they can be away from the action and without good windows. Try to check the accommodations for your particular line. Either way, most kids find that sleeping quarters add to the adventure and fun of travel.

- Pack wisely and lightly. Large bags are often stored in the lower level of the train, even for people in the largest sleeping compartments. They're usually accessible, but it can be a pain to get into them, so pack what you want with you on the train in smaller overnight bags. Bring medications, snacks, activities, books, cosmetics, and sleep items with you.

- Wear shoes on the train because the moving plates between the cars can trap toes. Be careful around the train tracks and stay near the train if you do exit during a stop so you can hear the conductor's cry of "All Aboard!" and re-board.

- Be prepared to be social. Trains are naturally social places, something most kids enjoy. If your family or group has fewer than four people, you may share dining-car meals, because trains generally offer tables for four. Many riders strike up friendly conversations in the observation and other group cars. You might find yourself doing puzzles or playing games with others. Some trains have cars that offer activities for kids.

- Most importantly, try to be flexible if the train isn't on time. While trains strive to keep their schedules, delays are common. Slow travelers enjoy the experience and the journey.

Travel by RV

When Anna was four years old, she was fascinated with "house cars," or recreational vehicles, and wondered about the people who traveled and lived in them. Anna's curiosity inspired us to rent an RV for our next vacation, and take to the road. Years later, that trip is still one of our fondest travel memories. We found it incredibly novel to travel by RV and really enjoyed the campgrounds we stayed in and the fellow RVers we met. RVing is a rewarding and adventurous way to see the country. It provides relative freedom of schedules (although we booked spots in campgrounds in advance) and allows you to cook all your own food, if you'd like. It is economical, and traveling in close quarters certainly bonds families. In addition, many RVs are nonmotorized and have adopted other green innovations, such as solar paneling and lightweight construction, so that RV vacations have a much lower carbon footprint than they used to.

Here's how to get started RVing:

Locate an RV rental outlet near you.

Learn about RV use. Your rental company will brief you on driving rules and electric and water connection and use at sites.

Consult books and maps to plan a scenic route that uses fairly major highways with interesting stops along the way.

Locate campgrounds or other places you'd like to stay. Many of these are physically stunning or offer family-friendly activities and amenities. We happened into one that boasted a thriving RV community, which we joined for "washerboards," an old-fashioned version of shuffleboard played with washers. There are many campground resources online and through RV rental agencies.

Pack as you would for car camping, including cookware and food, clothing layers, first-aid items, car insurance information, flashlights, lawn chairs, and other practical items and creature comforts. There are checklists available online for packing, driving, cooking, and safety. See the Resources section for some sources.

When in doubt, ask fellow RVers for advice. Many are seasoned and enjoy the community aspect of their hobby and welcome the chance to lend tips to newer travelers.

Slow Snippet: At one of our RV camping spots, four-year-old Anna was curious about the campers at the next campground, so we watched as she went over to say hello. Upon her return a few minutes later, we asked how it was and she replied, "Oh, I'm just coming back to get my chair." We still have her miniature camp chair and the friends we made, thanks to our daughter's outgoing nature.

10

Everyday Slow

Slowing down is an act and a habit that can be woven into every part of our lives, not just the times when we choose to partake in a slow activity. Bringing the intention of slowing to all the parts of our lives infuses them with a sense of richness and meaning that we tend to miss when we're rushing around. Life's textures, and ultimately memories, are woven from the many small acts and microrituals that come together, moment by moment, to add up to our days, weeks, and ultimately lifetimes.

"It's the little things," we say a lot in our family, and you may too. Whether a small gesture, an appreciation, a joke, a shared intimacy, or a moment of truly experiencing the wonder and awe of nature and feeling just a little bit more alive, the little things serve as soft cushions of warmth, memory, and delight. It's a gift to provide them for our children and ourselves.

We tend to pay a lot of attention to celebrations and vacations, but according to parent educator Riley Miller and others, daily life has an extremely powerful impact on the way children feel and the things they will remember most. My childhood family was playful and it is indeed the small things I remember: laughing together at mealtimes and outings, telling funny stories with extended family and friends. My parents did magic tricks for us kids during Sunday dinners, just as Michael and I later did puppet shows and sang for Anna. As a child, I thought it was fun just to run errands with my dad. We didn't have to go anywhere special. My daughter has said she feels the same way. We are a family that notes together when the clock hits 12:34.

Most of us are born with a healthy sense of wonder and the joy of being alive. Babies are inherently curious and delighted. The challenge for busy parents and families is keeping that sense of awe, gratitude, and joy in our and our children's lives as they grow older.

In traditional cultures, the marking of natural, seasonal, and life events brought elements of sacredness and awe to daily life and helped people connect to forces larger than themselves. Because we are surrounded by rhythm in nature and in our bodies, appreciating the rhythms of daily life remains a powerful way to fuse the spiritual with the everyday. Having a regular rhythm at home, enhanced by a bit of ritual or songs for young children, can transform a hectic family life into a peaceful one. Mealtime, bedtime, and morning blessings and practices, such as quiet hugging time or holding up a child to greet the first light of day, can all add up to a richer and more fulfilling family experience. Many children and parents who practice predictable routines report greater stability and satisfaction with family life.

Imbuing everyday moments with individuality and intention helps bond families and lets children know that they are important family members. My family and I have seen firsthand how vital the small moments are. They can mean a great deal to a child and be a means of strengthening family ties, and they occur when given space and love.

✳ Have a Morning Ritual

Our mornings can set the tone for the whole day. It's wonderful to greet the day with gratitude and enthusiasm. Thank the sun for rising; the air we breathe; the beautiful trees, neighborhood, neighbors, or family members. It's especially great to let younger family members know that they are greeted along with the day. It can be fun to integrate a little movement into the morning routine—some gentle stretching, or hugging and cuddling. Or perhaps a happy good-morning song. Just as with bedtimes, mornings can provide a quiet, almost sacred time to just be together as a family.

Good-Morning Song

Good morning to you,
Good morning to you,
We're all in our places,
With bright shiny faces,
Is this not the way
To start a new day?

Good Morning (Traditional Waldorf Verse and Movements)

Good morning, dear earth (lower hands toward floor)
Good morning, dear sun (raise arms into the air)
Good morning, dear stones (place hands one atop the other)
And the plants, every one (open out hands, as if blossoming)
Good morning, dear bees (move hand around in flying motion)
And the birds in the trees (move fingers like fluttering wings)
Good morning to you (hands out to others)
And good morning to me! (hands across own chest)

✳ Eat as Many Meals as Possible Together

By the time a child is eighteen, if he or she is lucky, there will have been approximately six thousand dinners, or breakfasts, with the family. Mealtimes are often the only times that busy families have together. It can be incredibly grounding to just sit down all together at the end of the day and share triumphs and thoughts. While it's always wonderful to hear how everyone's day went, sometimes more unusual questions really get people talking and sharing. One family I know asks everyone to share something funny that happened during the day. Others may want to share something they learned or something they're thankful for. Sometimes more unusual questions bring out responses. My family likes to ask, "What color was today?" You can write funny or interesting questions on cards, or papers that you put in a jar and then draw and answer when the mood is right. Try these conversation starters:

What animal was today?
What flower was today?
What cartoon character was today?
What ice cream flavor was today?
What number was today?
Do you have a lucky number?
What's your favorite thing right now?
What did you dream about last night?
If you could go anywhere in the world, where would you go?
If you could be invisible, what would you do?
Would you rather travel in outer space or under the sea?
What one thing would you change about the world?

As kids get older and perhaps busier, it can take some planning to find the time between activities and work for everyone to come together, as well as the time to plan and prepare meals. If you enjoy cooking, doing so as a family can provide fun bonding time. If not, aim to keep weeknight meals simple and to buy what you need for a few meals at once, to keep cooking and shopping times down, as well as costs. You can also make double batches of food and have the leftovers the next night. Or pick up takeout food on your way back into the house.

Home-cooked meals are great, but the time spent together is even more vital.

✳ Have Children Help Prepare Meals

Often we segregate jobs when doing them together can augment everyone's joy. Most children are highly aware of and interested in food—preschoolers tend to enjoy play cooking, shopping, and eating. Meal preparation provides terrific opportunities for fun family bonding, for kids to learn a little about cooking, and most important, to allow family members to feel and be useful. Most young children like feeling that their contributions matter. At age-appropriate levels, have them help pick recipes and plan meals, brainstorm and write shopping lists, go shopping, wash fruit, help make sandwiches, measure or cut food, or set and clear the table. Older children can make a dish for a family pot-luck or create their own special meal. Kids might also enjoy creating special table settings, by collecting and displaying seasonal objects, making simple napkin rings with beads and wire, or making construction-paper place cards to honor special guests (fold paper in half lengthwise and write the guest's name on one half). These touches go a long way toward helping children honor a meal and those who are gathered.

✳ Have a Mealtime Blessing or Ritual

Often mealtimes represent a transition from previous activities. It can be extremely grounding to take a moment when first at the table to enjoy being together again and to really connect physically with family members and the beautiful food. This may be through a deep breath, a silent moment, reaching out and holding hands, lighting a candle, or saying a blessing, religious or not—to thank the Creator, or Mother Earth, your own or a farmer's garden, or the cook and preparers of the food, and to express gratitude to the gathered for being at the table. Food is elemental and nourishes body and soul, and expressing gratitude for the ground where it was grown, the person who made it, and the company with whom we enjoy it can be a simple but profoundly rewarding, connecting, and slowing act.

You may have blessings and graces that have been passed down through your family or spiritual community. There are many simple, child-friendly, Earth-based blessings that you can also adopt.

Waldorf Blessing

Earth who gives to us this food,
Sun who makes it ripe and good,
Dearest Earth and dearest Sun,
Joy and love for all you've done.

Mother Earth Gratitude

For the golden corn and the apple on the tree,
For the golden butter and the honey from the bees,
For the fruits and nuts and berries we gather on our way,
We praise the loving Mother Earth and thank her every day.

Johnny Appleseed

The Earth is good to me
And so I thank the Earth
For giving me
The things I need
The sun, the rain, and the appleseed.
The Earth is good to me.

✳ Sing While Doing Chores

The seven dwarves may have been onto something when they sang "Whistle While You Work." Singing, marching, and playing instruments is joyful at chore time and any time. Besides being bonding, natural, and joyous—and helping tasks go faster—repeated singing rituals can help young children feel secure and transition between activities. You can repeat these simple, workman-like rhymes throughout the task at hand.

Cleanup Song

Clean up, clean up,
Everybody, everywhere.
Clean up, clean up,
Everybody do your share.

Let's Clean Up (to the tune of "The Farmer in the Dell")

Let's clean up today.
Let's clean up today.
We've had our fun.
Our day is done.
So, let's clean up today.

A helper I will be.
A helper I will be.
There's work to do.
There's work to do.
A helper I will be.

This Is the Way We Wash Our Hands (to the tune of "Here We Go Round the Mulberry Bush")

This is the way we wash our hands,
Wash our hands,
Wash our hands.
This is the way we wash our hands,
Early in the morning.

If you'd like, substitute a day of the week, such as "On a Tuesday morning."

There are also many lyrics you can add to this song that help with self-care routines, getting dressed, and performing household chores. You can also make up your own.

> **This is the way we:**
> **Wash our face**
> **Brush our teeth**
> **Brush our hair**
> **Put on clothes**
> **Tie our shoes**
> **Sweep the floor**
> **Wash our clothes**
> **Bake our bread**

✳ Make Time to Put Things Away When Done

Sometimes visual clutter can add to conscious and subconscious feelings of being overwhelmed, for people of all ages, and that can work against efforts to appreciate and enjoy what we have. Children who get in the habit of putting things away when they're done with them experience satisfaction and completion. They learn to care for their space and their things. Don't forget to sing a cleanup song as you go!

Having fewer things, and having those things be of good quality, can help us appreciate the craftsmanship that went into making the objects. Caring for and storing things properly can give us a sense of joy and appreciation and help make our spaces calming and pleasing. Sometimes that care involves handwork and tradition. When we polish the silver that was handed down from my parents, it offers an opportunity to tell Anna about family meals and other memories. Children may get joy from polishing their toys or proudly displaying a collection. If you have a lot of toys, consider rotating the ones that are in play, either by interest or by season, or having special toys that come out for rainy or sick days.

✳ Find Adventure in Your Daily Rounds

The attitude that life is an adventure is one of the most important ones to have. Every day is an adventure to a young child. There are things we can do to foster that feeling and bring even more joy to our activities. Whether you're in a rural, suburban, or urban area, whether it's a weekday or a weekend, the day has a natural rhythm to it. It may be based on agriculture, commerce, nature, or something else, and we can enjoy much of that during devoted time or while we're getting other things done. When Anna was young, we loved getting up early and visiting businesses—a lot happens in the morning! Produce and eggs are delivered to markets and restaurants; bakers create bagels and bread and decorate cakes, often in view of customers. Construction sites start up, often with bulldozers and other heavy machinery that's interesting to watch. When a house was being built next door to Anna's preschool, the school replaced a wooden fence with Plexiglas so the fascinated kids could watch the construction. Truly early risers in certain areas might take in a fish or flower market or visit a busy downtown or bustling neighborhood. Our closest city, San Francisco, offers the early morning ritual of people practicing tai chi in the park.

Other places and times of day might lend themselves to different adventures. When Anna was small, her nap time roughly coincided with cow-milking time at a local dairy. Often we planned to take the forty-five-minute ride during her nap, so she would be able to wake up and watch the cows being milked from the viewing area. We thank the farm for providing a milking barn with a viewing area! Of course, once we were in farm country, we'd take the opportunity to visit farms and pick food in season, enjoying the farms' beauty and bounty and bringing home apples, blueberries, pumpkins, honey, vegetables in season, and more, which we could then eat or make wonderful jams and other items with. There is something especially satisfying about getting food from a farm or farmer and then creating something delicious. It completes a circle and helps children know where their food comes from. We also paid visits to the dairy where our own milk comes from, to have a connection to that land, to thank the cows, and to make the freshest butter possible right on the spot.

Another way to enhance your daily experience is to stop and say hello to neighbors, shopkeepers, mail carriers, and others who are on their own daily rounds. Feeling a part of the neighborhood and community are very important to children's senses of security. Being out in the neighborhood enhances their own safety, as they get to know the members and map of their community, and your family does its part to make streets safer for others to follow in your footsteps. Slowing the pace and really seeing the neighborhood also helps children feel grounded in and part of a specific place, as well as time.

> ***Slow Snippet:*** We began weekly milk delivery when Anna was small, partly as a way to lend rhythm to the week. Many years later, we still enjoy waiting outside for our delivery of farm-fresh milk, and the small degree of fullness it lends to our week and our lives.

✳ Read Bedtime Stories or Have a Bedtime Ritual

Bedtime is an extremely important time for children. It's a time for bonding and connecting with family, for winding down and saying good-bye to the day in a peaceful way that sets the tone for calm, restful, and rejuvenating sleep. Because many children have sleep issues, consistency and repetition at bedtime can be vital. With older kids, bedtime can be a time when their guard is down enough to share their experiences and feelings in a meaningful way and gain your closeness and support. You'll want to leave enough time for your child to regroup after sharing and get a good night's sleep.

Reading stories is a timeless and wonderful way to slow down at bedtime and have a calm routine that also allows for imagination and the beauty of language and pictures. The stories themselves can be whimsical, adventurous, or poetic, from picture books or chapter books. You might want to start a session with light or funny stories and end with calm stories in which characters experience the end of a full day, get sleepy, and fall asleep. There's a reason one of our favorite family books, *Good Night, Moon,* is so popular. It uses gentle repetition to allow a child to imagine saying good night to all his or her familiar objects and people. The act of saying good night has a calming finality to it and lets children have closure to their day.

Bedtime reading also allows for physical closeness. Reading

can be done while cuddling or touching, or being otherwise physically close. Showing pictures in picture books naturally slows our pace. And people of all ages usually enjoy being read to. Both Michael and I read to Anna every night, until about the middle of elementary school, when she began to want to read by herself in bed sometimes. That time was incredibly bonding and calming for our family. We usually let Anna choose the books. Inexplicably, at the age of two, she routinely asked for a book that was actually a face-painting instruction manual. I guess she really enjoyed the bright colors and designs. It was a challenge to make up stories to go with the faces, but we did! Later, we read a mixture of picture books and chapter books. We still talk fondly about many of our favorites, like Pantaloon, the baking poodle; Scuppers, the salty sailor dog; Curious George; Richard Scarry's busy animals; and many others.

In addition to reading, you may want to ritualize other aspects of bedtime and nighttime. It's very helpful to have a regular bedtime that is predictable and allows enough time to wind down and enough time to sleep. Lots of children are given baths to help create routine and calm. Often rooms are quiet and bedrooms and bedtimes electronics-free. Lots of parents enjoy singing gentle lullabies. The actual tucking in can also be done the same way each night, which helps children feel especially secure. You needn't stay with children until they are fast asleep. In fact, it can be helpful for them to be relaxed enough to be able to put themselves to sleep.

✴ Create Fun Bath Games and Rituals

Bathing provides another opportunity for ritual, calming, bonding, and fun. Note that some children find bathing energizing, in which case you might want to leave extra time at night or bathe at a different time.

Most children, once used to the water, enjoy being in it. There are lots of toys designed to make bath time fun and creative for kids, such as bath paint and crayons, or foam pieces to stick on the tub's wall, which allow for child-directed play while a parent watches. As with many things, the best toys may be free, inexpensive, or recycled. Anna loved holding tea parties in the tub, which involved repeatedly filling and emptying plastic teacups and pots, along with measuring cups and spoons. She finger-painted with small amounts of shaving cream and later snorkeled, complete with mask. For a long time we sang campfire songs at bath time. And we did washcloth puppet shows, which I wrote about in the introduction. We had routines for shampooing, as simple as having Anna pretend to look up at an airplane, which made that go easier, as well.

Slow Parenting

When we desire or envision slowing down, what most of us really yearn for is to have more joy in our lives. We want to enjoy the large triumphs and the small moments. This calls for fully participating in things when they happen, as well as some shifts in our relationships with time. Many of us live in a state of relative anxiety. The to-do list is long and beckoning. We try to accomplish a great deal and give our children many opportunities, yet we often fail to make peace with time.

Because modern life can be poor at marking milestones, honoring free play, and allowing balance and rest, we need to create those things for ourselves. It can be a challenge to say no to all the activities and obligations of a hectic schedule, year-round and particularly at the especially frenzied holiday season, end of the school year, and back-to-school time in the fall. A few intentional changes can help slow your family so you can experience more harmony, joy, quality time, and fond memories.

Manage Time

✳ Evaluate Your Own Desires

Are you signing your child up for activities you would have liked for yourself? Although exposure to many things is delightful and, indeed, a luxury, too much of a good thing can backfire. Try to be clear about whether your own needs or anxieties about your child's achievement are fueling a desire to overschedule activities. Often what children want, when asked, is simply more unstructured time with their siblings, friends, or parents.

✳ Make Time for Yourself and Your Spouse

Making time for yourself is often the first thing that gets bumped off the to-do list. Exhausted adults have no resources left for their children and, for everyone's health and benefit, need to break away and recharge. If need be, schedule time to spend alone, as a couple or with friends, even if it's only once a month. Consider doing more family activities that, though age-appropriate, are not necessarily child focused. Sometimes children come along on our activities more readily than we expect them to, and the results can be rewarding for everyone.

✳ Get Enough Sleep

Missing out on sleep puts everyone in a bad mood, which can add to daily stress. Try to have a regular bedtime for children and for yourself. If work remains to be done into the night, tell yourself that it can wait until tomorrow. If there's time, a nice routine before bed, such as reading out loud (to children of any age) can be calming and put a nice cap on the day, which helps everyone get to sleep better.

✳ Stop Running a Taxi Service

Many of us spend a great deal of time in the car, shuttling our children from one activity to the next. Although it's wonderful to provide our children with enriching opportunities, something is also lost when we spend too much time "lost in transportation." Sometimes a small shift can give you back precious time. Consider arranging a carpool, which offers social benefits for kids while freeing up some parental time (and helping the planet), or sacrifice the first-choice activity to choose one that is closer to home. Combine errands or incorporate them into your rounds to limit car trips, or take kids on an errand and then do something more fun. We found time together by parking a few blocks from school and walking in and out. The time we take back in small ways can really add up.

✳ Pool Resources and Ask for Help

These twin ideas speak to our modern, often solitary, way of life and the difficulty many of us have asking for help. While not everything can be shared, some things truly benefit from it. When Anna was young, our family was in a forty-family babysitting co-op. Families were screened for membership by co-op members, to ensure homes were babyproofed and safe. We met regularly, so members could get to know one another. When a family needed a sitter, they would call someone from the list, and that person would receive credit for hours of sitting, while the recipient family got hours subtracted. This was a wonderful approach to an age-old problem. Families got sitters for free and time to pursue outside activities. Children and adults got to know one another and create a thriving community. When kids got older, some of the members turned to one another to barter goods and services. The co-op showed us firsthand that arrangements that imitate villages can be helpful, comforting, and fun beyond measure.

✳ Give Your Electronics the Day Off

Electronic media are so incredibly seductive for people of all ages that sometimes we literally need to unplug to experience our families, selves, and time. You might want to follow the direction of many world religions and cultures and call a formal and scheduled time of rest each week, for a day or even for a night. Most people who do this find it incredibly restorative, as they are able to give their full attention to the activity at hand and to their companions and themselves. Even though we may be available to work and to our wide circles of friends every waking hour, we don't have to be. If you're constantly plugged in, it can be very instructive to see what happens when you get quiet and what happens when you do get back to media. It is usually emergency-free and easy to get back into the flow of work and communication. The messages can wait.

In addition, because many television shows contain images and messages that can be anxiety provoking, the opposite of relaxing and slowing, a TV and news media diet can prove very rewarding, as well. Even cutting out a show a day and substituting it with a family walk or game can add time and joy to your life.

✳ Say No to More Things

We don't have to volunteer to take on more at work or to serve on every school committee that needs us. Periodically assess your needs and your output and, if something is out of balance, readjust. Likewise, children don't have to sign up for a lot of activities. Often children are overscheduled to the point of creating stress for the whole family. Perhaps explore one or two activities at a time, and carefully consider the costs and benefits of each before adding any new ones. It may help to assure yourself that it is usually not the last opportunity for your child to enjoy ballet or soccer. More pleasure may come from devotion to one thing at a time and to free play rather than organized activity.

✳ Limit Choices

There is a famous study in which shoppers were able to sample from a table with either twenty-four jars of jam or six jars. The people who sampled from the larger table were ten times less likely to actually choose a jam and buy it. They were overwhelmed and ultimately paralyzed by having so many choices. A paradox of modern life is that we often have so many choices that not only is it difficult to choose one, but the choice can also be painful and fraught with indecision, dissatisfaction, and doubt. For children, we can help by limiting their choices, reducing activities, and eliminating or rotating toys and other clutter in the home. Adults can attempt to make peace with the fact that we can't do everything, and try to let go of those things that don't make the first cut.

Create Joy

✳ Give Your Kids Some Downtime

There are multiple benefits to unstructured, spontaneous time, individually and as a family—in every area of psychological, physical, and spiritual health. Children who have unstructured time and play are more creative, flexible, self-aware, and calm. Families who have unstructured time and play are joyful and close. It may take practice to put the same value on downtime that we do on organized, goal-oriented activity. It may be uncomfortable at first to be idle. If you have to schedule this time in a calendar, do so.

Don't be afraid to let your child have downtime; to play, daydream, or explore on his or her own—even to be bored. Every activity doesn't have to lead to a future goal. And every moment doesn't have to provide outside entertainment. In fact, our tendency to over-schedule and overstimulate children can create undue stress for them, as well as the inability to simply entertain themselves, play freely, tolerate stillness, or discover their own inner compasses—who they are and what they like to do.

Sometimes we forget what it is like to be a child. Childhood lasts about eighteen years, which leaves plenty of time for structured activities. When Anna was young, soccer fever was in full force in our town. Once pee-wee soccer ended, the teams began to require a time commitment that seemed to us above the hobby and play level that we thought appropriate for young children. Because she didn't love the sport, we didn't pursue it, which left room for activities that could be done on a more casual basis. Anna tried different musical instruments and acted in local children's theater, and she had free time with friends and family. Those Saturday mornings when she wasn't at soccer practice allowed us to play, hike, bike, cook, and make art. In high school, Anna became a serious year-round team athlete, putting age-appropriate time into activities she chose personally. She didn't suffer because she didn't pursue soccer at the age of six. Conversely, she's a great team member with an unbridled enthusiasm for sports and a wonderful sense of play and of herself.

✳ Embrace Imperfection

Sometimes over-scheduling and busyness arise from our fears about not being perfect parents. As a result, we can overattend to the perceived needs of our children and hover and plan to a degree that doesn't help anyone: children miss out on the crucial development and competence that comes with meeting challenges, and parents continue to feel inadequate, because we can never live up to an ideal. Our feelings of inadequacy can spread to our children, who get the message that things—and perhaps they themselves—aren't good enough. Acknowledging and embracing imperfection allows us to live in the moment and experience the kind of spontaneous play and joy that is most beneficial and bonding for kids and families.

✴ Cultivate Friendships with a Variety of People

Welcome people into your life who are different ages than you, or whom you don't know through your child. Sometimes, as parents, we need to connect with people who reflect different or dormant interests or parts of ourselves. People who are in a different phase of life may be less harried themselves, so that you can't help but slow down in their presence. Perhaps there is a neighbor or friend with whom your family would enjoy taking a walk or doing a craft. Especially if there are no grandparents nearby, a relationship with someone older can be a wonderful, life-enlarging experience for a child. Many senior facilities welcome young visitors with a parent. Performing a service, such as visiting a shut-in, is an excellent way to slow down, gain perspective, and make a friend.

✴ Be a Tourist in Your Town

Have you ever noticed how tourists are usually delighted? Granted, they're on vacation together and have come to their destination to have fun. But they also see everything with fresh eyes. Things are novel and waiting to be explored. Even if you've lived somewhere your whole life, there may be new things to see or do if you decide to do so like a tourist. We regularly have days when we play tourist in our town.

☀ Try Something New

Just as tourists see with new eyes, trying something new, individually or as a family, can rejuvenate your mind, body, and spirit. Many of us have something we've always wanted to try—the time may be now. As we learn, we also model for our children that it's good to experiment, and okay to be a beginner and even fail. Trying new things keeps life interesting, playful, and fun.

☀ Get Physical

Laugh, sing, and dance together. Play, walk, and exercise together. There's a time to get out of the way and leave children to their play and there's a time to get physical with them, something many adults don't do very often. Don't be afraid to look silly. You and your children will remember the episodes fondly. In addition, wrestle and roughhouse, with girls as well as boys. Experts tell us that active physical play makes kids smart, flexible, likable, joyful, and fit. Writes Dr. Rudolf Dreikurs, coauthor of the popular book, *Children: The Challenge*, "Parents are so concerned with providing what's best for their children that they neglect to join them."

☀ Practice Gratitude

Researchers have found that an "attitude of gratitude" is highly calming and beneficial to our bodies and minds. It might take practice to regularly bring gratitude to the forefront and exchange negative emotions for positive ones. It may help to keep a gratitude journal, say blessings at mealtimes, or let those around us know how much we treasure them.

✺ Perform Service

Like gratitude, service is an enriching act that helps our minds and bodies in countless ways. Service can help us remember to count our own blessings and share them with others. Service reminds us, especially children, that the world is larger than our experience of it. Performing service as a family is tremendously rewarding. It's not difficult to find an agency, event, or individual in your area who would welcome your help, whether for one time or on an ongoing basis. School, scout, youth, and community groups may have organized outings you can join. Or gather family and friends and create your own. We regularly visited a local senior facility with Anna's scout troop. Our favorite activity was bringing cheery flowers and arranging them with the women. That gave everyone something to do and opened up avenues for conversation. We also did puzzles and simple crafts. Other times, we served outdoors by collecting trash and pulling weeds in local parks and at shores. Those actions connected us to each other as well as to the people and nature around us.

✺ Be in the Present Moment and Do One Thing at a Time

Many of us are so good at regretting the past or worrying about or planning the future that we miss what's right in front of us. We can learn from our children in this area—they are often uniquely present. Being present brings us greater joy, appreciation, and a feeling of the fullness of life. Single tasking, or bringing one's whole mind to any endeavor, is a hallmark of being present. Not only does it make us more truly efficient; it also makes us calmer and less scattered than we are when we try to do many things at once. As we become more present, our awareness is strengthened, and the more small things we notice, the more we experience and enjoy. People who live in the present also tend to forgive themselves and others, and to love and laugh readily. They are ready to greet challenges and curveballs, as well as delights, and will find themselves trading frenzy for fun.

Resources

Writing this book brought to mind many of the cherished books that line our shelves, each of which has meant a great deal to me, while adding depth to our family life. Although this list only hints at the many wonderful resources for slowing families, I hope some of the reading mentioned will help you during your own further explorations. In addition, a more wide-ranging and up-to-date treasure of resources, news, and blogs about the slow movement and its many aspects is available on my website, www.slowfamilyonline.com. I've noted the publishing years of my books, some of which are available in newer or older editions.

Frenzy and Slowing

Alliance for Childhood. www.allianceforchildhood.org. Resources and advocacy to support children's healthy and joyful development.

Babauta, Leo. *The Power of Less: The Fine Art of Limiting Yourself to the Essential…in Business and in Life.* New York: Hyperion, 2008.

Briggs, Dorothy Corkille. *Your Child's Self-Esteem.* New York: Doubleday, 1970.

Carter, Christine. *Raising Happiness: 10 Simple Steps for More Joyful Kids and Happier Parents.* New York: Ballantine Books, 2010.

Catalfo, Phil. *Raising Spiritual Children in a Material World.* New York: Berkley Books, 1997.

Cohen, Lawrence J, PhD. *Playful Parenting.* New York: Ballantine Books, 2002.

Dancy, Rahima Baldwin. *You Are Your Child's First Teacher: What Parents Can Do With and For Their Children from Birth to Age Six.* Berkeley: Celestial Arts, 2000.

Dreikurs, Rudolf, MD and Vicki Soltz. *Children: The Challenge.* New York: Penguin Books, 1990.

Elkind, David, PhD. *The Hurried Child: Growing Up Too Fast Too Soon.* Cambridge: Perseus, 2001.

————. *The Power of Play: Learning What Comes Naturally.* Philadelphia: Da Capo Press, 2007.

Ginsburg, Kenneth R., MD. *Building Resilience in Children and Teens: Giving Kids Roots and Wings.* Elk Grove Village, IL: American Academy of Pediatrics, 2011.

Hirsh-Pasek, Kathy, PhD, Roberta Michnick Golinkoff, PhD, and Diane Eyer, PhD. *Einstein Never Used Flashcards: How Our Children Really Learn—and Why They Need to Play More and Memorize Less.* Rodale Books, 2004.

Hohlbaum, Christine Louise. *The Power of Slow: 101 Ways to Save Time in Our 24/7 World.* New York: St. Martin's Press, 2009.

Honoré, Carl. *In Praise of Slowness: Challenging the Cult of Speed*. New York: HarperCollins, 2004.

————. *Under Pressure: Rescuing our Children from the Culture of Hyper-Parenting*. New York: HarperCollins, 2008.

Kabat-Zinn, Myla, and Jon Kabat-Zinn. *Everyday Blessings, The Inner Work of Mindful Parenting*. New York: Hyperion, 1998.

Kenison, Katrina. *The Gift of an Ordinary Day: A Mother's Memoir*. New York: Grand Central Publishing, 2009.

Kohn, Alfie. *The Homework Myth: Why Our Kids Get Too Much of a Bad Thing*. Philadelphia: Da Capo Press, 2007.

Lodding, Linda Ravin. *The Busy Life of Ernestine Buckmeister*. Brooklyn: Flashlight Press, 2011.

McMahon, Regan. *Revolution in the Bleachers: How Parents Can Take Back Family Life in a World Gone Crazy Over Youth Sports*. New York: Gotham Books, 2007.

Moore, Thomas. *Care of the Soul: A Guide for Cultivating Depth and Sacredness in Everyday Life*. New York: HarperCollins, 1992.

Payne, Kim John, M.Ed, and Lisa M. Ross. *Simplicity Parenting: Using the Extraordinary Power of Less to Raise Calmer, Happier, and More Secure Kids*. New York: Ballantine Books, 2009.

Rethinking Childhood. http://rethinkingchildhood.com. Writings on the changing nature of childhood.

Rosenfeld, Alvin, MD and Nicole Wise. *The Over-Scheduled Child: Avoiding the Hyper-Parenting Trap*. St. Martin's Griffin, 2001.

Skenazy, Lenore. *Free-Range Kids: Giving Our Children the Freedom We Had Without Going Nuts with Worry*. San Francisco: Jossey-Bass, 2009.

Slow Family Living. http://slowfamilyliving.com. Classes, workshops, and coaching to help families slow down.

U.S. Play Coalition. http://usplaycoalition.clemson.edu. News and resources to promote the value of play throughout life.

Warner, Judith. *Perfect Madness: Motherhood in the Age of Anxiety*. New York: Riverhead Books, 2005.

Welwood, John. *Ordinary Magic: Everyday Life as Spiritual Path*. Boston: Shambhala, 1992.

Family, Community, Seasons, and Celebrations

Aveni, Anthony. *The Book of the Year: A Brief History of Our Seasonal Holidays*. New York: Oxford University Press, 2003.

Baker, Diane, Anne Hill, and Starhawk. *Circle Round: Raising Children in Goddess Traditions*. New York: Bantam Books, 1998.

Charles, Cheryl and Bob Samples. *Coming Home: Community, Creativity and Consciousness*. Fawnskin: Personhood Press, 2004.

Dalby, Liza. *East Wind Melts the Ice: A Memoir through the Seasons*. Berkeley: University of California Press, 2009.

Darian, Shea. *Seven Times the Sun: Guiding Your Child Through the Rhythms of the Day*. Philadelphia: Innisfree Press, 1994.

Erdrich, Louise. *The Blue Jay's Dance: A Memoir of Early Motherhood*. New York: HarperCollins, 1995.

Greenwood, Barbara. *A Pioneer Sampler: The Daily Life of a Pioneer Family in 1840*. New York: Houghton Mifflin, 1995.

Keats, Ezra Jack. *The Snowy Day*. New York: Viking Press, 1962.

McCloskey, Robert. *One Morning In Maine*. New York: Viking Press, 1952.

Polacco, Patricia. *The Keeping Quilt*. New York: Simon & Schuster, 1998.

Rhythm of the Home. http://rhythmofthehome.com. Online magazine featuring seasonal and family celebrations, food, and crafts.

Whitmyer, Claude, ed. *In the Company of Others: Making Community in the Modern World*. New York: Tarcher/Putnam, 1993.

Our Built Environment

Dannenberg, Andrew L., Howard Frumkin, and Richard J. Jackson. *Making Healthy Places: Designing and Building for Health, Well-being, and Sustainability*. Washington, D.C.: Island Press, 2011.

Hammond, Darell. *KABOOM! How One Man Built a Movement to Save Play*. New York: Rodale, 2011.

Jacobs, Jane. *The Death and Life of Great American Cities*. New York: Random House, 1961.

Kellert, Stephen R. *Building for Life: Designing and Understanding the Human-Nature Connection*. Washington, D.C.: Island Press, 2005.

Kunstler, James Howard. *The Geography of Nowhere: The Rise and Decline of America's Man-Made Landscape*. New York: Simon & Schuster, 1993.

———. *Home From Nowhere: Remaking Our Everyday World for the 21st Century*. New York: Touchstone, 1998.

Lanza, Mike. *Playborhood: Turn Your Neighborhood into a Place for Play*. Menlo Park: Free Play Press, 2012.

Gardening and Nature

Active Kids Club. www.activekidsclub.com. Resources for outdoor play.

Audubon Guides. www.audubonguides.com. Mobile field guides to nature.

Audubon Society Field Guides. www.audubon.org. Field guides and nature information from the Audubon Society.

Butterfly Site. www.thebutterflysite.com/create-butter fly-garden.shtml. Butterfly habitat information.

Butterfly Website. butterflywebsite.com/butterflygardening .cfm. Butterfly habitat information.

Caro and Co. www.caroandco.com.au. Nature crafts, play, and more.

Carson, Rachel. *The Sense of Wonder*. New York: Harper & Row, 1956.

Children & Nature Network. http://www.childrenandnature .org/. News and resources about the international movement to reconnect children with nature.

Clarkson, Rosetta E. *Magic Gardens: A Modern Chronicle of Herbs and Savory Seeds*. New York: Collier Books, 1992.

Cohen, Rebecca P. *15 Minutes Outside: 365 Ways to Get Out of the House and Connect with Your Kids*. Naperville: Sourcebooks, 2011.

Cornell, Joseph. *Sharing Nature with Children*. Nevada City: Dawn Publications, 1998.

Damrosch, Barbara. *The Garden Primer*. New York: Workman Publishing, 2003.

Enature. www.enature.com. Wildlife guides and nature and gardening information.

Enchanted Learning. www.enchantedlearning.com. Nature information and projects.

Go Explore Nature. www.goexplorenature.com. Resources for nature fun.

Grass Stain Guru. http://grassstainguru.com. Information about nature and play.

Hummingbird Guide. http://www.hummingbird-guide.com. Hummingbird habitat information.

Ladybird Johnson Wildflower Center. www.wildflower.org. Wildflower and native garden information.

Let the Children Play. http://progressiveearlychildhood education.blogspot.com. Early childhood outdoor and other play.

Louv, Richard. *Last Child in the Woods: Saving Our Children from Nature-Deficit Disorder*. Chapel Hill: Algonquin Books, 2005.

———. *The Nature Principle: Reconnecting with Life in a Virtual Age*. Chapel Hill: Algonquin Books, 2012.

Outside with Marghanita. http://marghanita.com. Inspiration about the wonders of nature.

National Wildlife Federation. www.nwf.org/gardenfor wildlife. Information on how to create and certify a habitat garden. www.beoutthere.org. Resources to help families spend more time outdoors.

Pollinator Partnership. http://pollinator.org. Nature conservation and habitat information.

Outdoor Afro. www.outdoorafro.com. A community that reconnects African Americans with nature.

Red, White & Grew. http://redwhiteandgrew.com. Gardening, cooking, and homeschooling fun.

Tallamy, Douglas W. *Bringing Nature Home: How You Can Sustain Wildlife with Native Plants*. Portland: Timber Press, 2007.

Cooking with Kids

Adams, Marcia. *Cooking from Quilt Country: Hearty Recipes from Amish and Mennonite Kitchens*. New York: Clarkson Potter, 1998.

Amendt, Linda J. *Blue Ribbon Preserves: Secrets to Award-Winning Jams, Jellies, Marmalades and More*. New York: HP Books, 2001.

Carden, Jennifer. *The Toddler Café: Fast, Healthy, and Fun Ways to Feed Even the Pickiest Eater*. San Francisco: Chronicle Books, 2008.

Editors of Sunset Books. *Home Canning*. Menlo Park: Lane
     Publishing, 1975.

Florence, Tyler. *Tyler Florence Family Meal: Bringing
     People Together Never Tasted Better*. Emmaus:
     Rodale Books, 2010.

Fobel, Jim. *Jim Fobel's Old-Fashioned Baking Book:
     Recipes from an American Childhood*. New York:
     Lake Isle Press, 1996.

Lukins, Sheila and Julee Rosso. *The Silver Palate Cookbook*.
     New York: Workman Publishing, 1979.

Lukins, Sheila and Julee Rosso. *The Silver Palate Good Times
     Cookbook*. New York: Workman Publishing, 1984.

National Center for Home Food Preservation. http://nchfp
     .uga.edu/publications/publications_usda.html.
     Multiple publications containing recipes and
     food-safety information.

Playful Pantry. http://playfulpantry.wordpress.com.
     Delightful recipes for all ages.

Prentice, Jessica. *Full Moon Feast: Food and the Hunger for
     Connection*. White River Junction: Chelsea Green
     Publishing, 2006.

Tannahill, Reay. *Food in History*. New York: Crown
     Publishers, 1998.

What's Cooking America. http://whatscookingamerica.net.
     Recipes, regional cooking, food history and more.

Williams, Chuck, ed. *Williams-Sonoma Kids Cookies: Scrumptious Recipes for Bakers Ages 9 to 13*. New York: Time-Life Books, 1998.

Crafts

Bramble Berry. www.brambleberry.com. Soap-making supplies and instructions.

Dharma Trading Company. www.dharmatrading.com. Textile craft supplies: fabric, yarn, clothing, books, and dyes.

Enchanted Learning. www.enchantedlearning.com. Wide variety of craft projects.

Juniper Tree. www.junipertreesupplies.com. Soap and candle supplies.

Noll, Bernadette and Kathie Sever. *Make Stuff Together: 24 Simple Projects to Create as a Family*. Hoboken: Wiley Publishing, 2011.

Paint, Cut, Paste. http://paintcutpaste.com. Fun craft projects.

Ross, Kathy. *Crafts to Make in the Fall*. Brookfield: Millbrook Press, 1998.

———. *Crafts to Make in the Spring*. Brookfield: Millbrook Press, 1998.

———.*Crafts to Make in the Summer*. Brookfield: Millbrook Press, 1999.

————. *Crafts to Make in the Winter*. Brookfield: Millbrook
    Press, 1999.

Schepp, Steven. *The Family Creative Workshop*. Vol 1–24.
    Plenary Publications, 1976.

Games and Activities

Games Kids Play. www.gameskidsplay.net. Rules to classic
    and other games.

Go Out and Play: Favorite Outdoor Games from KaBOOM!
    Somerville: Candlewick Press, 2012.

LeFevre, Dale N. *Best New Games: 77 Games and 7 Trust
    Activities for All Ages and Abilities*. Champaign:
    Human Kinetics, 2002.

Scoutorama. www.scoutorama.com. Games and activities for
    many ages and situations.

Songs

Blood, Peter and Annie Patterson. *Rise Up Singing: The
    Group Singing Songbook*. Bethlehem: Sing Out
    Publications, 2005.

Scoutorama. www.scoutorama.com/song. Words to classic
    and other songs.

RV Travel

Go RVing. http://www.gorving.com/locator/campgrounds
    .aspx. Information and resources about RV travel.

Books and Studies Cited in the Introduction

These are listed in the order of appearance.

Jayson, Sharon. "Working at Home: Family-Friendly?"
March 16, 2010. *USA Today*. http://www.usatoday
.com/life/lifestyle/2010-04-15-1Afamilytime15_
CV_N.htm.

"The Joys of Doing Nothing." *Scholastic*, 2009. http://www
.scholastic.com/resources/article/
the-joys-of-doing-nothing.

Ginsburg, Kenneth R, MD. *Building Resilience in Children
and Teens: Giving Kids Roots and Wings*. Elk Grove
Village, IL: American Academy of Pediatrics, 2011.

Ginsburg, Kenneth R., MD, MSEd, the Committee
on Communications, and the Committee on
Psychosocial Aspects of Child and Family Health.
*The Importance of Play in Promoting Healthy Child
Development and Maintaining Strong Parent-Child
Bonds*. Elk Grove Village: American Academy of
Pediatrics, 2006.

Kellert, Stephen R. *Building for Life: Designing and
Understanding the Human-Nature Connection*.
Washington, D.C.: Island Press, 2005.

Burdette, Hillery L, MD, MS, and Robert C. Whitaker, MD,
MPH. "Resurrecting Free Play in Young Children:
Looking Beyond Fitness and Fatness to Attention,

Affiliation and Affect." *Pediatrics & Adolescent Medicine*. 159:1 (January 2005). http://archpedi .ama-assn.org/cgi/content/abstract/159/1/46.

Cohen, Lawrence J, PhD. *Playful Parenting*. New York: Ballantine Books, 2002.

Rebekah A. Richert, PhD, et al. "Word Learning From Baby Videos." *Pediatrics & Adolescents*. 164:5 (May 2010). http://archpedi.jamanctwork.com/article .aspx?articleid=383151.

Hart, Betty, PhD, and Todd R. Risley, PhD. *Meaningful Differences in the Everyday Experience of Young American Children*. Baltimore: Paul H. Brookes Publishing, 2005.

"Generation M2: Media in the Lives of 8- to 18-Year-Olds." *Kaiser Family Foundation*. 2010. http://www.kff .org/entmedia/8010.cfm.

Turkle, Sherry. *Alone Together: Why We Expect More of Technology and Less of Each Other*. New York: Basic Books, 2011.

Moore, Thomas. *A Life at Work: The Joy of Discovering What You Were Born to Do*. New York: Three Rivers Press, 2009.

Payne, Kim John , M.Ed, and Lisa M. Ross. *Simplicity Parenting: Using the Extraordinary Power of Less to Raise Calmer, Happier, and More Secure Kids*. New York: Ballantine Books, 2009.

Carson, Rachel. *The Sense of Wonder*. New York: Harper & Row, 1956.

Dancy, Rahima Baldwin. *You Are Your Child's First Teacher: What Parents Can Do With and For Their Children from Birth to Age Six*. New York: Celestial Arts, 2000.

"The Importance of Family Dinners IV." *The National Center on Addiction and Substance Abuse at Columbia University*. September 2007. www.casa columbia.org/templates/publications_reports.aspx.

Fiese, Barbara, PhD, and Mary Spagnola, PhD. "Family Routines and Rituals: A Context for Development in the Lives of Young Children." *Infants & Young Children*. 20(4): 284-299 (Oct/Nov 2007). www.nursingcenter.com/library/JournalArticle .asp?Article_ID=744471.

E. W. Jensen, et al. "The Family Routines Inventory: Development and Validation." *Social Science and Medicine*. 17(4): 201-11 (1983). www.ncbi.nlm .nih.gov/pubmed/6844952.

Acknowledgments

Any book about family and community is naturally going to contain the loving input of a great many wonderful souls. I have many people to thank for their unwavering belief in, enthusiasm for, and contributions to this project. I am grateful to:

Andrea Somberg at Harvey Klinger Agency and Shana Drehs at Sourcebooks for seeing the potential of a book on Slow Parenting.

Kelly Bale, for her careful editing and kind shepherding of the book through the publishing process.

Dear friends and writers Anji Brenner, Katy Butler, Julie Carlson, Molly Coomber, Caroline Craig, Nicole Daspit, Andi T. DeMars, Rachel Gaunt, Andrea Halperin, Elise Hoogsteden-Roberts, Yolanda Kondonassis, Patty LaDuke, Bettina Mow, Paige O'Donohue, Cynthia Palmer, Shelly Peppel, Gail Reitano, Barbara Tannenbaum, Victoria Vogel-Rudolph, and Heather Young, who offered warm and insightful input at just the right moments, as well as their cheers throughout the writing.

Girl Scout coleader of many years Ruth Chavez, and fellow scout parents Cullyn Vaeth and Victoria Vogel-Rudolph, who taught me much about scouting and sisterhood.

Wende Kumara and all the teachers at Kumara School, whose vision for preschool and early childhood helped set our family on its slow, thoughtful, and delightful course.

My elders, mentors, and neighbors, many of whose warm

and wonderful insights and practices are sprinkled throughout the book.

Fellow family, nature, garden, cooking, and craft bloggers, for their continuing friendship, inspiration, and enthusiasm, and for making the online world feel as warm and personal as it would if we were having coffee across a kitchen table.

Slow Family Online contributors and readers, whose ongoing enthusiasm and feedback amazes and humbles me every day.

Fellow members of the long-standing online community, *The Well*, who cheered the many stages of the book and collectively arrived at its subtitle.

Richard Louv, Cheryl Charles, Amy Pertschuk, Avery Cleary, Juan Martinez, Rue Mapp, Jackie Green, and all my colleagues at the Children & Nature Network, for welcoming me into the fold and for offering a trail map for engaging others in the organic movement to reconnect children with the natural world.

The pioneering authors and thinkers at the forefront of the Slow Movement and all of its wonderful offshoots, many of whose work will be found in the Resources section.

My beautiful daughter, Anna, who has enthusiastically embraced our family adventures for sixteen years, from rising in the middle of the night to see volcanoes, meteor showers, or tide pools to diving into a session of baking pretzels, tie-dyeing clothes, or making jam.

My sweetheart and life partner, Michael, for his unwavering support, dedication, vision, clarity, and humor, and for being a fabulous parent and partner who has created the most loving home imaginable and makes me feel lucky and loved every day.

About the Author

Susan Sachs Lipman (Suz) is a parenting and family expert who blogs at the award-winning *Slow Family™ Online*, the Christian Science Monitor's *Modern Parenthood* blog, and numerous other outlets. She is the Social Media Director for the international Children & Nature Network. She has served on many boards and commissions and was named local "Girl Scout Leader of the Year." Suz lives with her husband and daughter

Photo: Jeanette Vonier

in Mill Valley, California, where she enjoys hiking, gardening, reading, soap crafting, and food canning. Her website is slowfamilyonline.com.

Lippy is a San Francisco Bay Area illustrator with a passion for line, movement, and the author! Keep up with his latest work at Lippy.com.